Identity and Ideology in Digital Food Discourse

Also available from Bloomsbury

Contemporary Critical Discourse Studies, edited by Christopher Hart and Piotr Cap
Discourse and Identity on Facebook, by Mariza Georgalou
Facebook and Conversation Analysis, by Matteo Farina
The Discourse of Online Consumer Reviews, by Camilla Vásquez
Searchable Talk, by Michele Zappavigna

Identity and Ideology in Digital Food Discourse

Social Media Interactions Across Cultural Contexts

Edited by Alla Tovares and Cynthia Gordon

BLOOMSBURY ACADEMIC
LONDON • NEW YORK • OXFORD • NEW DELHI • SYDNEY

BLOOMSBURY ACADEMIC
Bloomsbury Publishing Plc
50 Bedford Square, London, WC1B 3DP, UK
1385 Broadway, New York, NY 10018, USA
29 Earlsfort Terrace, Dublin 2, Ireland

BLOOMSBURY, BLOOMSBURY ACADEMIC and the Diana logo are trademarks of Bloomsbury Publishing Plc

First published in Great Britain 2021
This paperback edition published in 2022

Copyright © Alla Tovares, Cynthia Gordon and Contributors, 2021

Alla Tovares and Cynthia Gordon have asserted their right under the Copyright, Designs and Patents Act, 1988, to be identified as Editors of this work.

For legal purposes the Acknowledgments on p. ix constitute an extension of this copyright page.

Cover design by Ben Anslow
Cover photograph © Koosen/Getty Images

All rights reserved. No part of this publication may be reproduced or transmitted in any form or by any means, electronic or mechanical, including photocopying, recording, or any information storage or retrieval system, without prior permission in writing from the publishers.

Bloomsbury Publishing Plc does not have any control over, or responsibility for, any third-party websites referred to or in this book. All internet addresses given in this book were correct at the time of going to press. The author and publisher regret any inconvenience caused if addresses have changed or sites have ceased to exist, but can accept no responsibility for any such changes.

A catalogue record for this book is available from the British Library.

Library of Congress Cataloging-in-Publication Data
Names: Tovares, Alla V., editor. | Gordon, Cynthia, 1975-editor.
Title: Identity and ideology in digital food discourse: social media interactions across cultural contexts / edited by Alla Tovares and Cynthia Gordon.
Description: London; New York: Bloomsbury Academic, 2020. | Includes bibliographical references and index.
Identifiers: LCCN 2020030968 (print) | LCCN 2020030969 (ebook) | ISBN 9781350119147 (hardback) | ISBN 9781350189249 (paperback) | ISBN 9781350119154 (ebook) | ISBN 9781350119161 (epub)
Subjects: LCSH: Food–Social aspects. | Food in popular culture. | Social media. | Online social networks.
Classification: LCC GT2850.I35 2020 (print) | LCC GT2850 (ebook) | DDC 394.1/2–dc23
LC record available at https://lccn.loc.gov/2020030968
LC ebook record available at https://lccn.loc.gov/2020030969

ISBN: HB: 978-1-3501-1914-7
PB: 978-1-3501-8924-9
ePDF: 978-1-3501-1915-4
eBook: 978-1-3501-1916-1

Typeset by RefineCatch Limited, Bungay, Suffolk

To find out more about our authors and books visit www.bloomsbury.com and sign up for our newsletters.

Contents

List of Figures	vii
List of Tables	viii
Acknowledgments	ix
Introduction *Cynthia Gordon and Alla Tovares*	1

Part One Negotiating Individual Identities in Online Food Contexts

1 "Vegetables as a Chore": Constructing and Problematizing a "Picky Eater" Identity Online *Didem İkizoğlu and Cynthia Gordon* — 13

2 The Multidimensionality of Eating in Contemporary Information Society: A Corpus-based Discourse Analysis of Online Audience Reactions to a TV Show About Food *Jana Declercq, Stéphan Tulkens, and Geert Jacobs* — 33

3 Mediatizing the Fashionable Eater in @nytfood #tbt Posts *Gwynne Mapes* — 59

Part Two (Re)constructing and (Re)imagining Existing Food-related Language, Practices, and Actions in Digital Environments

4 Constructing Veganism Against the Backdrop of Omnivore Cuisine: The Use of Adjectives and Modifiers in Vegan Food Blogs *Cornelia Gerhardt* — 87

5 What if the Customer is Wrong?: Debates About Food on Yelp and TripAdvisor *Camilla Vásquez* — 111

6 Mukbang as Your Digital Tablemate: Creating Commensality Online *Hanwool Choe* — 137

Part Three Using Food as a Discursive and Material Resource for Online Activism and Political Engagement

7   Growing Online: Activist Identities in the "Grow Your Own" English Blogging Community *Nadine Pierce, Isidoropaolo Casteltrione, and Ana Tominc* 171

8   Food, Activism, and Chips Oman on Twitter *Najma Al Zidjaly, Einas Al Moqbali, and Ahad Al Hinai* 197

9   Parmesan and Patriotism on YouTube: Food as Ideology in Today's Russia *Alla Tovares* 225

Afterword: Food, Language, and Social Media: Past, Present, and Future *Alla Tovares and Cynthia Gordon* 251

Notes on Contributors 259
Index 263

Figures

3.1	@nytfood post from 19 Feb. 2015 (their fourteenth #tbt post). The featured image was originally printed in 1949 issue of the NYT; it pictures a chopped chicken mousse. User comments have been blurred to preserve anonymity.	67
3.2	Contemporary photo (@nytfood). Craig Lee © 2020 The New York Times Company.	68
3.3 – 3.5	Posts featuring women's hands with polished nails. © 2020 The New York Times Company.	71
3.6	Case study written caption (as seen in Fig. 3.1)	72
3.7	Nail painting emoji with hashtag	74
3.8	User comments (reproduced from Fig. 3.1)	75
6.1	BJ Haetnim reading chat messages during mukbang	144

Tables

1.1	Foods that picky eaters report that they do eat and do not eat, by number of mentions	21
2.1	Top 30 keywords of the keyness analysis	39
2.2	Top 10 collocations with the word "fristi/Fristi"	46
2.3	The top emoji/emoticons from the top 30 keyness list. The list contains both Twitter and Facebook rendering of emoji, as emoji are different across platforms	49
3.1	Characteristics of @nytfood #tbt posts	65
5.1	Typical moves in businesses' responses to complaints in online consumer reviews	115
5.2	Examples of evaluative adjectival phrases occurring in general food complaints	119
5.3	Evaluative adjectival phrases occurring in complaints about specific dishes or food items	124
7.1	"Environment" category by blog identifier	180
7.2	"Economics" category by blog identifier	181
7.3	"Food & Health" category by blog identifier	182
9.1	YouTube comments about the actor that construct polarization	235
9.2	YouTube comments about the cheesemaker that construct non-confrontation	239

Acknowledgments

This volume grew from a panel on "Food for Thought and Social Action" organized for the 15th International Pragmatics Association (IPrA) Conference. We are grateful to audience members for their comments and questions, and to Deborah Tannen for her feedback on our proposal for this volume. We are thankful for our colleagues' and students' enthusiasm regarding our research-in-progress on food and digital discourse, especially to students in the "Language and Food" courses we have been fortunate enough to teach at our respective institutions. Our gratitude goes to Andrew Wardell and Becky Holland at Bloomsbury for their support and guidance through the various stages of this project. We also thank Merv Honeywood at RefineCatch for his attention to detail. Alla Tovares extends special thanks to the late Raul Tovares, a true partner and best friend, who was an enthusiastic supporter of this book idea and who is sorely missed.

Introduction

Cynthia Gordon and Alla Tovares

Food has always been imbued with both material and ideological significance. What we buy and eat and how we talk about and around food are influenced not only by our personal tastes and preferences, but also – and to a larger degree – by cultural, economic, and sociopolitical factors (e.g., Cook 2004; Nestle 2007; Paarlberg 2013; Anderson 2014; Poulain 2017). Put differently, food is more than sustenance; talk about food conveys more than taste; and through both food and language, people index and negotiate identities and ideologies related to class, ethnicity, age, gender, culture, religion, and politics. Furthermore, new media (social media in particular) have become part of everyday communication, and are a notable site for food-related communication as well.

This volume explores food-related interactions in various digital and cultural contexts to demonstrate how users mobilize language, images, and videos – and food as a discursive resource – to accomplish actions of social, cultural, and political consequence, thereby constructing identities and ideologies that encompass, and transcend, food. Specifically, it illuminates the relationship between discourse, action, and ideology by examining the intersection of two areas of growing interest in linguistics and related fields – interaction about food and digital communication, especially on social media. Each area has been studied separately; for example, several volumes, including edited collections, have explored *Food and Language* (Lavric & Konzett 2009), *Culinary Linguistics* (Gerhardt, Frobenius & Ley 2013), and *Language and Food* (Szatrowski 2014) on the one hand, and *Digital Discourse* (Thurlow & Mroczek 2011), *Language Online* (Barton & Lee 2013), *Discourse 2.0* (Tannen & Trester 2013), and *Searchable Talk* (Zappavigna 2018) on the other. Increasingly, however, these areas intersect.

The studies presented in this volume draw on various discourse analytic frameworks to illuminate the intersection between food and digital discourse. They examine food-related discourse on a number of social media platforms (e.g., blogs, discussion boards, Facebook, Instagram, Twitter, and YouTube) as well as in diverse linguistic and cultural contexts. Specifically, the chapters explore food-related communication in Arabic, Dutch, French, German, Korean, Russian, and English (its American, British, and Canadian varieties) and in a variety of countries, from Belgium to the United States. In this introductory chapter, we contextualize the volume within the three main bodies of research to which it contributes: the study of food-related communication, the analysis of digital discourse, and theorizing on how identities and ideologies are linguistically and multimodally constructed and conveyed. By briefly reviewing key studies in these areas, and at their various intersections, we highlight themes that cut across the volume's chapters: Food serves as a fundamental resource for the processes of meaning-making, ideological production, and identity construction; with their rich, multimodal, and collaborative environment, digital media provide an ideal site to enact and examine such processes; and people use language and other symbolic resources in productive and creative ways to engage in them.

Food – its politics and policies, material and symbolic values – has recently been of increased interest not only in linguistics but also in cognate disciplines, including political science, communication studies, rhetorical studies, sociology, and anthropology (e.g., Frye & Bruner 2012; Pilcher 2012; Paarlberg 2013; Boerboom 2015; Vercelloni 2016; Chrzan & Brett 2017; Martschukat & Simon 2017; Poulain 2017; LeBesco & Naccarato 2018; Riley & Paugh 2019). In *Everyone Eats* (2014), anthropologist Eugene Anderson observes that all societies use food to communicate messages. Social scientists of various stripes have examined how food is used to communicate group identity and solidarity (e.g., Kerner, Chou & Warmind 2015), as well as about "status, gender, role, ethnicity, religion, identity, and other socially constructed regimes" (Anderson 2014: 6). Linguists, discourse analysts in particular, have addressed similar questions by focusing on communication *about* and/or *around* food. For instance, using a critical lens, Cook (2004) examines how stakeholders on both sides of the genetically modified foods debate use linguistic strategies to index their underlying values and beliefs. The papers in Szatrowski's (2014) edited volume analyze the interplay of language and food in naturally occurring conversations to demonstrate not only the co-construction of cultural identities, assessments, and categories, but also social activities and socialization. The chapters comprising Gerhardt, Frobenius, and Ley's (2013) edited book offer a broad exploration of the interconnections between food and language from a variety of theoretical and methodological perspectives and in diverse contexts, ranging from cookbooks, recipes, and drinking toasts to language classes and food blogs. These and other studies (e.g., Lavric & Konzett 2009; Jurafsky 2014; Diederich 2015; Cavanaugh & Riley 2017) underscore food and language as fundamental components of human experience and their intersection as a productive site to explore actions and ideologies, social structures, and human communication.

Digital media technologies offer new communicative opportunities and possibilities, and Web 2.0 – often dubbed the social or interactive Web – has transformed its users from consumers of information into "prosumers," or both producers and consumers of information (e.g., Rousseau 2012; Seargeant & Tagg 2014; Vásquez 2014). Moreover, new media affordances allow people with no offline or direct online connections to form virtual "ambient" groupings, with emerging social relationships that are "generated and influenced by unfolding linguistic patterns" (Zappavigna 2013: 2). At the same time, researchers have argued that it would be unproductive to view social media practices as devoid of antecedents and/or as detached from the offline world (e.g., Herring 2013; Jenkins, Ford & Green 2013; Locher, Bolander & Höhn 2015; Humphreys 2016). In this regard, Barton and Lee (2013), building on Kress (2003), observe that while digital technologies transform all facets of life, these transformations are not isolated but rather are ingrained in larger social changes that in turn influence technologies. They go on to suggest that notwithstanding technological changes, language remains central to understanding online communication because it "is essential in shaping changes in life and our lived experiences" and is simultaneously "affected and transformed by these changes" (Barton & Lee 2013: 3). As recent studies indicate (e.g., Blackburn, Yilmaz & Boyd 2018; Schneider et al. 2018), the topic of food continues to gain prominence in online communication; thus, it offers a productive site to explore not only the linkages between various genres and modalities of discourse, and existing and emerging approaches to discourse analysis, but also to delve into the sociocultural and ideological underpinnings of communication about food.

The chapters that comprise this volume contribute to the relatively small, but rapidly growing, body of existing studies that consider food-related digital communication (e.g., Sneijder & te Molder 2005; Brandt & Jenks 2011; Jurafsky et al. 2014; Rousseau 2012; Diemer, Brunner & Schmidt 2014; Zappavigna 2014; Vásquez & Chik 2015; Chik & Vásquez 2017), while also extending research on conversational discourse that shows how communicating about food (and drink) not only creates tastes and preferences, but also accomplishes social and ideological work (e.g., Ochs, Pontecorvo & Fasulo 1996; Gonçalves 2013; Wiggins 2013; Dominguez-Whitehead & Whitehead 2014; Karrebæk 2014, 2017; Forchtner & Tominc 2017). Our contributors draw on various discourse-based approaches to digital communication (e.g., those outlined in Herring 2004; Barton & Lee 2013; Page et al. 2014) to illuminate food-related interaction across a range of cultural, linguistic, and digital contexts. The chapters individually and collectively contribute to understanding forms and functions of food-related communication and digital discourse, and, extending prior research (e.g., Ochs 1993; Bucholtz & Hall 2005; Jaworski & Thurlow 2009; Machin & van Leeuwen 2016), how identities and ideologies are linguistically and multimodally constructed and conveyed.

The book's nine analytical chapters can be read either sequentially or independently; each chapter presents a different study and can be understood on its own. The organization of the book reflects the range of digital food discourse studies, which spans from investigating individual identity construction to exploring nation-building. The book consists of three parts. The first, Chapters 1 through 3, focuses on how individual identities are negotiated against larger – often conflicting – ideologies of health, nutrition, and (good) taste. In Chapter 1, Didem İkizoğlu and Cynthia Gordon draw on computer-mediated discourse analysis (Herring 2004) to investigate English-language discussion threads started by adult "picky eaters" (i.e., people who reject many types of foods) on a predominantly U.S. American online health and weight loss discussion board. They show how posters discursively construct this identity, problematize it, and indicate their efforts to change, thereby indexing, and reifying, master narratives or ideologies that construct "picky eating" as unacceptable for adults and food consumption as an individual, morally loaded choice. In Chapter 2, Jana Declercq, Stéphan Tulkens, and Geert Jacobs consider how an online audience reacts to a Belgian Dutch-language infotainment TV show about food that focuses on health and nutrition on the one hand, and food production on the other. Through a combination of content analysis and corpus linguistic analysis of Twitter and Facebook reactions to the TV show, the authors explore audience participation in knowledge production about food as well as the multidimensionality of food discourses, including taste, health, and ethical and environmental considerations. Chapter 3, by Gwynne Mapes, centers on "throwback Thursday" (#tbt) posts from the *New York Times* food section's Instagram account (@*nytfood*) to identify orders of elitist stancetaking (Jaworski & Thurlow 2009). Mapes argues that mediatized representations of food by a prominent American newspaper are instrumental in teaching people how to attain and manage status and that by mocking antiquated food practices, @*nytfood* followers assert their own fashionable modernity-cum-superiority. Her analysis also suggests how deceptively democratic and inclusive digital platforms can be spaces of, and for, social hierarchy where privileged standards of good taste and fashionable eating are (re)produced.

Chapters 4, 5, and 6, comprising the second part of the volume, tackle the (re)construction and (re)imagination of existing food-related language, practices, and actions in digital environments (i.e., food lexicon, customer-restaurant representative interaction, and eating, respectively). Cornelia Gerhardt (Chapter 4) demonstrates how the analysis of lexical choices in food blogs can shed light on the construction of veganism as a lifestyle. By zeroing in on how adjectives and pre- and post-nominal modifiers are mobilized to describe vegan recipes and ingredients in English, German, and French – and in three different countries (Canada, Germany, and France) – this study reveals the tension between veganism as a global phenomenon and its (linguistic) construction against the backdrop of omnivore cuisine and its language. In Chapter 5, Camilla Vásquez examines how U.S. American businesses respond to negative food-related reviews on Yelp and TripAdvisor, two popular reviewing sites. The analysis focuses on discursive strategies such as apologies, counter claims, and pronominal choices that restaurants deploy in their responses to diners' complaints; in so doing, it offers valuable insights into how contemporary businesses manage their online reputations. Hanwool Choe (Chapter 6) turns attention to the process of eating by examining mukbang, a Korean livestream in which a host eats while interacting with viewers – the eater speaks (on video) to the viewers while eating and viewers type (in a chat box) to each other and to the eater. Her analysis illuminates how the mundane social activity of eating is performed online via discursive and multimodal resources, while also demonstrating how mukbang interaction creates a sense of commensality, thereby realizing a Korean cultural value that involves not only sharing a table but also sharing food from the same plate.

The final part of the collection, Chapters 7–9, centers on food as a discursive and material resource for online activism and political engagement, specifically regarding alternative food-growing, international conflicts, and grassroots nation-building. In Chapter 7, Nadine Pierce, Isidoropaolo Casteltrione, and Ana Tominc analyze how writers from an English blogging community, Grow Your Own (GYO), discursively construct activist identities through online promotion of alternative practices of growing and consuming food. Using the lens of critical discourse analysis (CDA), they demonstrate how GYO bloggers construct themselves, in contrast to others, as active, responsible, self-sufficient, and common-sense environmentalists, with the power to change current harmful practices in food production, transportation, and consumption. Najma Al Zidjaly,

Einas Al Moqbali, and Ahad Al Hinai, in Chapter 8, integrate theorizing on indirectness, stance, and morality to investigate Arabic-language Twitter messages tagged with a hashtag naming a popular Omani snack food (#Chips_Oman). Their analysis shows that while #Chips_Oman was initially created by Omani citizens negatively reacting to their national snack being used as a piñata by children in a video taken in the United Arab Emirates, it also became a resource for airing internal grievances and negotiating national moral orders. In other words, the food-related hashtag was used to express political dissent pertaining to international as well as country-internal conflicts. In Chapter 9, Alla Tovares provides an account of the intersection of digital discourse, food, and politics by focusing on how Russia's ban on imported Western foods is discussed on YouTube. Analyzing Russian-language written comments posted in reaction to YouTube videos about Parmesan, an ideologically charged food item in Russia, the author demonstrates how gastronomy is constructed as ideology against the backdrop of the Russian/Ukrainian geopolitical conflict.

In the Afterword, we discuss the chapters' collective contributions regarding how food-related communication in digital contexts accomplishes key social activities – among them circulating information, drawing social and cultural boundaries, and conveying political and activist stances – that are central to the construction of meanings, identities, and ideologies. We also take stock of recent developments in digital food discourse and related fields and map out directions for future research.

References

Anderson, Eugene N. (2014), *Everyone Eats: Understanding Food and Culture*, 2nd edn, New York: New York University Press.

Barton, David and Carmen Lee (2013), *Language Online: Investigating Digital Texts and Practices*, London: Routledge.

Blackburn, Kate G., Gamze Yilmaz and Ryan L. Boyd (2018), 'Food for Thought: Exploring How People Think and Talk about Food Online', *Appetite*, 123: 390–401.

Boerboom, Samuel, ed. (2015), *The Political Language of Food*, Lanham, MD: Lexington Books.

Brandt, Adam and Christopher Jenks (2011), '"Is it Okay to Eat a Dog in Korea ... Like China?" Assumptions of National Food-Eating Practices in Intercultural Interaction', *Language and Intercultural Communication*, 11(1): 41–58.

Bucholtz, Mary and Kira Hall (2005), 'Identity and Interaction: A Sociocultural Linguistic Approach', *Discourse Studies*, 7(4–5): 585–614.

Cavanaugh, Jillian R. and Kathleen C. Riley, eds. (2017), 'The Semiotics of Food-and-Language', Special Issue, *Semiotic Review*, 5. Available online: https://www.semioticreview.com/ojs/index.php/sr/issue/view/1.

Chik, Alice and Camilla Vásquez (2017), 'A Comparative Multimodal Analysis of Restaurant Reviews from Two Geographical Contexts', *Visual Communication*, 16(1): 3–26.

Chrzan, Janet and John Brett (2017), *Food Culture: Anthropology, Linguistics and Food Studies*, New York: Berghahn.

Cook, Guy (2004), *Genetically Modified Language: The Discourse of Arguments for GM Crops and Food*, New York: Routledge.

Diederich, Catherine (2015), *Sensory Adjectives in the Discourse of Food: A Frame-Semantic Approach to Language and Perception*, Amsterdam and Philadelphia: John Benjamins.

Diemer, Stefan, Marie-Louise Brunner and Selina Schmidt (2014), '"Like, Pasta, Pizza and Stuff" – New Trends in Online Food Discourse', *CuiZine: The Journal of Canadian Food Cultures*, 5(2). Available online: https://www.erudit.org/en/journals/cuizine/2014-v5-n2-cuizine01533/1026769ar/

Dominguez-Whitehead, Yasmine and Kevin A. Whitehead (2014), 'Food Talk: A Window into Inequality among University Students', *Text & Talk*, 34(1): 49–68.

Forchtner, Bernhard and Ana Tominc (2017), 'Kalashnikov and Cooking-Spoon: Neo-Nazism, Veganism and a Lifestyle Cooking Show on YouTube', *Food, Culture & Society*, 20(3): 415–441.

Frye, Joshua and Michael Bruner, eds. (2012), *The Rhetoric of Food: Discourse, Materiality, and Power*, New York: Routledge.

Gerhardt, Cornelia, Maximiliane Frobenius and Susanne Ley, eds. (2013), *Culinary Linguistics: The Chef's Special*, Amsterdam and Philadelphia: John Benjamins Publishing Company.

Gonçalves, Kellie (2013), '"Cooking Lunch, that's Swiss": Constructing Hybrid Identities Based on Socio-Cultural Practices', *Multilingua*, 32(4): 527–547.

Herring, Susan (2004), 'Computer-Mediated Discourse Analysis: An Approach to Researching Online Behavior', in Sasha Barab, Rob Kling and James H. Gray (eds), *Designing for Virtual Communities in the Service of Learning*, 338–376, New York: Cambridge University Press.

Herring, Susan (2013), 'Discourse in Web 2.0: Familiar, Reconfigured, and Emergent', in Deborah Tannen and Anna Marie Trester (eds), *Discourse 2.0: Language and New Media*, 1–25, Washington, DC: Georgetown University Press.

Humphreys, Ashlee (2016), *Social Media: Enduring Principles*, New York: Oxford University Press.

Jaworski, Adam and Crispin Thurlow (2009), 'Taking an Elitist Stance: Ideology and Discursive Production of Social Distinction', in Alexandra Jaffe (ed), *Stance: Sociolinguistic Perspectives*, 195–226, New York: Oxford University Press.

Jenkins, Henry, Sam Ford and Joshua Green (2013), *Spreadable Media: Creating Value and Meaning in a Networked Culture*, New York: New York University Press.

Jurafsky, Dan (2014), *The Language of Food: A Linguist Reads the Menu*, New York: W.W. Norton & Company.

Jurafsky, Dan, Victor Chahuneau, Bryan R. Routledge and Noah A. Smith (2014), 'Narrative Framing of Consumer Sentiment in Online Restaurant Reviews', *First Monday*, 19. Available online: http://firstmonday.org/ojs/index.php/fm/article/view/4944

Karrebæk, Martha Sif (2014), 'Rye Bread and Halal: Enregisterment of Food Practices in the Primary Classroom', *Language & Communication*, 34: 17–34.

Karrebæk, Martha Sif (2017), 'Pigs and Pork in Denmark: Meaning Change, Morality and Traditional Foods', Paper 230, *Working Papers in Urban Language & Literacies*. Available online: http://ku-dk.academia.edu/MarthaKarreb%C3%A6k

Kerner, Susanne, Cynthia Chou and Morten Warmind, eds. (2015), *Commensality: From Everyday Food to Feast*, London: Bloomsbury.

Kress, Gunther (2003), *Literacy in the New Media Age*, New York: Routledge.

Lavric, Eva and Carmen Konzett, eds. (2009), *Food and Language/ Sprache und Essen*, Frankfurt: Peter Lang.

LeBesco, Kathleen and Pater Naccarato, eds. (2018), *The Bloomsbury Handbook of Food and Popular Culture*, London: Bloomsbury Academic.

Locher, Miriam A., Brook Bolander and Nicole Höhn, eds. (2015), 'Relational Work in Facebook and Discussion Boards/Fora', Special Issue, *Pragmatics*, 21(1).

Machin, David and Theo van Leeuwen, eds. (2016), 'Multimodality, Politics and Ideology', Special Issue, *Journal of Language and Politics*, 15(3).

Martschukat, Jürgen and Bryant Simon, eds. (2017), *Food, Power, & Agency*, New York: Bloomsbury.

Nestle, Marion (2007), *Food Politics: How the Food Industry Influences Nutrition and Health*, Berkeley, CA: University of California Press.

Ochs, Elinor (1993), 'Constructing Social Identity: A Language Socialization Perspective', *Research on Language and Social Interaction*, 26(3): 287–306.

Ochs, Elinor, Clotilde Pontecorvo and Alessandra Fasulo (1996), 'Socializing taste', *Ethnos*, 61(1-2): 7–46.

Paarlberg, Robert (2013), *Food Politics: What Everyone Needs to Know*, 2nd edn, New York: Oxford University Press.

Page, Ruth, David Barton, Johann Wolfgang Unger and Michele Zappavigna (2014), *Researching Language and Social Media: A Student Guide*, New York: Routledge.

Pilcher, Jeffrey M., ed. (2012), *The Oxford Handbook of Food History*, New York: Oxford University Press.

Poulain, Jean-Pierre (2017), *The Sociology of Food: Eating and the Place of Food in Society*, trans. Augusta Dörr, New York: Bloomsbury.

Riley, Kathleen C. and Amy L. Paugh (2019), *Food and Language: Discourses and Foodways across Cultures*, New York: Routledge.

Rousseau, Signe (2012), *Food and Social Media: You Are What You Tweet*, Lanham, MD: AltaMira Press.

Schneider, Tanja, Karin Eli, Catherine Dolan and Stanley Ulijaszek, eds. (2018), *Digital Food Activism*, New York: Routledge.

Seargeant, Philip and Caroline Tagg, eds. (2014), *The Language of Social Media: Identity and Community on the Internet*, Basingstoke: Palgrave Macmillan.

Sneijder, Petra and Hedwig F.M. te Molder (2005), 'Moral Logic and Logical Morality: Attributions of Responsibility and Blame in Online Discourse on Veganism', *Discourse & Society*, 16(5):675–696.

Szatrowski, Polly E., ed. (2014), *Language and Food: Verbal and Nonverbal Experiences*. Amsterdam and Philadelphia: John Benjamins Publishing Company.

Tannen, Deborah and Anna Marie Trester, eds. (2013), *Discourse 2.0: Language and New Media*, Washington, DC: Georgetown University Press.

Thurlow, Crispin and Kristine Mroczek, eds. (2011), *Digital Discourse: Language in the New Media*, New York: Oxford University Press.

Vásquez, Camilla (2014), *The Discourse of Online Consumer Reviews*, London: Bloomsbury.

Vásquez, Camilla and Alice Chik (2015), '"I am not a foodie...": Culinary Capital in Online Reviews of Michelin Restaurants', *Food and Foodways*, 23(4): 231–250.

Vercelloni, Luca (2016), *The Invention of Taste: A Cultural Account of Desire, Delight and Disgust in Fashion, Food and Art*, trans. Kate Singleton, New York: Bloomsbury.

Wiggins, Sally (2013), 'The Social Life of "Eugh": Disgust as Assessment in Family Mealtimes', *British Journal of Social Psychology*, 52(3): 489–509.

Zappavigna, Michele (2013), *Discourse of Twitter and Social Media: How We Use Language to Create Affiliation on the Web*, New York: Bloomsbury.

Zappavigna, Michele (2014), 'CoffeeTweets: Bonding Around the Bean on Twitter', in Philip Seargeant and Caroline Tagg (eds), *The Language of Social Media: Identity and Community on the Internet*, 139–160, Basingstoke: Palgrave Macmillan.

Zappavigna, Michele (2018), *Searchable Talk: Hashtags and Social Media Metadiscourse*, New York: Bloomsbury.

Part One

Negotiating Individual Identities in Online Food Contexts

1

"Vegetables as a Chore": Constructing and Problematizing a "Picky Eater" Identity Online

Didem İkizoğlu and Cynthia Gordon

1 Introduction

Food and eating practices are loaded with symbolic, moral, and social meanings that are continually enacted and negotiated in everyday interactions, including those that occur in digital contexts. In this paper, we use computer-mediated discourse analysis (Herring 2004) to investigate posts from an online health and weight loss discussion forum where users seek and share advice about improving their diets. Specifically, we consider how posters create a "picky eater" identity for themselves (as well as for others), how they problematize this identity, and how they indicate their efforts to change their eating habits and move themselves out of this identity category. While there is no one definition of "picky eating," it is generally understood as restricting intake to some small set of familiar foods, and a lack of willingness to try new foods, as noted by Taylor et al. (2015) and Fish (2005), among others. Such studies also observe that "picky" or "fussy" eating is usually associated with children, for instance a toddler who refuses to eat vegetables and will only eat "beige food" such as noodles with butter, and point out that picky eating is considered a problem that needs to be overcome, both for children and adults. Kauer et al. (2015) found that adult picky eaters were more likely than non-picky adults to self-identify as unhealthy eaters, for example (though Taylor et al. 2015 note that little is known about the actual health outcomes of picky eating).

In addition to health and nutrition concerns, choices related to food and eating often take on social and moral dimensions: Studies have shown that healthy foods – such as the green vegetables, fish, and whole grains that many picky eaters avoid – are associated with higher incomes (Block, Scribner & DeSalvo 2004), higher levels of educational attainment (Darmon & Drenowski

2008), and affluence (Wills et al. 2011). Further, as pointed out by Sneijder and te Molder (2006) and Karrebæk (2012), making healthy food choices is a way of demonstrating rationality, morality, and self-control. We summarize the broad cultural ideology, or what Tannen (2008) calls a "master narrative," regarding adult picky eating as follows: Consuming a diet that consists predominantly of carbohydrates (e.g., white-flour-based baked goods, potatoes) and other bland foods (in color and/or flavor) is typically viewed as a problem that adults need to solve, and it can be solved through individual determination and active engagement. With this as a backdrop, it is not surprising that picky eaters might aim to change their dietary preferences, and therefore seek out advice and support online.

In this chapter, we examine five discussion threads that focus on adult picky eating that took place in an English-language online discussion board on a website affiliated with a popular weight-loss application (app) developed in the United States that we call "FriendInFitness" (or "FIF," as users often abbreviate the name). Our analysis demonstrates how posters construct their identities by claiming, to use Sacks's (1972, 1989) terms, the "membership category" label of "picky eater" and by invoking what he calls "category-bound activities," specifically the activities of eating some (limited set of) foods while avoiding others (notably, vegetables). To do this, posters use negation, modals (especially abilitative), and negative emotion verbs. Participants' descriptions of their strictly limited eating habits contribute to their problematizing of the picky eater identity in that they index master narratives about food and eating, especially the ideology that picky eating is expected of children but is not acceptable for adults. We also show how posters use discourse to imagine a transformation which involves a split of the current picky eater self and the desired rational self who will train the picky eater self to enjoy eating healthier and more diverse foods. To do this, they use reflexives, action verbs that presume a knowledge state difference between the agent and the patient, and the stacking of modals and modifiers to create a sense of "hyper hedging" that separates the poster's current self from the disliked foods, as well as the poster's current self from the desired reformed self.

In what follows, we first briefly review previous research on stances, acts, and identities, as well as research on self-transformation, including theorizing by Goffman (1971). Next, we introduce our data and methods in more detail. We then turn to the analysis, focusing on the creation of, problematizing of, and plans to escape the "picky eater" identity. In the conclusion, we address contributions our study makes to the study of food-related identities and ideologies online.

2 Background

2.1 Stances, acts, and identity categories

As Ochs (1992, 1993) demonstrates, interlocutors index identities in discourse by performing certain acts and taking up stances. She defines stance as a "display of a socially recognized point of view or attitude," which includes displays of certainty/uncertainty and intensity, as well as type of emotion or affect toward referents (1993: 288). Sacks's (1972, 1989) notion of membership categorization also links actions and identities. It highlights expectations people have regarding the actions performed by members of particular groups of people, or identity categories. For instance, in middle-class American culture (as in many cultures), it is expected that a person who belongs to a category of "mother" would comfort her crying baby. Thus, as Schegloff (2007: 470) describes it, by mentioning that some person engages in what Sacks calls a "category-bound activity" (such as comforting a crying baby), a speaker can "allude to" that person's category membership (such as "mother").

Previous research on the discourse of online support demonstrates that acts, stances, and membership categorization are important in online contexts and in regard to food. For example, Stommel and Koole (2010) show how, in order to attain membership in an online support group for people with eating disorders (most of whom are women in their study), a poster must display the point of view that she is ill; she cannot show alignment with people who glamorize disordered eating. Sneijder and te Molder (2009) demonstrate how posters in online discussions about veganism create their identities as vegans by defining vegan meals as ordinary and simple, and by constructing methods of avoiding vitamin deficiencies, such as taking supplements, as routine. In other words, they use language to "resist negative inferences about the vegan lifestyle" (Sneijder & te Molder 2009: 622), and engaging in this activity is part of what constitutes their identities as vegans.

In Gordon and İkizoğlu (2017), we draw on the concepts of membership categorization and stance to examine one thread (drawn from the same data source we use for the current analysis – a FriendInFitness discussion board). In this thread, the original poster asks for diet and health advice on behalf of her boyfriend (a phenomenon we refer to as "asking for another," following Schiffrin's 1993 notion of "speaking for another"). In how the original poster "asks for" her boyfriend in her opening post, she (inadvertently) evokes two identities that other posters to the thread comment on: The original poster is construed as a nagging mother-figure and her boyfriend as a childish victim of nagging. We demonstrate how two linguistic features in the original post index these identities. First, the original poster's uses of extreme case formulations (Pomerantz 1986), realized via adjectives and adverbs, lead others to orient to her as inappropriately controlling, and to her boyfriend as immature. Second, the details she provides about her boyfriend's diet, realized via nouns and adjectives pertaining to food and identity, link him to the category of "child" – she portrays him as a picky eater who eats items such as French fries, pancakes, plain crackers, and processed foods, while avoiding vegetables and fruit. The theme of gravitating to some foods while shunning others, and the utility of the notions of acts, stances, and membership categories in analyzing online identity construction, emerge in the threads we examine here as well.

2.2 Self transformation

As mentioned, some food-related communication involves a focus on transformation, such as changing ones' orientation to extreme calorie restriction and other unhealthy practices (e.g., Stommel & Koole 2010). One common way that people show that they have transformed is by apologizing, and we thus draw on Goffman's (1971) theorizing on this phenomenon. As Goffman notes, in issuing an apology, "an individual splits himself into two parts, the part that's guilty of an offense and the part that dissociates itself from the delict and affirms a belief in the offended rule" (1971: 113). In uttering something like, "I apologize," a woman for example splits herself as a new changed person (the "I" who issues the apology) from her past self (the "I" who misbehaved). Sidnell (2016: 2), who specifically emphasizes the idea of transformation in the context of food, uses the term "askesis" to refer to "the various techniques by which a person attempts to close the gap between what he or she is and what he or she hopes to be"; he also notes that "food choices and one's dietary regimen are seen as part of an *askesis* or set of exercises by which an individual seeks to effect various transformations." Indeed, numerous scholars have demonstrated how improving one's diet is discursively and multimodally constructed as creating not only a healthier, but also a more moral, and more upwardly social mobile, self. For example, Gordon's (2015) analysis of a family health makeover reality TV show demonstrates how the show's expert nutritionist's replacement of items from the families' diets like pizza and fried chicken with items like bok choy and smoked salmon simultaneously serves as a nutrition and health makeover and as a means of acculturating them toward middle-class values. Underlying reality shows like this one, as well as other food-related infotainment shows (see Declercq, Tulkens & Jacobs, this volume), and indeed an entire dieting and weight-loss industry (which includes diet apps like FriendInFitness and their discussion boards), is the idea that self-transformation when it comes to food consumption is both desirable and possible.

3 Data and Methods

The threads we analyze here are extracted from the health and nutrition discussion boards hosted by the application (app) we call FriendInFitness or FIF (in this chapter, we have changed the name of the app/website and use pseudonymous usernames; see Gordon forthcoming for an in-depth discussion of this decision). The app, which was founded in the United States in 2005, facilitates, through an individual smartphone- or computer-based "logging" function, users' recording of their food consumption (i.e., calorie intake) and exercise (i.e., calorie expenditure). The app, along with its accompanying website, which hosts message boards on topics such as "General Weight Loss and Diet Help," "Food and Nutrition," and "Motivation and Support," is freely available online. While many discussion threads on these boards focus specifically on weight loss, others also consider topics such as gaining weight, fitness and exercise, recipes, and even fun and games. Both the logging and discussion board components of FIF are similar to other popular weight-loss, health, and fitness apps, including SuperTracker and Lose It! The main site of FriendInFitness is in English, though discussion boards in other languages are also available. The threads we consider are drawn from the English-language "Food and Nutrition" board.

We draw broadly on Herring's (2004) computer-mediated discourse analysis to examine five individual discussion threads about picky eating. These five threads all use "picky eater" or "fussy eater" in their titles. The original posters name these threads "Picky eaters," "Help ... I hate veggies! Super picky eater!," "Extremely fussy eater," "any picky eaters out there?" and "Extreamly Adult Picky Eaters" (note that in these thread titles and in all of our data excerpts, grammar and spelling appear in the original). All of the threads showed activity in 2015 and/or 2016; the oldest thread ("Help ... I hate veggies! Super picky eater!") was started in 2012 and the newest ("any picky eaters out there?") was started in September 2016 and was active for only two days. The "Picky eaters," "Help ... I hate veggies! Super picky eater!," and "Extremely fussy eater" threads are composed of 31 posts each. The threads titled "any picky eaters out there?" and

"Extreamly Adult Picky Eaters" are 6 and 17 posts long respectively. In each thread, the original poster describes picky eating as a problem and asks for advice on how to change.

4 Analysis

4.1 Constructing and problematizing picky eater identities

We first show how the picky eater identity is constructed through direct identity claims. This occurs (1) when posters name the identity category of "picky eater" (or, less often, "fussy eater") and use it to refer to themselves and (2) when they categorize the foods into two groups based on whether they can or cannot eat them. They thus not only name their identity categorization explicitly, but also indicate the category-bound activities in which they engage. Specifically, they describe avoiding certain foods using the linguistic strategies of negation, modals (mainly abilitative), and verbs of emotion that index their negative affective stances toward such foods. Second, we discuss how the participants' descriptions of their strictly limited eating habits contribute to problematizing the picky eater identity by indexing master narratives about food and eating. This allows the participants to orient to picky eating as an issue that needs to be solved. Third, we demonstrate how the transformation process, changing from a picky eater into a person who can eat and appreciate a wider range of foods, especially healthy foods, is identified as one that requires effort, determination, and a splitting of the self, where the rational adult self takes control over the picky-eating self and re-trains that self to eat vegetables through strategies that include teaching, forcing, and tricking. We highlight how posters use reflexives, action verbs that assume a difference in the knowledge state between the agent and the patient, and stacking of modals and modifiers to create a sense of "hyper hedging," in order to create the split self that is required for transformation, as well as to distance the poster from the food that they are not yet willing or able to consume.

4.1.1 Constructing the picky eater identity through direct identity claims and category-bound activities

Participants create picky eater identities through direct identity claims and by indicating foods that they do and do not eat. By direct identity claims, we mean instances where participants explicitly refer to themselves as picky eaters. In membership categorization analysis literature, this is referred to as using "category labels" (Moerman 1988). Direct identity claims often occur at the very beginning of posts when participants introduce themselves. In the case of the original post (the post that initiates a thread), the claim is in the title of the post and is repeated in the post's body. Direct identity claims are usually supported and expanded by the other strategies, such as citing category-bound activities or indexing master narratives about picky eating. For instance, JonnaXD in the post titled "any picky eaters out there?" continues with "I am a very picky adult eater." A poster named xosarahduh opens her thread "Picky Eaters!" with "I am a super picky eater I.E. not a big fan of most fruits and veggies." Here she also uses the second strategy we identify – naming foods that she does not like (which we will discuss in more detail later). Soehlerking, in her response to previous posters who had discussed how they hate vegetables and gag when trying to eat them, states, "I have found my real family! My parents are convinced that my taste buds stopped developing at age 5." This identity claim is less direct – it does not use a label (though the use of the category labels "family" and "parents" are interesting, they are beyond the scope of the present chapter). Instead, soehlerking draws an alignment between herself and previously self-identified picky eaters who have expressed food avoidance. These posts also index wider cultural ideologies that link picky eating to something typically practiced by children, working to problematize this shared identity.

In addition to naming the identity category of "picky eater," posters also indicate category-bound activities that constitute it. The main category-bound activity that defines the picky eater identity is, not surprisingly, eating, but the object of this transitive verb is more significant than the verb itself in constructing the activity. Participants list the limited set of foods that they do eat, and emphasize that the list is exhaustive, thus indicating the severity of their situation. For instance, devilboy1592 notes "I'm 37 and I was a very picky eater, to the point where all I ate was hot dogs, burgers, waffles and Doritos 5 days a week, no water just Pop," providing a five-item list (of four foods and one beverage) that he claims constituted his entire diet. Echoing findings from our previous study (Gordon & İkizoğlu 2017), these preferences are stated in an extreme way ("all I ate"; "no"; "just") which heightens the seriousness of the situation. Another poster, ericbechtel, describes the picky-eating habits of other people: "I've had lots of girlfriends in my life who lived on the 'chicken finger' diet (Chicken fingers, french fries, ranch)." This again indicates extremely limited eating habits, consisting of consumption of fast-food menu items.

While posters name what they (or others) as picky eaters do eat, it is more frequent for them to name the foods that they do not eat (the term "cannot" or "can't" is often used). This practice is in line with how we defined picky eating at the beginning of this chapter; picky eating is mostly about restriction and avoidance (see also Gerhardt, this volume, on "ex negativo" understandings of taste). Various posts in the threads we examined illustrate this point. For instance, Kell1980 in the thread titled "Picky Eaters!" states "I have some absolute no's (uncooked meat as in sushi, just can't wrap my mind around it)." She uses the negative form "absolute no's" (and an extreme one in "absolute"), and a negative of the abilitative modal *can* as she describes her avoidance of sushi. Likewise, skinbeauty20 in the "Extremely fussy eater" thread reports, "I refuse to eat eggs, seafood, yogurt, and most fruits and veggies." Here she negates the action of eating using another strong verb, "refuse," and gives a list of things she does not eat. The list includes category-level items such as fruits and vegetables, which restrict her food options. She goes on to note that she ended up canceling a meal delivery service she had signed up for when she realized that "there was no way" she would eat "90% of what was on it"; describing this cancellation and in this manner emphasizes her level of food avoidance. Likewise, Colorscheme posts in the "any picky eaters out there?" thread, "I'm very picky. I won't eat veggies cooked, only raw except for potatoes. I also don't eat meat, and I cannot have eggs [I am allergic]." She uses "cannot" in a different way, to refer to a food allergy, but also indicates what she "won't" eat because she's "very picky."

In Colorscheme's post we also see that she differentiates between preparation methods, pointing out that she consumes vegetables only if they are raw. Preparation emerged in some of the other picky eaters' posts as well; for example, metropolisbean, in the thread "any picky eaters out there?" proclaims, "I have always hated broccoli rabe with a passion" but indicates a newly discovered ability to consume it if it is cooked in a particular way (being salted, briefly boiled, and then sauteed in garlic). While some posters emphasize preparation, others point out that they react to the texture of foods. For example, Nicole Stanton in the "Help ... I hate veggies! Super picky eater!" thread comments, "I've never been able to eat fruits or veggies or most whole grains. The texture gets me long before the taste does. I can eat something that tastes bad, I cannot for the life of me keep something down that is mushy, grainy, crunchy, or slimy." Other posters, such as guruonamou, prioritize taste: "I don't like many bitter flavours eg. most vegetables, dark chocolate, alcohol etc." Although different participants seem to have different restrictions and preferences, there are many overlaps. Table 1.1 below gives a snapshot of how posters categorize foods in these threads (as foods they do eat and do not eat) and provides the number of mentions of each food.

"Vegetables as a Chore"   21

Table 1.1 Foods that picky eaters report that they do eat and do not eat, by number of mentions

Foods they DO eat	Mentions	Foods they DO NOT eat
	26	(Raw/plain/steamed) veggies/vegetables
	7	Fruit
	6	Spinach; eggs
	5	(Plain/Greek) yogurt; (dark) meat (on a bone)
Chicken nuggets/tenders/fingers; Lays/chips/Doritos/crisps	4	(Leafy) greens; broccoli; carrots; tomato(es); onions; seafood; cauliflower; lettuce
Carrots (sticks or shaved); toast; corn; (plain/cheese) burger	3	Salad; mushrooms/fungus; avocado; (sugar) beets
(French) fries; crackers; (vanilla) ice cream; (canned) beans; (grilled) veggies	2	Brussels sprouts; asparagus; (dark) chocolate; cheese; chicken
Zucchini; pumpkin soup; sweet potatoes chili; soup; processed junk; eggs; cheese ravioli; salad; cheese; raw onions; tomato soup; mushy broccoli; canned green beans; carrots; potatoes; bananas; apples; chicken; macaroni and cheese; beige foods; popcorn; pasta; hot dogs; waffles; tacos with just meat and cheese; pancake; grilled cheese sandwich; chocolate cereal; milkshake, Greek yogurt; rolls; butter; pizza; tinned chicken; cauliflower; spinach; spaghetti squash; tuna salad; lettuce	1	Banana; broccoli rabe; radish; kale; corn; artichoke; peanut butter; alcohol; whole grains; olives; pickles; water; sweet potatoes; zucchini; pasta; steak; sausages; turkey; bacon; beef; pork; peppers; peas; grapefruit; mangoes; casseroles; kale; milk products

This table highlights how the "picky eater" identity is created in these threads primarily by declaring avoidance, especially of vegetables as a larger category (there are 26 mentions of "vegetables" and "veggies"), but also of types of vegetables (e.g., "greens" received 4 mentions), as well as specific vegetables (e.g., "spinach" was mentioned 6 times; and "beets" 3 times). With 7 mentions, fruit is also constructed as a broad category of avoidance. In contrast, the foods that picky eaters do eat are mentioned less frequently, with the most commonly mentioned items, processed chicken products and chips/crisps, receiving only 4 mentions each. French fries, crackers, and toast are among other foods that are mentioned more than once. Notably, these are "beige foods" that picky children often choose (e.g., Fish 2005).

The list of preferred and avoided foods listed in Table 1.1 gives a sense of the practices of picky eaters. However, this list is provided out of context. In some of the mentions of foods that picky eaters will eat, for instance, they are described as being discovered to be edible relatively late in life or only when they are prepared in very specific ways. It is thus also important to consider how exactly picky eaters situate these foods in their everyday lives, as reflected in longer extracts from their posts.

As posters describe their eating habits, they often list these food items using negation, modals (mainly abilitative), and verbs of emotion. Through these strategies, they index their strong affective stances towards these foods, which – according to them – basically make it impossible for them to consume such foods. Stephernie's post – "I'm pretty good about eating fruit, but really hate most veggies." – in the "Picky eaters!" thread illustrates the use of the prototypical affective verb "hate" (which is a very extreme verb). Likewise, Gotham Veggie writes, "I detest cauliflower when it is not cooked enough," illustrating a similar affective stance toward cauliflower. In another example, kim_mc, the original poster who started the "Help! I hate veggies! Super picky eater!" thread, notes, "I can't eat a piece of lettuce without gagging!" Here we see a modal relating to ability and a negative; "gagging" is also an affectively-laden verb as it implies disgust.

The use of the abilitative modal verb allows this poster and others to express their lack of flexibility in engaging in the action of eating certain foods. In other words, they cannot bring themselves to carry out the action of eating. As pointed out by Enfield (2017), lack of flexibility is correlated with lack of accountability. That is, not eating these foods is framed not as a choice made by these posters, but as the result of something that is beyond their control. (This notion will become more significant in the third section of the analysis, where we discuss how picky eaters conceptualize a split sense of self as they discuss improving their diets.) In response to kim_mc's thread-starting post indicating she "can't" eat even a piece of lettuce, LBachynsky observes, "You are my veggie hating twin!!! I can count on one hand the veggies I will eat. Lettuce ruins everything for me and I can't continue eating." She thus aligns with the original poster through her use of the emotion verb "hate" and her use of abilitative modal verb marked with negation (she "can't" continue eating). In the same thread, RonanByrne observes, "Lettuce was one thing I couldn't face," expressing negative affect towards lettuce using the same strategies of abilitative modal verb combined with negative marking. In addition to the modal marking of this sentence, the verb "face" expresses the negative, confrontational nature of the picky eater's encounter with the hated vegetable (we typically "face" our fears and our enemies, but not our successes and our positive relationships). The sustained negative affective stance toward foods is represented as a confrontational relationship by other users as well. Gotham Veggie, in the "any picky eaters out there?" thread, explains, "My mortal enemy, the radish also recently surprised me," humorously personifying the vegetable while describing learning to appreciate it.

To sum up, in this section we have discussed the strategies used by the posters to construct themselves as picky eaters. These strategies include naming the membership category explicitly by referring to themselves as picky eaters, and by describing the primary category-bound activity that characterizes picky eaters (eating a very limited set of foods and avoiding a multitude of foods, particularly vegetables). In constructing this category-bound activity, they list the food items they do and do not eat in ways that emphasize the small number and narrow variety of edible foods and the vastness of the restricted foods, and they take up highly negative affective stances toward foods through the use of modal verbs, negation, and affective verbs and modifiers; some posters also use personification. As participants emphasize the foods they do not eat and express their stances toward them, they pave the way for problematizing their eating habits. We discuss how this takes place in the next section.

4.1.2 Problematizing the picky eater identity

As we have shown, picky eating is constructed in the discussion threads we examine primarily through discourse about the inability to eat particular foods (which are negatively evaluated). We now turn to how posters construct picky eating as a problem that needs to be overcome. When original posters begin their threads and ask for advice and support, they are necessarily problematizing their current "picky" identities and practices. The thread posted in the Food and Nutrition board titled "Help … I hate veggies! Super picky eater!" started by kim_mc, as shown below, is a case in point.

> **Excerpt (1)**
> I want to eat veggies so bad! I am jealous of people that can fill their plates with veggies and eat all that food for such low cals and all kinds of healthy vitamins!
>
> I have hated veggies all my life and I'm a super picky eater!

After several sentences (already discussed) wherein kim_mc describes how she "can't eat a piece of lettuce without gagging," she explains how she avoids salads and crunchy foods, and then closes her post with, "So does anybody have any suggestions or is anyone a picky eater like me? Is [if] so, what do you do????".

This poster problematizes her eating practices and asks for help incorporating vegetables into her diet. Her main concern is to limit her calorie intake (a common preoccupation of users of the discussion boards) while at the same time consuming more foods and increasing the nutritional value of what she consumes, which she expresses is possible with a vegetable-rich diet. This constructs picky eating as a potential health problem. Indeed, posters who respond to calls for help like the one from kim_mc also describe picky eating as a problem. This is especially the case with people who report being former picky eaters. In the "any picky eaters out there?" thread, newlaofofbread joins the discussion and introduces herself as follows: "I'm a recovering picky eater, yes, it DOES get easier eventually." She thus orients to picky eating as a disorder that takes time and effort to manage and surmount (her use of "recovering picky eater" can be intertextually linked to the common phrase "recovering alcoholic").

In addition to highlighting caloric and nutritional concerns, posts about being an adult picky eater also problematize the identity in more indirect ways that index the master narrative that adults should not be picky eaters (and that picky eating is childish). As mentioned in the previous sections, the foods picky eaters commonly eat index child identities, and the foods they avoid index adult and healthy eater identities. In the "Picky Eaters!" thread, brandonharri responds to that original poster's call for help:

Excerpt (2)
I'm also a super picky eater. My wife accuses me of eating like a 4 year old. That's probably a big part of why I'm overweight, though. I tend to skip the salad when we're out to eat somewhere and go straight for the rolls and butter and my entre is normally fried chicken tenders and fries with loads of ketchup and bbq sauce. Delicious.

...

As an adult picky eater trying to eat better than I have in the past 33 years, I've Googled so many variations of "healthy foods for picky eaters". The results I find are mostly "How to hide healthy foods in your kids' meals" or "put the veggies on a stick, kids love eating things off a stick". If not pointed at picky five year olds, it's someone on a forum saying "suck it up and eat your veggies," and that's not really helpful at all.

Here, brandonharri paraphrases what his wife has told him (that he eats "like a 4 year old"), which serves to explicitly connect his picky eater identity and the identity of a young child. In using the term "accused," he indirectly suggests that his picky eating may be a thorny issue in their relationship. He illustrates the point that he is a childlike and "super picky" eater by providing an example of a food that he avoids (salad, often associated with adult tastes) and listing the children's foods that he prefers (rolls, butter, fried chicken tenders, fries, ketchup and barbecue sauce), which predominantly are beige foods. In these ways, brandonharri evokes the ideology that picky eating is children's practice, and is not appropriate for adults. He mentions that his online searches to find information about how to address his picky eating yielded results that target kids and were not helpful (indeed, scholarly research has only recently begun to consider adult picky eating, as noted by Thompson et al. 2015). In part, brandonharri's searches may be motivated by the fact that he links picky eating to his being "overweight." They also serve as evidence of the ideology that picky eating can be overcome.

Similar to brandonharri's response to the original poster in the "Picky eaters!" thread, soehlerking, in responding to kim_mc's post in "Help . . . I hate veggies! Super picky eater!" makes the point that, "My parents are convinced that my taste buds stopped developing at age 5. Let me know if you figure out some way of not seeing vegetables as a chore!" This too connects the picky eater and child identities, and also indicates a need for transforming dietary habits. The act of eating vegetables, referred to here as "a chore," indexes both the poster's moral stance towards eating healthful foods and especially vegetables (these are things one must eat as an obligation) and, perhaps more indirectly, the child identity (chores are imposed upon children by their parents). Here healthy eating is imposed upon the picky eater by herself, which brings us to the phenomenon we explore in the next section: Posters construct a split self, which is a strategy that is required for reform and change.

In summary, posters, once they construct a picky eater identity for themselves, approach this identity as a problem that needs to be solved. They do this by describing the problems picky eating is reportedly causing them in terms of health (missing certain nutrients and being overweight), relationships (with loved ones identifying their eating as abnormal), and by appealing to the master narrative that picky eating is not acceptable for adults. Their asking for advice to change their ways contributes to the construction of picky eating as a problem.

4.2 Transforming self from picky eater to healthy eater

Similar to the users of many support boards on the FIF website, including those for weight loss, health, and exercise, the picky-eating posters whose discourse we examine seek to improve and change. As indicated by previous work by Goffman (1971) and Sidnell (2016), negotiating and demonstrating a transformation is based on splitting the self as the current reformed, or wanting-to-reform, agent (who claims the transformation) and the past misbehaving self (who is forced, tricked, or socialized into this transformation). We have seen in the previous section that the picky eater self is described as guided not by reason but by impulsive and uncontrollable reactions caused by particular foods. In this section we will see that this self is grammatically separated from the rational self who wants to reform; this splitting is brought into discourse through reflexives and through the stacking of verbs.

It should be noted that a common strategy used by parents to get their picky-eating young children to eat vegetables and other healthy foods is to "hide" these healthy foods in familiar dishes. This is evidenced, for instance, by the New York Times Bestseller, *The Sneaky Chef: Simple Strategies for Hiding Healthy Foods in Kids' Favorite Meals*, by Missy Chase Lapine, and by brandonharri's mention in his post that his internet searches about picky eating resulted in hits such as "How to hide healthy foods in your kids' meals" (as was shown in Excerpt 2). In a parallel way, adult picky eaters who aim to self-reform separate the self who wants to change from the self who is a picky eater.

This split is observed in the methods the picky eaters use to overcome their problem and the linguistic means they use to describe these methods. A very common way of linguistically showing this sense of split self is describing the measures that the reasonable self will carry out using transitive verbs, where the agentive subject is expressed with "I" and the picky-eating self is expressed with the reflexive pronoun "myself" as the direct object of the sentence. For example, in the "Extremely fussy eater" thread, one woman observes that she got used to plain (rather than highly sweetened) yogurt after "One week of 'forcing' myself to have plain greek yogurt in the morning with fresh fruit." She continues, "I now prefer it over the sweetened kind with more calories and sugar." In this extract, the self that wants to transform forces the picky-eating self to eat something different, and the picky-eating self comes to comply. Similarly, in the "any picky eaters out there?" thread, the original poster explains, "I've tried to 'teach' myself not to be" a picky eater. The verb "teach" inherently involves two people, where one person is presumably superior to the other in terms of knowledge and skills (in Sacks's 1972, 1989 terms, as Schegloff 2007 explains, this constitutes a collection of categories, or categories that "go together" – teacher and student). In this case, the superior one is the rational self, who knows better about what and how to eat. A similar formulation of this phenomenon is observed in a post by the former picky eater minmolk in "Help . . . I hate veggies! Super picky eater!" where he advises his fellow picky eaters to "Take the time to train yourself and stop thinking of yourself as picky. That's treating yourself like a child, your an adult and you can take a little bit of discomfort to reap benifits." Here again, the poster invokes the master narrative that suggests picky eating is for children. He also describes the transformation as a process that takes time and effort, which can be undertaken by rational adults. Issuing an imperative, minmolk indicates that the adult self needs to "train" the picky-eating self. Another post that illustrates the use of reflexives is where Ronanbyrne remarks that in trying to overcome picky eating, "I had to remind myself to add new things and keep increasing the serving sizes of things had already tried." Here the self that wants to change is "reminding" the picky eater self, which again implies that the child-like picky eater self forgets or ignores previously made decisions, and indicates that the rational self, mentally and/or morally superior, needs to take on this task.

Another way of expressing reflexivity between the agentive and rational self and the impulsive picky eater self is to describe solutions that involve "tricking" the picky eater self into eating certain foods. These posts reinforce that the rational self knows, plans, and acts, while the picky eater self responds to physical stimuli, i.e., the tastes and textures of foods. For example, in the "Help! I hate veggies! Super picky eater!" thread, katsmo explains, "I would try sneaking things in here and there like drinking a glass of V8 [vegetable juice] (Diet V8 Splash is actually really good) or throwing a handful of spinach or avocado into a smoothie. Slip in a serving or two of veggies that way." A poster named smallsunflower125 posts, "You can try creating recipes that hide the veggies (you can puree them into just about any recipe, and hide their taste and texture)." Likewise, Gotham Veggie remarks, "I've also found that I can blend things into a smoothie that I don't like (like a number of leafy greens & blueberries) with fruits I do like & yogurt to make a wonderful drink." In these examples, the reflexivity does not show as a pronoun, but instead is implied (e.g., "You can try creating recipes that hide the veggies" has an implied "from yourself" that is not explicitly stated). Here too, the self who wants to reform, acting separately from the picky eater self, will "slip in," "puree," or "blend," the desired healthy food into something else in order to "sneak" and "hide" its taste or texture.

Verb stacking is the second strategy that contributes to the splitting of selves that is required for self-transformation. This serves as an iconic separation between the two selves – it linguistically (and, onscreen, visually) distances the subject "I" and the desired act (our use of bold font below draws attention to this separation). It also creates a greater distance between the "I" who wants to change and the problematic food item. Verb stacking also seems to function as a kind of "hyper hedging," minimizing any accountability that the picky eater might create by expressing a plan to change. In line with this, this is a strategy that is mainly used by current picky eaters, rather those who are "recovered" or "in recovery." For example, a poster to the "Help I hate veggies" thread explains, "I understand that there are some things you just can't learn to like no matter how you try. I **would love to be able** to eat bananas." Notice the distance between "I" who wants to change and the "I" who will eat bananas – the verbal elements "would," "love," and "be able" separate the two. This also creates a great deal of distance between the "I" who wants to change and the bananas themselves. In these ways, there is a weakening of the expressed commitment to actually eating bananas. Another poster in the same thread indicates, "I **may have to start** trying the whole 'food processor mash of veggies snuck into food' thing." In addition to constructing a rational self who wants to reform using the "sneaking" strategy to fool the picky-eating self, we see a separation between the "I" that wants to reform and the actual eating practice, as well as a weak commitment on the part of the picky eater self. Instead of, for example, using the "will" and stating, "I will try the whole 'food processor mash of veggies snuck into food' thing," the poster uses "may have to start." A poster to the "Extremely fussy eater" thread likewise observes "I**'ve been working on overcoming** my tendency to reject unfamiliar greens out of hand"; the stacking here distances the picky-eating "I" from the "I" who is reforming and no longer rejecting leafy green vegetables. In these examples too the verbs create iconic distance between the "I" who wants to transform and the foods ("veggies" and "unfamiliar greens").

In summary, we have shown that picky eaters describe the process of surmounting picky eating as one that requires a splitting of the self into two: A current (childlike) picky eater who acts in the form of impulsive reactions based on perception of taste and texture of foods, and a more adult self who has helped, or will help, the picky eater self to overcome the eating problem through reason, determination, and, where necessary, manipulation. This split is reflected in how the posters use language. Specifically, as they describe the strategies for overcoming picky eating, they use reflexive constructions where the agentive (adult) self is in the subject position and the picky eater (childlike) self is in the direct object position, which assume a split in terms of knowledge between the mentioned selves: The agentive self knows what to do and tricks the picky eater self into eating healthy foods by hiding those foods in other foods. We also observed in posts by current picky eaters a stacking of verbal constructions that renders a hyper hedging effect. This minimizes accountability for actually implementing the required changes to the diet and creates iconic distance between the current picky-eating self who wants to change and the action – and challenging foods – that will transform the problematic self into the desired self.

5 Conclusion

We have shown how a "picky eater" identity is constructed and problematized in five online food and nutrition discussion threads initiated by adults seeking advice regarding how to reform their picky-eating practices. We have demonstrated how the membership category of "picky eater" is evoked directly by bringing up the category label, and by mentioning the primary category-bound activities of group members – avoiding (and discursively taking up negative affective stances toward) many healthy foods (notably vegetables and leafy greens) that previous research suggests carry with them associations of maturity and affluence, while expressing preference for what have been commonly recognized as "beige" and childlike foods. Strategies involved in this include negation (because for picky eaters what they restrict is more defining than what they actually eat), modals (mainly abilitatives that indicate that restricting food is not a choice but a matter of inability to consume it), and verbs of emotion (that denote the poster's negative affective stance toward the rejected foods). In evoking a picky eater identity, the identity of "child" is also indexed, both directly and indirectly. This contributes to the "picky eater" identity being problematized; the master narrative, or ideology that is evoked, is that eating this way is inappropriate for adults, and that they can and should fix the problem. Indeed, that and how these posters turned to the discussion boards is undergirded by the idea that picky eating is a problem to be overcome, and for reasons that are both nutritional and social. Lastly, via reflexives and the stacking of verbs, the posters manifest a splitting of the self that is required for transformation. This iconically marks the distance between the current self and the desired future self who is no longer a picky-eating adult; it also distances the current self from the presently unpalatable foods.

These findings contribute to our understanding of the discursive strategies and linguistic features used by online forum participants to accomplish food-related identity work, thus complementing and extending existing research on online communication among various types of eaters, such as vegans (e.g., Sneijder & te Molder 2004; Gerhardt, this volume), people interested in weight loss (e.g.,

Gordon forthcoming), and people who experience disordered eating (e.g., Stommel & Koole 2010). It highlights how food avoidance figures centrally into picky eaters' identities, which echoes Bourdieu's (1984) observation that asserting taste for all eaters is accomplished in large part by refusal (see also Gerhardt, this volume). In addition, our study identifies online discussion boards as an important site for producing and reifying food-related ideologies. Specifically, it sheds light onto how ideological connections are discursively made between members of a category of people who interact online and the foods they avoid, and what these connections mean: There are different expectations regarding how adults versus children should eat; there are ways to eat that are more mature, healthful, moral, and socially acceptable than others; and individual eaters are expected to plan, act, and transform according to these ideologies.

Acknowledgments

The authors thank Alla Tovares for her feedback on our chapter. This study also benefitted from comments by audience members at IPrA 2017 in Belfast, Northern Ireland, as well as by other presenters who were part of the "Food for Thought and Social Action" panel. We appreciate feedback on our early ideas from members of the InLab data workshopping group in Georgetown University's Department of Linguistics.

References

Block, Jason P., Richard A. Scribner and Karen B. DeSalvo (2004), 'Fast Food, Race/Ethnicity, and Income', *American Journal of Preventive Medicine*, 27(3): 211–217.

Bourdieu, Pierre (1984), *Distinction: A Social Critique of the Judgement of Taste*, Cambridge: Harvard University Press.

Darmon, Nicole and Adam Drewnowski (2008), 'Does Social Class Predict Diet Quality?', *American Journal of Clinical Nutrition*, 87(5): 1107–1117.

Enfield, Nick J. (2017), 'Elements of Agency', in Nick J. Enfield and Paul Kockelman (eds), *Distributed Agency*, 3–8, New York: Oxford University Press.

Fish, Donna (2005), *Take the Fight out of Food: How to Prevent and Solve Your Child's Eating Problems: For Children Aged Nine Months to Nine Years*, New York: Atria Books.

Goffman, Erving (1971), *Relations in Public: Microstudies of the Social Order*, London: Allen Lane.

Gordon, Cynthia (forthcoming), Intertextuality 2.0: Metadiscourse and Meaning-Making in Online Weight Loss Discussion Boards.

Gordon, Cynthia (2015), '"We were Introduced to Foods I Never Even Heard of": Parents as Consumers on Reality Television', in Anne Teresa Demo, Jennifer L. Borda, and Charlotte H. Kroløkke (eds), *The Motherhood Business: Consumption, Communication, and Privilege*, 95–120, Tuscaloosa: University of Alabama Press.

Gordon, Cynthia and Didem İkizoğlu (2017), '"Asking for Another" Online: Membership Categorization and Identity Construction on a Food and Nutrition Discussion Board', *Discourse Studies*, 19(3): 253–271.

Herring, Susan C. (2004), 'Computer-Mediated Discourse Analysis: An Approach to Researching Online Behavior', in Sasha Barab, Rob Kling and James H. Gray (eds), *Designing for Virtual Communities in the Service of Learning*, 338–376, New York: Cambridge University Press.

Karrebæk, Martha Sif (2012), '"What's in Your Lunch Box Today?" Health, Respectability, and Ethnicity in the Primary Classroom', *Journal of Linguistic Anthropology*, 22(1): 1–22.

Kauer, Jane, Marcia L. Pelchat, Paul Rozin and Hanah F. Zickgraf (2015), 'Adult Picky Eating. Phenomenology, Taste Sensitivity, and Psychological Correlates', *Appetite*, 90(1): 219–228.

Moerman, Michael (1988), *Talking Culture: Ethnography and Conversation Analysis*, Philadelphia: University of Pennsylvania Press.

Ochs, Elinor (1992), 'Indexing Gender', in Alessandro Duranti and Charles Goodwin (eds), *Rethinking Context: Language as an Interactive Phenomenon*, 335–358, Cambridge: Cambridge University Press.

Ochs, Elinor (1993), 'Constructing Social Identity: A Language Socialization Perspective', *Research on Language and Social Interaction*, 26(3): 287–306.

Pomerantz, Anita (1986), 'Extreme Case Formulations: A Way of Legitimizing Claims', Human Studies, 9: 219–229.

Sacks, Harvey (1972), 'On the Analyzability of Stories by Children', in John J. Gumperz and Dell Hymes (eds), *Directions in Sociolinguistics: The Ethnography of Communication*, 325–345, New York: Holt, Rinehart and Winston.

Sacks, Harvey (1989), 'Lecture Six: The MIR Membership Categorization Device', *Human Studies*, 12(3): 271–281.

Schegloff, Emanuel A. (2007), 'A Tutorial on Membership Categorization', *Journal of Pragmatics*, 39(3): 462–482.

Schiffrin, Deborah (1993), '"Speaking for Another" in Sociolinguistic Interviews: Alignments, Identities, and Frames', in Deborah Tannen (ed), *Framing in Discourse*, 231–255, New York: Oxford University Press.

Sidnell, Jack (2016), 'Askesis and the Ethics of Eating at a Yoga School in South India', Gastronomy, Culture, and the Arts: A Scholarly Exchange of Epic Proportions Proceedings, 1–22. Available online: http://library2.utm.utoronto.ca/italianopentext/content/session-41-askesis-and-ethics-eating-yoga-school-south-india

Sneijder, Petra and Hedwig F. M. te Molder (2004), '"Health Should not Have to Be a Problem": Talking Health and Accountability in an Internet Forum on Veganism', *Journal of Health Psychology,* 9(4): 599–616.

Sneijder, Petra and Hedwig F. M. te Molder (2006), 'Disputing Taste: Food Pleasure as an Achievement in Interaction', *Appetite,* 46(1): 107–116.

Sneijder, Petra and Hedwig F. M. te Molder (2009), 'Normalizing Ideological Food Choice and Eating Practices: Identity Work in Online Discussions on Veganism', *Appetite,* 52(3): 621–630.

Stommel, Wyke and Tom Koole (2010), 'The Online Support Group as a Community: A Micro-Analysis of the Interaction with a New Member', *Discourse Studies,* 12(3): 357–378.

Tannen, Deborah (2008), '"We're Never Been Close, We're Very Different": Three Narrative Types in Sister Discourse', *Narrative Inquiry,* 18(2): 206–229.

Taylor, Caroline M, Susan M. Wernimont, Kate Northstone and Pauline M. Emmett (2015), 'Picky/Fussy Eating in Children: Review of Definitions, Assessment, Prevalence and Dietary Intakes', *Appetite,* 95: 349–359.

Thompson, Claire, Steven Cummins, Tim Brown and Rosemary Kyle (2015), 'What Does It Mean to Be a "Picky Eater"? A Qualitative Study of Food Related Practices and Identities', *Appetite,* 84: 235–239.

Wills, Wendy, Kathryn Backett-Milburn, Mei-Li Roberts and Julia Lawton (2011), 'The Framing of Social Class Distinctions Through Family Food and Eating Practices', *The Sociological Review,* 59(4): 725–740.

2

The Multidimensionality of Eating in Contemporary Information Society: A Corpus-based Discourse Analysis of Online Audience Reactions to a TV Show About Food

Jana Declercq, Stéphan Tulkens, and Geert Jacobs

1 Introduction

Food plays a central role in human life; it is essential to survive, but also fulfils a plethora of social functions. According to McIntosh (1996: 3), "many relationships between individuals are created and maintained by food"; food choices reflect and construct ethical, cultural and religious ideas, personal memories and preferences, financial considerations, and peer pressure (McIntosh 1996; Niva 2007; Deliens et al. 2014). For example, Alba (1990) found that for self-identified "white ethnics," i.e., Americans with European ancestry such as Italians or Poles, food was the primary way to reconstruct and confirm their ethnic identity. Food was even more important than using phrases from the language of their heritage, or upholding customs and traditions. Food products can also be symbols for certain countries or regions, like lobster for Maine in the United States (McIntosh 1996). Additionally, certain types of food serve as symbols of wealth as they construct social and economic prestige, like red meat (Macdiarmid, Douglas & Campbell 2016). At the same time, (red) meat is avoided by some for health or religious reasons, or because of concerns for animal rights and the environment.

In this regard, health and nutrition increasingly become key considerations in food choices. Coveney (2000: 1) points out that nutrition, or the science of food and eating

> serves as the basis for many of the judgements we make about ourselves and others as eaters. That is to say, the moral decisions we make of ourselves (as 'good' or 'bad') are directly related to the technical and rational knowledge of science.

Being healthy is seen as an individual responsibility today; consequently, there is a strong moral imperative to live healthily (Clarke et al. 2003; Niva 2007; Declercq 2018). As eating is seen as a primary gateway to healthy living, attention to healthy eating has increased in public spheres (Conrad & Barker 2010; Declercq 2018).

Food thus fulfils wide-ranging roles, and consequently "consumer food culture is immensely complex, being multidimensional and constantly changing: food patterns, tastes and beliefs are now in a permanent state of transition; existing and older food cultures are semi-permanently under assault" (Lang & Heasman 2004: 186). This trend is also strengthened by that fact that, in Western societies, food is cheap and easily accessible for many consumers (Lang & Heasman 2004), and food options have multiplied. Consequently, what we eat has become diversified and personal, and food becomes a site for identity work, endowed with symbolic meaning (Stringfellow et al. 2013). For instance, identities as a health vegetarian (Fox & Ward 2008), or as a food lover (Bisogni et al. 2002), and group dynamics among adolescents, in which healthy eating is seen as "uncool" (Stead et al. 2011), all have become pervasive aspects of our lifestyle.

This chapter examines how audiences cope with the complex multidimensionality of food and eating. We analyze how social media users react to information from an infotainment TV show about food – more specifically about health, nutrition, and food production – aired by Belgium's Dutch-language public broadcaster. We focus on how audiences react to information broadcast on this TV show for three reasons, because of 1) the currently persistent need of consumers for more information on food, 2) the central role of TV and media in this dissemination of knowledge, and 3) the multidimensional take on food in the program. Each argument will be discussed more in-depth below.

First, according to Verbeke (2008: 281), "consumers seem to want information to help them derive more pleasure from food, to achieve a better diet, to avoid certain allergens or to know the origin and environmental, ethical and technological conditions under which the food has been produced and processed." Verbeke's (2008) observation ties in with in Webster's (2006) more general concept of the information society. Webster (2006) argues that, first, because of technological and economic changes, information in general has become a central part of our lives. It is an increasingly important cornerstone of many economies, and thus has become a commodity. Additionally, information is easily accessible via new technologies and media, and has become a lot more important in our social circulation and cultural lives. Consequently, information on (almost) anything is more ubiquitous than ever, including on food, and it is an important aspect of our lives.

Second, more specifically, television played, and still plays, an important role as one of the first impactful contributors to the information society, making information widely available. However, TV does more than just distributing information; it sets the agenda, frames issues, directs public debate and influences policy (e.g., Harcup 2015; Declercq 2018). TV also fulfils these roles in relation to food; the amount of food-related television has risen in Western societies since the beginning of the twenty-first century (de Solier 2005; Phillipov 2013). For every dimension of food and eating, there are specific TV formats: for tasting and cooking (Phillipov 2013), such as *Master Chef*; for slimming and dieting (Sukhan 2012), such as *The Last 10 Pounds Bootcamp*; for exploring new cultures and food traditions (Stringfellow et al. 2013), such as Jamie Oliver's *Jamie's Great Italian Escape*. Food is mediagenic and newsworthy, and TV and other legacy media have strongly contributed to the mediatization of food. In doing so, TV has produced, and still produces, impactful normative ideas of good eating (Eskjær 2013).

At the same time, the way the public watches television has undergone changes as it is now increasingly engaged in online dialogue; viewers discuss TV content online, both live and after broadcasting, by (live) tweeting, posting on a broadcaster's or program's Facebook page, in Facebook groups, in Instagram stories and posts, and so on. We are therefore interested in how food-related social media content is produced in dialogue with traditional media content.

Finally, the TV show that we focus on provides an interesting case to study the dialogue between TV and social media content because the show discusses a wide range of food dimensions, but evidently still is selective in what aspects are highlighted and how they are framed. Reactively produced content can provide insights into how audiences engage with these frames and highlights, whether they reproduce or add to these, and/or whether they bring in other considerations and dimensions than those discussed in the show. It shows how the audience participates in knowledge production about food in contemporary information societies. In our analysis, we focus on the public's take on this multidimensionality of food discourses in our information society. Instead of analyzing one or two dimensions of food, as often happens in research, we show that multiple dimensions are entangled in complex ways, how they compete with one another, and how they need to be understood as such.

In the next section, we will discuss the bottom-up corpus-based discourse analysis methodology we used to learn more about how audiences deal with the show's discourse on food.

2 Methodology

2.1 Data set and context

The show under scrutiny was a primetime infotainment show produced by Belgium's Dutch-language broadcasting channel, one whose main aim was to inform a broad audience about health and nutrition, food production and marketing. The show combined an entertaining style with elements from watchdog journalism, focusing on fact-checking and revealing potentially controversial issues relating to food and nutrition. The season consisted of eight 45-minute episodes, including five elements: 1) a health-focused story, focusing on nutritional aspects of a type of food, like smoothies; 2) a day in the life of a celebrity, focusing on their food choices; 3) a visual rendition of the entire production process of certain foods, showing the process played backwards, for instance of black pudding; 4) a segment on the production or marketing of food, for instance on children's marketing, and, when relevant, consequences for one's health; and 5) a quiz question on food.

For the study presented here we look at tweets and Facebook reactions posted during the broadcasting of the season in March–June 2016 (starting 6 weeks before the first episode and 6 days after the last episode). The tweets were collected by mining all tweets with the show's hashtag; Facebook reactions were collected on the show's official page, underneath videos and posts from the editors. In the case of Twitter, we collected tweets through an exhaustive search of the show's hashtag on the Twitter website, and then programmatically extracted tweets from the search results. After data collection, we manually removed unrelated tweets, for example from Twitter bots, resulting in a final set of 1,181 tweets. Facebook data were collected using the Pattern Python Package (De Smedt & Daelemans 2012). We scraped all posts from the page and extracted all comments and replies to comments. This resulted in a set of 4,787 comments. We collected 44,662 words of Facebook data and 15,000 words of Twitter data, resulting in a total of 59,662 words.

The show was in Dutch, and the social media data set is mainly in Dutch too. However, as all varieties of Dutch have an extensive tradition of borrowing from English in a range of contexts and genres, such as instant messaging (Lettinga, Wijk & Broeder 2017), and in reality TV (Zenner, Speelman & Geeraerts 2015), the data set also contains a number of English words and expressions, such as "omg." A limited number of reactions were in foreign languages, which were removed from the data set.

2.2 Data preparation and analysis

This analysis draws on corpus-based discourse analysis, or corpus-assisted discourse studies (CADS) (Baker 2010; Partington, Duguid & Taylor 2013; Hunt & Harvey 2015). CADS is an approach that combines corpus linguistics and discourse analysis techniques. Corpus approaches allow for systematically detecting trends in big bodies of data. In CADS, the primary techniques are keyness analyses and the analysis of dispersion, collocation, and concordances. In a keyness analysis, the most frequent words of the corpus under scrutiny are compared to the most frequent words in a more general corpus, which is called the reference corpus, to examine which words occur significantly more in the corpus under analysis. The trends in the keyness analysis are further explored by analyzing how words are distributed in a text (dispersion); which and how words co-occur frequently (collocations); and how words appear in context, by manually looking at the strings of words in which they occur (concordances). In CADS approaches, these corpus findings are further contextualized by a detailed qualitative discourse analysis of a set of selected examples.

For this CADS, the Antconc software package was used (Anthony 2018). As a reference corpus, we used the Twitter subset of the *Sonar* new media corpus (Oostdijk et al. 2013). This 2011–2012 Dutch-language corpus consists of tweets submitted by Twitter users themselves, as well as tweets that the researchers collected themselves. This corpus thus is a social media corpus, but not topic-specific, and therefore allows for proper comparison with our corpus, which is a topic-specific social media corpus. Of the total of 23,197,211 tokens, we randomly sampled the first 10,000 tweets, resulting in a set of 74,608 tokens.

Several preprocessing steps were applied. Punctuation was removed to ensure tokens were recognized properly, except for combinations of punctuation markers that make up emoticons, such as ;) or :(. To make sure that emoji renderings of emoticons (like " ") were recognized as the same token, we converted both emoji and emoticons to their shortcodes. We ensured that the shortcodes were not recognized as separate words by removing spaces in the shortcodes. After a preliminary keyness analysis, certain items in the list of keywords were found to be alternative spellings for high-frequency words, like "da" for "dat" (*this*) and "gwn" for "gewoon" (*just*). As such variation is not of interest in this study, we normalized these forms to their standard forms. Similarly, we normalized all expressions of laughter, such as "hahah," "hahahah," to a uniform "haha."

3 Analysis

To learn more about the trends in the main corpus in a bottom-up fashion, we started with a keyness analysis (see Table 2.1). We used the log-likelihood ratio test with an alpha of p<.05, corrected for multiple comparisons using Bonferroni correction, which yielded a list of 141 keywords, i.e., words that occur significantly more in our corpus than in the reference corpus. In what follows, relevant trends within the top 20 (when relevant extended to top 30) of this keyword list will be analyzed. Several keywords were excluded from the analysis, for various reasons. First, the top keyword is the name of the show, which was also used as the hashtag. Similarly, numbers 6, 10 and 13 are the presenters' names. The concordances of these items showed that these occurrences are mainly audience members tagging the presenters, or that these reactions discussed the presenters' appearance and language; they are therefore also not further discussed. Keyword 18 "el" is a common particle of surnames of people that were tagged, and therefore also excluded. We will focus on the remaining words in this top 20, which are clustered in three sections: 1) eating healthily, 2) eating animals, and 3) the emotions of eating, in which we analyze the use of emoji in the data. This bottom-up approach takes the analysis into different directions, but it is exactly this approach that allows for uncovering the complex, multidimensional nature of the food discourses in our data set.

3.1 Eating healthily

A first relevant keyword is "gezond" (*healthy*) (25), as it explicitly refers to a specific dimension of eating. It occurs 75 times; however, a combined search of all forms of the adjective "gezond" (*healthy*) and the noun "gezondheid" (*health*) yields a higher number of occurrences, specifically, 131. Talking about health does not always entail using these words, so the keyword list cannot tell us how big the share of health-related social media reactions actually is. However, it provides a first indication that it is a dimension of eating that the audience is interested in and likes being informed about. Audience members sometimes just used the word in reactions such as "niet gezond dus" ("*so not healthy*"), sometimes tagging a friend, which points to the fact that the health aspect as such raised their interest and was considered relevant enough to share with a friend. A number of reactions containing the words "gezond(heid)" (*health(y)*) also show that health is a primary consideration for consumers (see excerpt 1).

Table 2.1 Top 30 keywords of the keyness analysis

Rank	Frequency	Keyness	Effect	Keyword Dutch	Translation (when relevant)
1	1179	1908.4	0.039	[showname]	
2	533	771.42	0.0178	😄	
3	322	506.14	0.0108	Fristi	Fristi (the brand name of a yogurt drink)
4	185	297.66	0.0062	😵	
5	260	254.53	0.0087	eten	to eat/food
6	143	230.03	0.0048	presenter	
7	141	183.79	0.0047	Eet	eat
8	113	181.74	0.0038	😐	
9	111	178.52	0.0037	😷	
10	102	164.04	0.0034	[presenter]	
11	369	161.11	0.0123	meer	more
12	111	154.33	0.0037	vlees	meat
13	93	149.56	0.0031	[presenter]	
14	127	126.27	0.0043	programma	program/show
15	161	125.99	0.0054	nooit	never
16	81	120.63	0.0027	suiker	sugar
17	84	112.53	0.0028	drink	drink
18	72	106.39	0.0024	El	
19	70	103.23	0.0024	fruit	fruit
20	98	99.34	0.0033	drinken	to drink/drink (plural form)
21	66	96.91	0.0022	omg	
22	58	93.25	0.002	luizen	lice
23	58	93.25	0.002	vegan	vegan
24	53	85.21	0.0018	😖	
25	67	81.69	0.0023	gezond	health(il)y
26	49	78.78	0.0017	😕	
27	60	75.91	0.002	😊	
28	47	75.56	0.0016	😄	
29	45	72.35	0.0015	voeding	food
30	44	70.74	0.0015	😳	

(1) A segment in the show explained that smoothies are not as healthy as often believed, because of high sugar levels and lack of fiber. A twitter user tweets this in response:

en ik maar denken dat ik gezond bezig was met mijn smoothies . . . #hashtagshow
and I was thinking I was being healthy drinking smoothies . . . #hashtagshow

The users express their disappointment when discovering that certain food choices motivated by health concerns turn out to be ineffective. The reactions also reflect the show's ambition to reveal information that audiences do not know but do want to know, and which is potentially shocking.

The concordances of this keyword also show audience members may have been intrinsically interested already in healthy eating before watching the show. In some reactions, they act as informed consumers who make authoritative statements and add extra insights about food and health:

(2) The smoothie item is also discussed on Facebook, to which one user adds:

Inderdaad smoothie is geen dieetproduct, maar wel nog steeds veel gezonder dan fris- of sportdrank.
True smoothies are not a dieting product, but still a lot healthier than fizzy or sports drinks.

This audience member agrees that smoothies are unhealthy, but assertively adds that they are still healthier than other drinks, adding to the perspective that the show offers. Users often add information themselves, sometimes in a less mild tone than the previous example:

(3) A Twitter user reacts to a quiz segment in which potatoes, quinoa, rice, and pasta need be ranked from fewest to most calories:

#hashtagshow Glycemische index aardappelen veel hoger dan quinoa, belangrijker dan calorieën. #vergetentemelden #zonde
#hashtagshow glycaemic index [of] potatoes is a lot higher than [of] quinoa, more important than calories. #forgottomentionthat #shame

This example adds information and at the same time critiques the show for being incomplete and not highlighting what is really important: the glycemic index of food. In doing so, the user seems to internalize and invoke the program's logic of revealing important and shocking information, with the hashtags at the end.

The examples above show that we live in an information society: Audiences seem to be, or act like they are, well-informed, or ask questions to become more well-informed. They use social media to look for and provide extra information. This is also confirmed by the fact that the most common collocate of health is "is" (*is*). The concordances in this case show people discuss what is (not) healthy, in factual, assertive statements, or questions.

However, although this keyword is interesting in terms of how the audience deals with one specific dimension, it does not show how different dimensions intersect. The following section looks at trends in the data relating to eating animals, and explores the multidimensional discussion of this topic.

3.2 Eating animals

3.2.1 *Eating meat in general*

"Vlees" (*meat*) is keyword 12 in the list (Table 2.1), and the concordances show that it is discussed in different ways; audience members bring up many aspects of eating meat, sometimes in the same (short) reaction. In what follows, we will list the dimensions that we found and explore them more in-depth with qualitative analysis of the concordances.

First, meat is discussed in terms of the health benefits of (not) eating it:

(4) In the show, a segment compared the number of calories and amount of fat in meat burgers and in veggie burgers. On the Facebook page, a movie clip of this segment was posted with the caption "Did you know meat substitutes are ten times fattier than normal meat?" to which a Facebook user reacts:

> en alle antibiotica in vlees? Die dan niet in veggie burgers zit?
> **and all of the antibiotics in meat? That veggie burgers don't contain?**

The user argues that healthy eating is not just about counting calories, but also avoiding food that contains harmful substances such as antibiotics, which are often present in meat. S/he highlights how even one specific dimension of food, i.e., health, is multidimensional and complex. Because of the multiple effects of food on many systems in our body, the answer to the question what healthy eating is, depends on many factors and, to a certain extent, personal priorities. The user also again adds information that is often constructed as shocking, following the show's practice to reveal information of such kind.

Second, eating meat is discussed in terms of ethics. More specifically, audience members discuss why eating meat is (un)acceptable from an animal rights perspective, and for environmental reasons. The following examples combine both considerations, constructing opposite arguments. Both examples are reactions to a segment in which a vegan celebrity was followed for a day, focusing on his food choices. Several movie clips of this segment were posted on the show's Facebook page. Under this post, a long discussion on eating meat ensued, such as:

(5)

> *Wat is er extreem aan een levensstijl die zo min mogelijk leed wil veroorzaken? Daar zou ik nu eens heel graag een antwoord op krijgen. En nee, je kan geen vlees eten en tegelijk goed zijn voor het milieu. Vleesproductie is de allergrootste oorzaak van milieuproblemen wereldwijd. Nog nooit Cowspiracy gezien?!*
> **What's so extreme about a lifestyle that wants to cause as little suffering as possible? I would love to hear an answer to that. And no, you can't eat meat and be good for the environment. Meat production is the biggest-ever cause of environmental problems globally. Have you never seen Cowspiracy?!**

In this example, the user advocates for a vegan lifestyle, combining several ethical subdimensions: animal suffering and the environment. The rhetorical question ("What's so extreme . . .") ventriloquizes an earlier reaction in which another user argued against "vegan extremists" and their "tendency" to impose their ideas on others. In her/his reaction, s/he thus questions whether arguing for less suffering is really that extreme. The "and no, you can't eat meat" ventriloquizes earlier reactions on environmental aspects of eating meat, answering the question whether meat is always bad for the environment. To make the claim more credible, s/he refers to the popular 2014 documentary, *Cowspiracy*, on animal agriculture and its impact on water use, deforestation, and greenhouse gas emissions.

In the following example, both dimensions are discussed as well, but with opposite conclusions:

(6)

> *Ik zou oppassen want fruit en groenten leven ook en doe je deze dan niet dood? Het zal mij een worst wezen,ik blijf genieten van mijn stukje vlees of vis. Zelfs eieren eten ze niet. Weet je wat vervuild? De industrie en overbevolking. [. . .] Ieder zijn ding en mijn ding blijft vlees eten.*
> **I'd be careful because fruit and vegetables are alive too and don't you kill those too? I don't care, I still enjoy my piece of meat or fish. Even eggs they don't eat. You know what is polluting? The industry and overpopulation. [. . .] to each his own, I keep eating meat.**

This user compares eating meat to eating plants, questioning whether there is a difference in the extent to which these organisms are alive and can be killed, to argue against the importance of animal suffering in food choices. The environmental aspect is addressed by saying that there are other causes of pollution than agriculture, implying that these are greater problems. Finally, an appeal to the idea of freedom of choice is made in the last sentence, in the "to each his own" phrase.

In this Facebook thread, ethical considerations thus are often combined, as is also the case in the following example:

(7)

> *Voor mij gaat er niets boven heerlijk grasgevoerd vlees. Heel gezond en ook milieuvriendelijk. Daar hoef je ook geen regenwoud voor te kappen.*
> **For me there's nothing better than delicious grass-fed meat. Very healthy and also environmentally friendly. For that you don't need to chop down rainforests.**

In this example, an ethical compromise is proposed; grass-fed meat is put forward as both a healthier and more sustainable alternative to industrially produced meat. Possibly, it is also considered a more humane form of animal agriculture, as the animals are not in stables when grass-fed.

Finally, meat is discussed in terms of taste and texture, and how personal preferences in relation to these aspects impact consumption, as well as how it intersects with other considerations. Meat eaters argue they miss the taste of meat, while vegan and vegetarians argue plant-based eating is the tastiest:

(8)

> *nooit vlees! Niets zo lekker als volledig plantaardig!*
> **never meat! Completely plant-based is the tastiest!**

These examples show that not only several ethical subdimensions are combined dynamically, but that other dimensions such as taste also appear in primarily ethical discussions. Audience members thus rationalize their choices in discussions on (not) eating meat by focusing on different aspects of the complex interplay between different dimensions of (not) eating meat.

The focus on ethics in our data also is particularly relevant as both animal suffering and the environment were never a topic in the TV show; veganism was only briefly explained in the celebrity item discussed above, and environmental concerns were only briefly addressed in two segments on vegetarianism. The arguments on antibiotics or grass-fed meat in the online reactions were not featured in the show. Audience members actively add information about many dimensions, including dimensions that are not discussed in the show, echoing wide-ranging ideologies on food, for instance on vegetarianism (Fox & Ward 2008). This is also apparent in the next section, in which trends on eating specific animals are discussed.

3.2.2 Eating specific animals: rabbits, lambs, and insects

Online discussions about eating rabbit, lamb, and insects reveal another set of considerations to evaluate eating animals. These discussions are almost always reactions to the weekly segment on how food is produced, including often graphic images of animals such as rabbits and lambs being butchered. For this analysis, we considered the tokens "konijn" (*rabbit*) and "lam" (*lamb*) in our corpus. The terms occur 75 times, and are usually accompanied by discussions on whether audience members will keep eating, or no longer eat rabbit and/or lamb meat, as in the following example:

> (9) A Twitter user live tweets when seeing the segment on how rabbit meat is produced:
>
> *daarom eet ik geen konijn met kippen heb ik wel geen medelijden #hashtagshow*
> **that's why I don't eat rabbit with chickens I have no compassion though**

The audience member says s/he does not eat rabbits, but explicitly adds s/he has no compassion for chickens. It is unclear whether s/he aims to be critical of her/his own categorization, but the comparison as such shows that there is at least an awareness of a categorization from which different eating patterns follow. Some audience members more clearly categorize rabbits as "cute," and as pets:

> (10) A Twitter user live tweets the following when seeing the segment on how rabbit meat is produced:
>
> *shit die konijnen seg ik had ooit ook een wit exemplaar #rip #hashtagshow*
> **shit those rabbits you know I once had my own white one #rip**

This audience member struggles with the double categorization of rabbits as both pets and food. Using the hashtag #rip (rest in peace), s/he expresses grief over the death of her/his own rabbit pet and/or the rabbits that are butchered in

The Multidimensionality of Eating in Contemporary Information Society 45

the show, assigning the anthropomorphic status of a loved one to the rabbit(s). The same is illustrated by the following example:

(11) In a reaction to a Facebook posts that contains the TV show's segment on the production of rabbit meat, a Facebook user reacts:

van lamsburger naar lam, eet geen dieren laat staan babies.
from lamb patty to lamb, don't eat animals let alone babies.

The term "baby" (*baby*) again is anthropomorphic, and personifies the lamb(s). This person considers eating young animals to be an even stronger offence than eating fully grown animals, much like how we culturally evaluate harming human babies worse than harming adults.

This pattern clearly shows that eating, and more specifically eating meat, is multidimensional. There are general ethical, environmental, health, and taste concerns, but also more specific cultural imperatives, constructions, and categories that come into play. These are sometimes much more emotional and, for instance, relate to categories of animals as pets, animals as food, and animals as pests, the aggravating circumstances of harming anything or anyone who is still an infant or child, and personal memories of pets.

The multidimensionality of eating animals becomes even more complex when further examining the word *Fristi*, number 2 in our keyword list (Table 2.1). Fristi is a milk-based, strawberry-flavored yogurt drink, sold in Belgium and the Netherlands. The TV show featured a segment about carmine, a red colorant that is widely used in food, such as in candy and this yogurt drink. Carmine is derived from the cochineal, a small insect. In Dutch, this translates as "cochinelleluis," which literally can be broken down as *cochineal louse*. This explains why "luizen" (*lice*) is keyword 22 in the keyness list.

Fristi was used as the prime example of carmine use in the show. The segment was, like many, constructed as a shocking reveal. It first featured one of the presenters opening a pot that was full of dead cochineal, followed by close-ups of the insects. Back in the studio, the other presenter squeezed one of the lice until the liquid colorant was released, after which he tried to put some of the bright red colorant on the face of the co-presenter, which made her scream. This was followed by an interview with the spokesperson of the Belgian consumer protection organization, who puts the use of carmine in perspective by saying that, while it was safe health-wise, it is also "a bit consumer fraud," as consumers expect the color comes from the strawberries. During the interview, one of the presenters said that "basically people are drinking lice juice without even knowing."

Table 2.2 Top 10 collocations with the word "fristi/Fristi"

Rank	Frequency	Statistic	Collocate	Translation (when relevant)
1	89	5.47218	meer	more
2	76	3.56484	Ik	I
3	75	4.69475	😂	😂
4	59	5.08916	geen	no/none
5	57	6.02590	nooit	never
6	42	3.02446	dat	that
7	38	4.80031	nog	still
8	37	3.18071	van	of
9	36	5.10140	lekker	tasty
10	33	5.95361	drinken	drink

The show thus framed consuming carmine, and eating insects, as disgusting and slightly fraudulent, and the information as shocking. To explore how the audience reacted to this, we analyzed the collocates of the word "fristi," i.e., which words co-occur most frequently in the five words right before and after each occurrence of "fristi." Table 2.2 list shows the top 10 collocates.

The collocates confirm that the framing of insects in Fristi as shocking resonated with the audience. The most frequent collocate is "meer" (*more*), which is almost exclusively used in the construction "I drink nooit **meer** fristi" (*I'm never drinking fristi* **anymore**), like in this example:

(12) Facebook user:

> *omg gatverrr nou kan k geen fristi drinken* 😱😱
> **omg dammit now I can't drink fristi anymore** 😱😱

The audience member uses the modal "kan" (*can*) to clarify that the new information about carmine makes it impossible for him/her to continue to consume Fristi. In line with this, people use the word "durven" (*to dare*), saying they don't *dare* to drink it anymore, or use it in constructions to challenge friends that they address on Facebook by tagging them. Because of the carmine, drinking Fristi becomes a challenge or even a frightening action. Audience members also express that they are happy they do not like or (hardly ever) drink it, such as this one:

(13) Facebook user:

> *wauuuuwwww gelukkig drink ik geen fristi*
> **wowwwwww fortunately I don't drink fristi**

The collocates "geen" (*no/none*), "nooit" (*never*) serve the same purpose as above and are used in reactions in which audience members say they will change their behavior. The second keyword is "ik" (*I*); the concordances show that this word again is used in reflection on behavior and the individual choice to no longer drink Fristi.

When audience members state they will keep drinking it, they almost always do it in constructions like this one:

(14) Facebook user:

> *net bekeken. k ga toch fristi blijven drinken mmm lekker*
> **just watched it. I'm still going to keep drinking fristi mmmm tasty**

Audience members express that despite the information about carmine, they will still consume it. However, the linguistic structure in the words "toch" (*still*) and "blijven" (*to keep/keeping*) shows that the information about carmine has the potential to change that point of view, but that they decided against actually making the change, as they will keep consuming it.

These examples show that the Fristi segment elicits a lot of reactions of disgust and reactions in which users discuss what to do in terms of Fristi consumption. In sum, both in the show and on social media, eating insects – especially when being tricked into doing so – is considered problematic. This is a culturally determined point of view: In many parts of the world, insects are a common source of protein. Interestingly, there are no occurrences in the corpus in which users discuss *why* consuming insects is problematic. The ethical aspect of killing insects is never raised, and eating insects is not seen as problematic because insects are considered cute or pet animals. Rather, insects are not attractive as food. Similarly, the health benefits or risks of eating insects never emerge in the data set, while previous research and our findings point to the importance of health imperatives in food choices.

Our analysis thus confirms, as also argued by Sealey and Charles (2013), that we construct different categories for insects and mammals, and that these classifications have different consequences for how we treat and view certain animals. In our data, the categorization is clear: Eating meat from mammals like cows is generally seen as pleasurable, although it requires reflection because of health, environmental, and animal rights. Eating insects is generally problematic because insects are unattractive as a food and can even ruin pleasurable consumption of food, for instance in the case of insect-based colorants. These trends point to two important findings: First, they show that audiences find it important to be informed about their food, and to be knowledgeable about the ingredients. Second, the data confirm that eating is multidimensional not only because of considerations that are directly and commonly associated with eating, such as health and sustainability, but also because it is entangled with broad social and cultural considerations, in this case which animals we consider to be food, pets, or vermin. In line with this, we see differentiated ways of how the audience deals with these dimensions. The discussions on meat are rational and complex, often debating different ethical aspects of meat-eating; in the case of Fristi and lambs and rabbits, the tone is more emotional, and the content mainly explores (dealing with) disgust. This brings us to the final trend in our keyness list: the abundant use of emojis. In the following section, we analyze the emojis that are used in the corpus to further explore the emotional aspects of eating.

3.3 The emotions of eating

A final dominant trend in the keyness list (Table 2.1) are the emoji and emoticons in the data set. The keyword top 30 contains 9 emoji/emoticons, of which 4 are in the top 10. These emoji are further explored in Table 2.3, in which the three left columns list the emoji/emoticons that appear in the top 30, while the right column provides an overview of the emotions, and phrases or words (indicated by quotation marks in the table) that these emoji are commonly associated with, as found in studies that performed corpus analyses of social media corpora, or that surveyed and questioned users about their associations.

There are several methodological reasons beyond our specific data set that can account for the prominence of (certain) emoji/emoticons in the list. In general, our corpus contains more emoji/emoticons (4.7 percent of all tokens) than the reference corpus (1.2 percent of all tokens). This has a twofold explanation. First, our reference corpus only consists of tweets, and does not contain Facebook data.[1] In our corpus, the number of emoji/emoticons is higher in the Facebook subcorpus (5.5 percent of all tokens) than in our Twitter subcorpus (2 percent). Emoji/emoticons thus seem to be used more on Facebook. And as our reference corpus only consists of Twitter data, the high keyness of emojis can be partly attributed to differences in medium.

However, when comparing these to the emoji/emoticons in the keyness list, we see a more specific trend in emoji/emoticon use in our corpus. The next

Table 2.3 The top emoji/emoticons from the top 30 keyness list. The list contains both Twitter and Facebook rendering of emoji, as emoji are different across platforms

#	Shortcode	Twitter	Facebook	Associated with (as found in literature)
2	Face with tears of joy			Distress, surprise, laughter (Miller et al. 2016); tears of joy, surprise (Annamalai & Salam 2017); happy, excited (Jaeger & Ares 2017)
4	Face screaming in fear			Terrified, scared, shocked, screaming (Annamalai & Salam 2017); surprised/shocked, scared/afraid (Jaeger & Ares 2017)
8	Face with medical mask			Sick, fever, having flu (Annamalai & Salam 2017)
9	Loudly crying face			Omfg, lmao, crying (Barbieri, Ronzano & Saggion 2016); crying, loudly crying (Annamalai & Salam 2017); grief/sorrow/distress/pain, sad, frustrated (Jaeger & Ares 2017)
24	Weary face			Tired, lazy, regret, irritated, weary, annoyed (Annamalai & Salam 2017); grief/sorrow/distress/pain, sad, frustrated, disappointed, depressed (Jaeger & Ares 2017)
26	Fearful face			Surprised, shocked, worried, nervous, scared (Annamalai & Salam 2017)
27	Flushed face			"Dying," "wtf," "nooo," "noo," "lmaooo" (Barbieri et al. 2016); surprised, flushed, shocked (Annamalai & Salam 2017); surprised, shocked (Jaeger & Ares 2017)
28	Beaming face with smiling eyes			Laugh, happy, feeling awesome, feeling good (Annamalai & Salam 2017); happy, excited, content/satisfied, pleasure, good (Jaeger & Ares 2017)
30	Crying face			"Ugh," "sad," "stomach," "miss," "nooooo" (Barbieri et al. 2016); crying (Annamalai & Salam 2017); grief/sorrow/distress/pain (Jaeger & Ares 2017)

section shows that the audience used emojis/emoticons in our corpus mostly to express negative emotions, such as disgust, fear, surprise and shock, which is unusual for social media and specifically for food discourses on social media, as argued below, but which matches the framing of the show.

The interpretation of emoji/emoticons can be challenging as their meanings are subject to change, various interpretation and misconstrual, and personal appropriations (Kelly & Watts 2015; Miller et al. 2016; Miller et al. 2017). In the case of emoji, this is partly because emoji are sometimes rendered differently across platforms (Miller et al. 2016) (see Table 2.3). However, there still is consensus on the lexical meaning and pragmatic use of most emoji/emoticons. Table 2.3 shows that almost all emojis/emoticons in our list are used and interpreted negatively, except for *face with tears of joy* 😂 (2) and *beaming face with smiling eyes* 😁 (28). The others are all unambiguously attributed meanings that relate to negative emotions, such as sadness, fear, disgust, and feeling shocked. The *face with tears of joy* emoji 😂 is a special case here, as this emoji is found to be ambiguous (Miller et al. 2016): It can mean or index distress or negative emotions, as well as indicating that something is funny or surprising. To find out how the emoji is mainly used in the specific context in our corpus, we looked at the collocates of this emoji in our data. First, the collocates indicate the emoji is often used several times in a row, as the main collocate is the emoji itself. Second, users most frequently mobilize it to express something to be funny, as collocate "haha" shows (113 occurrences). The second most frequent collocate is "ik" (*I*) (94 occurrences), and again, the concordances show that this "ik" (*I*) is often used to report on the author's behavior. More precisely, the audience member discusses what he or she luckily did not consume, does not want to consume anymore, or will keep consuming although there are potential reasons for not doing so. The following examples are all reactions to the information on carmine as a colorant in Fristi:

(15) Facebook user:

haha wat ben ik blij dat ik dat echt niet lust 😂
haha I am so happy I don't eat that 😂

(16) Facebook user:

ik ga dood denk ik 😂 *ik ben echt kapot bang voor insecten* 🐛
I'm dying I think 😂 **I am crazy scared of insects** 🐛

(17) Facebook user:

ieuwww ik drink dat zo graag 😩
ewww I love drinking that 😩

In these concordances, the more contextual use and meaning of both the emoji and the collocate "haha" becomes clear: Although both can have a positive meaning and use, it is associated with a positive feeling (such as relief) about something negative, or it expresses the nervous laughter that comes with surprise and distress.

In short, although interpreting emoji/emoticons requires tentativeness, most emoji/emoticons in our keyword list express negative emotions, such as fear, sadness, disgust, and shock. This trend of audience members expressing disgust is confirmed by a search for words that typically express disgust in Dutch such as "ieuw" *(eww)*, "bah," and "bweuk" *(yuck, eww)*. There are 158 occurrences of these words and their spelling variations. Because of the spelling variation, these tokens do not show up in the keyword list (Table 2.1). In contrast, the reference corpus contains 6 instances of these tokens expressing disgust. Moreover, the Facebook and Twitter corpora combined only contain 47 word tokens used to express that something is tasty, such as "mmm" (and all variations), and "yummie."

However, other research shows that both in general for emoji use on social media (Novak et al. 2015; Ljubešić & Fišer 2016), and also specifically when Twitter users discuss food (Vidal, Ares & Jaeger 2016), emoji/emoticons tend to have positive meanings and/or add positive sentiment. For food-related tweets, Vidal, Ares and Jaeger (2016) found that emoji usually highlight hedonistic aspects of eating, of savoring good food (often in good company). The negative sentiments that the emoji/emoticons are associated with in our sample thus contradict this general trend, showing that the specific context of the show elicits different reactions to food than those usually produced on social media. This suggests that the framing of the information on food in the show as controversial resonates with the audience. The information on food creates tensions and/or negative emotions, as it foregrounds aspects of eating that go against the hedonistic, pleasurable sentiment that is usually associated with publicly available discussions on food and eating on Twitter and Facebook.

Interestingly, the negative emotions do not apply to every aspect of the data set. As part of the exploration of the top 20 keywords, we analyzed the use of the word "programma" *(program/show)* (number 14; 127 occurrences). The collocates show a number of positive words that were used frequently, such as "super" (*great*) (17 occurrences), "goed" (*good*) (21), "interessant" (*interesting*) (13), and "leuk" (*fun*) (13). To ensure these words were not used in combination with any form of negation, or in an ironic sense, all 127 occurrences of the word programma/program were manually coded for positive evaluation, negative evaluation, and no evaluation. Out of 127 occurrences, 21 were not evaluative. Of 106 evaluative occurrences of the word program, 15 were negative (11.8 percent), while 91 were positive (85.9 percent). This analysis shows that audience members tend to evaluate the show positively on social media. Interpreting these findings requires caution as the number of evaluations is limited, but it is a striking trend in relation to the trends described above. Even though the audience members find the information on the show difficult to digest, they do seem to appreciate being informed. This suggests that they like to learn more about food, and to be informed.

This tension can be accounted for in two ways. First, many television shows center around being, and liking to be, shocked (Biltereyst 2004; Gordon 2011). This was also the aim of the show under investigation, as discussed above, which seems successful in this regard. Second, as a result of the multidimensional nature of eating in information societies, audiences face competing interests and motivations in eating. They want to be well-informed, rational consumers on the one hand, but are also surrounded with pervasive cultural, social and psychological considerations on eating, and the emotions associated with them.

4 Conclusion

This chapter investigated online discourses of eating in the context of audience social media reactions to a TV show about food to explore how audiences deal with the multidimensionality of food, and (new) information about these dimensions. Our data point to several trends. First, our study confirms that (the discourse on) eating is highly multidimensional, and that this creates tensions for consumers. This multidimensionality has multiple levels: Some dimensions are primarily and explicitly associated with eating, such as taste, health, and the ethics of environmental damage and killing animals. Sections 3.1–3.2 show that audiences are interested in in-depth discussions and extensive information on these dimensions. However, other cultural imperatives come into play that do not relate only to eating, but, for instance, to how societies categorize animals as food or pets. Despite the tensions these create, the audience shows a pro-active engagement to add information, and to contribute to informing each other. This increases the multidimensionality of the discourses on food and indicates how important audience members find participating in the information society as they tend to bring in new and/or more complex arguments and considerations.

At the same time, audiences also struggle with this multidimensionality and its tensions. For instance, in the Fristi case, the audience generally does not want to consume insect-derived products, but for those who like Fristi, the taste consideration can overrule their apprehension, or even disgust. The tense intersection of some dimensions is also confirmed by our emoji analysis. It showed that much of the actual information on the show is associated with emotions of shock, disgust, sadness, and fear, and that changing behaviors because of these tensions and emotions is a frequent topic of discussion in the data set.

Second, our analysis shows that some dimensions are approached rationally, reflexively, and persuasively in complex discussions, but that the audience sometimes responds mainly emotionally to (information on) certain dimensions. This is accounted for by the fact that our corpus consists of reactions to a consumer television show in which segments are often constructed to be shocking, and to impact behavior. This seems to work, as the audience often expresses shock, and discusses their consumption of certain foods.

Finally, our analysis shows that online discourses need to be understood in context, and more specifically in the context of the discourses they react to. Like any discourse, online discourses entextualize and mobilize other (mediated) discourses (Angermuller 2012), in our case the TV show discourses. Sometimes, audiences follow how information is framed, but they also add new elements, build on it, and produce counterdiscourses. In the case of looking at social media data that topicalize current affairs, it is important to consider how these topics have recently been discussed by traditional media. This is relevant even when the relation between the social media post and the traditional media content is less direct than in our case, for instance in the case of migration discourses, or discourses on big mediatized events such as Brexit. As mentioned above, traditional media continue to play an important role in our society as agenda-setters, framers, directing public debate and influencing policy (Harcup 2015; Declercq 2018). Although online discourses are growing in scope and prominence and deserve proper attention in academia, it is worth exploring whether certain trends can be explained more in-depth by comparing them with discourses on the same topic that are produced by traditional media.

Notes

1 There is no Dutch corpus of Facebook discourse, and for reasons of privacy and public availability, composing one is not feasible.

References

Alba, Richard (1990), *Ethnic Identity: The Transformation of White America*, New Haven: Yale University Press.

Angermuller, Johannes (2012), 'Fixing Meaning: The Many Voices of the Post-liberal Hegemony in Russia', *Journal of Language and Politics*, 11(1): 115–134, https://doi.org/10.1075/jlp.11.1.06ang.

Annamalai, Subashini and Sobihatun Nur Abdul Salam (2017), 'Undergraduates' Interpretation on WhatsApp Smiley Emoji', *Jurnal Komunikasi, Malaysian Journal of Communication*, 33(4): 89–103, https://doi.org/10.17576/JKMJC-2017-3304-06.

Anthony, Laurence (2018), *Antconc Version 3.5.6. [Computer Software]*, Tokyo, Waseda University.

Baker, Paul (2010), *Sociolinguistics and Corpus Linguistics*, Edinburgh: Edinburgh University Press.

Barbieri, Francesco, Francesco Ronzano and Horacio Saggion (2016), 'What Does this Emoji Mean? A Vector Space Skip-Gram Model for Twitter Emojis', *Proceedings of Language Resources and Evaluation Conference*, 3967–3972, https://doi.org/10.12011/1000-6788(2016)07-1744-09.

Biltereyst, Daniel (2004), 'Media Audiences and the Game of Controversy: On Reality TV, Moral Panic and Controversial Media Stories', *Journal of Media Practice*, 5(1): 7–24, https://doi.org/10.1386/jmpr.5.1.7/0.

Bisogni, Carole A., Margaret Connors, Carol M. Devine and Jeffery Sobal (2002), 'Who We Are and How We Eat: A Qualitative Study of Identities in Food Choice', *Journal of Nutrition Education and Behavior*, 34: 128–139, https://doi.org/10.1016/S1499-4046(06)60082-1.

Clarke, Adele E., Janet K. Shim, Laura Mamo, Jennifer Ruth Fosket and Jennifer R. Fishman (2003), 'Biomedicalization: Technoscientific Transformations of Health, Illness, and U.S. Biomedicine', *American Sociological Review*, 68(2): 161–194, https://doi.org/10.2307/1519765.

Conrad, Peter and Kristin K. Barker (2010), 'The Social Construction of Illness: Key Insights and Policy Implications', *Journal of Health and Social Behavior*, 51(S): S67–S79, https://doi.org/10.1177/0022146510383495.

Coveney, John (2000), *Food, Morals and Meaning: The Pleasure and Anxiety of Eating*, Oxon and New York: Routledge.

De Smedt, Tom and Walter Daelemans (2012), 'Pattern for Python', *Journal of Machine Learning Research*, 13: 2063–2067.

de Solier, Isabelle (2005), 'TV Dinners: Culinary Television, Education and Distinction', *Continuum*, 19(4): 465–481, https://doi.org/10.1080/10304310500322727.

Declercq, Jana (2018), '(De)Constructing the Discourse of Health News: A Linguistic Ethnographic Enquiry', PhD diss., Ghent University.

Deliens, Tom, Peter Clarys, Ilse De Bourdeaudhuij and Benedicte Deforche (2014), 'Determinants of Eating Behaviour in University Students', *BioMed Central Public Health*, 14(53). Available online: doi:10.1186/1471-2458-14-53.

Eskjær, Mikkel Fugl (2013), 'The Mediatization of Ethical Consumption', *MedieKultur: Journal of Media and Communication Research*, 29(54): 21–46.

Fox, Nick and Katie Ward (2008), 'You Are What You Eat? Vegetarianism, Health and Identity', *Social Science and Medicine*, 66(12): 2585–2595, https://doi.org/10.1016/j.socscimed.2008.02.011.

Gordon, Cynthia (2011), 'Impression Management on Reality TV: Emotion in Parental Accounts'. *Journal of Pragmatics*, 43(14): 3551–3564, https://doi.org/10.1016/j.pragma.2011.08.004.

Harcup, Tony (2015), *Journalism: Principles and Practice*, Los Angeles: Sage.

Hunt, Daniel and Kevin Harvey (2015), 'Health Communication and Corpus Linguistics', in Anthony McEnery and Paul Baker (eds), *Corpora and Discourse Studies*, 134–154, https://doi.org/10.1057/9781137431738_7.

Jaeger, Sara R. and Gastón Ares (2017), 'Dominant Meanings of Facial Emoji: Insights from Chinese Consumers and Comparison with Meanings from Internet Resources', *Food Quality and Preference*, 62 (March): 275–283, https://doi.org/10.1016/j.foodqual.2017.04.009.

Kelly, Ryan and Leon Watts (2015), 'Characterising the Inventive Appropriation of Emoji as Relationally Meaningful in Mediated Close Personal Relationships', *Experiences of Technology Appropriation: Unanticipated Users, Usage, Circumstances, and Design*. Paper presented at Experiences of Technology Appropriation: Unanticipated Users, Usage, Circumstances, and Design, Oslo, Norway, 20/09/15 - 20/09/15.

Lang, Tim and Michael Heasman (2004), *Food Wars: The Global Battle for Mouths, Minds and Markets*, London: Earthscan.

Lettinga, Aafke, Carel van Wijk and Peter Broeder (2017), 'The Use of English in Dutch Text Messages as a Function of Communicative Constraints', *Taal En Tongval*, 69(1): 71–88.

Ljubešić, Nikola and Darja Fišer (2016), 'A Global Analysis of Emoji Usage', *Proceedings of the 10th Web as Corpus Workshop*, 82–89, https://doi.org/10.18653/v1/W16-2610.

Macdiarmid, Jennie, Flora Douglas and Jonina Campbell (2016), 'Eating Like There's no Tomorrow: Public Awareness of the Environmental Impact of Food and Reluctance to Eat Less Meat as Part of a Sustainable Diet', *Appetite*, 96: 487–493, https://doi.org/10.1016/j.appet.2015.10.011.

McIntosh, Wm. Alex (1996), *Sociologies of Food and Nutrition*, New York: Springer Science, Business Media.

Miller, Hanna, Daniel Kluver, Jacob Thebault-Spieker, Loren Terveen and Brent Hecht (2017), 'Understanding Emoji Ambiguity in Context: The Role of Text in Emoji-Related Miscommunication', *Proceedings of the Eleventh International AAAI Conference on Web and Social Media*, 152–161.

Miller, Hanna, Jacob Thebault-Spieker, Shuo Chang, Isaac Johnson, Loren Terveen and Brent Hecht (2016), '"Blissfully Happy" or "Ready to Fight": Varying Interpretations of Emoji', *International AAAI Conference on Web and Social Media*, 259–268, https://doi.org/10.1089/cyber.2011.0179.

Niva, Mari (2007), '"All Foods Affect Health": Understandings of Functional Foods and Healthy Eating among Health-Oriented Finns', *Appetite*, 48: 384–393. https://doi.org/10.1016/j.appet.2006.10.006.

Novak, Petra Kralj, Jasmina Smailović, Borut Sluban and Igor Mozetič (2015), 'Sentiment of Emojis', *PLoS ONE*, 10 (12): 1–22, https://doi.org/10.1371/journal.pone.0144296

Oostdijk, Nelleke, Martin Reynaert, Véronique Hoste and Henk van den Heuvel (2013), *SoNaR User Documentation*. Available online: https://ticclops.uvt.nl/SoNaR_end-user_documentation_v.1.0.4.pdf.

Partington, Alan, Alison Duguid and Charlotte Taylor (2013), *Patterns and Meanings in Discourse: Theory and Practice in Corpus-ssisted Discourse Studies (CADS)*, Amsterdam: John Benjamins.

Phillipov, Michelle (2013), 'Mastering Obesity: *MasterChef Australia* and the Resistance to Public Health Nutrition', *Media, Culture & Society*, 35(4): 506–515, https://doi.org/10.1177/0163443712474615.

Sealey, Alison and Nickie Charles (2013), '"What Do Animals Mean to You?": Naming and Relating to Nonhuman Animals', *Anthrozoos*, 26(4): 485–503, https://doi.org/10.2752/175303713X13795775535652.

Stead, Martine, Laura McDermott, Anne Marie MacKintosh and Ashley Adamson (2011), 'Why Healthy Eating is Bad for Young People's Health: Identity, Belonging and Food', *Social Science and Medicine*, 72(7): 1131–1139, https://doi.org/10.1016/j.socscimed.2010.12.029.

Stringfellow, Lindsay, Andrew MacLaren, Mairi Maclean and Kevin O'Gorman (2013), 'Conceptualizing Taste: Food, Culture and Celebrities', *Tourism Management*, 37: 77–85, https://doi.org/10.1016/j.tourman.2012.12.016.

Sukhan, Tiara (2012), 'Bootcamp, Brides, and BMI: Biopedagogical Narratives of Health and Beloning on Canadian Size-Transformation Television', *Television & New Media*, 14(3): 194–210, https://doi.org/10.1177/1527476412457995.

Verbeke, Wim (2008), 'Impact of Communication on Consumers' Food Choices', *Proceedings of the Nutrition Society*, 67(3): 281–288, https://doi.org/10.1017/S0029665108007179.

Vidal, Leticia, Gáston Ares and Sara R. Jaeger (2016), 'Use of Emoticon and Emoji in Tweets for Food-Related Emotional Expression', *Food Quality and Preference*, 49: 119–128, https://doi.org/10.1016/j.foodqual.2015.12.002.

Webster, Frank (2006), *Theories of the Information Society*, 3rd edn, Oxon: Routledge.

Zenner, Eline, Dirk Speelman and Dirk Geeraerts (2015), 'A Sociolinguistic Analysis of Borrowing in Weak Contact Situations: English Loanwords and Phrases in Expressive Utterances in a Dutch Reality TV Show', *International Journal of Bilingualism*, 19(3): 333–346, https://doi.org/10.1177/1367006914521699.

3

Mediatizing the Fashionable Eater in @nytfood #tbt Posts

Gwynne Mapes

1 Introduction: What *not* to eat

A "new"/social media platform such as Instagram might seem an unlikely site for a discussion of historical eating practices; however, the complex fusion of time and space is particularly noticeable in this explicitly modern and mediatized setting. Indeed, Bakhtin's (1981) famous notion of the "chronotope," in the quotation below, is well-suited for considering the problematic ways "this intersection of axes" comes to be embodied and portrayed in digital discourse, and how time "takes on flesh":

> Time, as it were, thickens, takes on flesh, becomes artistically visible; likewise, space becomes charged and responsive to the movement of time, plot and history. This intersection of axes and fusion of indicators characterizes the artistic chronotope.
>
> Bakhtin 1981: 85

More specifically, I am interested in how antiquated food representations on social media are implicated in the construction and maintenance of contemporary elite status. To this end, I examine a dataset comprised of *New York Times* (hereafter, NYT) food section #tbt ("throwback Thursday") Instagram posts, all of which feature real photographs from decades-old NYT articles. Serving as perfect foils to what many have come to value in our contemporary consumerist practices, these outdated photographs and accompanying captions effectively teach us – and we, as (Western) Instagram users, teach each other – how and what not to eat, if we want to be considered modern and sophisticated, and if we seek the distinction Bourdieu (1984) associated with consuming fashionable food.

As many scholars have established, and as this edited volume attests, the intersection of food, language, and cultural/social practice across various material and discursive domains is a particularly ripe site for analysis (e.g., Jurafsky 2014; Cavanaugh & Riley 2017). Furthermore, the increasingly digitized nature of our world heightens and accentuates these relationships. My thinking here stems from recent scholarship concerning *mediatization* (e.g., Agha 2011; Androutsopoulos 2014), a term which captures the ways in which cultural texts and practices are elaborately co-produced, and are co-constitutive. As Jaworski and Thurlow (2017: 277), following (Krotz 2009), observe, mediatization "has been identified as a long-term process of the emergence of institutionalized media and its relevance for and influence on the construction of social life." In this regard, mediatization research is not about technology *per se*, but rather focuses on the (re)contextualization and (re)circulation of texts – and especially the ways in which they "hail" each of us as dialogical, co-constructive subjects (see Althusser 1971). Likewise, Jaworski and Thurlow (2017: 277) also attest to the disciplining function of mediatized representations in contemporary society, suggesting that they uphold rather than disrupt "the nexus of status, privilege and power, while also obfuscating inequality." It is the subtle schooling of consumers into particular, elite behaviors that is the primary focus of the present study. In considering how an emphatically contemporary, mediatized engagement with historical food images can also foster the co-production of superiority, I expand on Jones, Chik, and Hafner's (2015: 13) conviction that digital practices seem to primarily facilitate "commercial practices and the promotion of dominant values of competition and conspicuous consumption" (see also Thurlow 2013). Against this backdrop, in what follows I demonstrate how the co-instruction and co-construction of distinction in NYT food section Instagram (@nytfood) #tbt posts exemplify a production and perpetuation of neoliberal cycles of social inequality. I argue that this occurs principally through the subtle discursive moves encapsulated in Jaworksi and Thurlow's (2009) notion of "elitist stancetaking."

2 Stance and elitist stancetaking

Stancetaking has been a relatively popular subject in sociolinguistics, as evidenced by Jaffe's (2009) and Englebretson's (2007) edited volumes, as well as the range of other studies extending Ochs's (1992) idea that taking up stances is a means of constructing identities and relationships in discourse. Following Du Bois (2007: 163), I take "stance" to be a public act by a social actor, achieved dialogically through overt communicative means (language, gesture, and other symbolic forms), through which social actors simultaneously evaluate objects, position subjects (themselves and others), and align with other subjects, with respect to any salient dimension of the sociocultural field.

The positioning of self and others in relation to the evaluated object is key to Du Bois's thinking on stance, and to his notion of "the stance triangle" (cf. Kiesling's 2018 update to this concept). In this vein, what separates stance from something like *sociolinguistic style* or *stylization* is its emphasis on interpersonal relationships – that is, the salience of alignment or dis-alignment with other subjects as they engage in various evaluative actions and practices. An interlocutor's *uptake* of another subject's stance act is revealed in their subsequent evaluative speech, gesture, or other bodily movements – and, in the case of social media like Instagram, in their written comments. Du Bois (2007: 61) calls this "stance follow". Crucially, one's stance follow might be more or less likely depending on the relative status or power of the participants; in many cases, and as the current study suggests, alignment with a particular stance is a normalized and naturalized, or taken for granted, response. Stancetaking behavior is thus linked to access (in terms of power relations) and socialization (see also Ochs 1992 on "indexing gender"). In other words, certain stance alignments are oftentimes predictable – and, as existing research demonstrates (e.g., Lempert 2009), specific stances are linked to particular identities. Rauniomaa (2003) captures this in the notion that stances "accrue," as does Damari (2010: 626) in her discussion of the "durable identity categories" speakers come to construct and latch onto. Taha (2017) takes this line of research a step further, considering how we might characterize these relatively less-tangible stance objects. She uses the term "shadow subject" to describe "projected sel[ves]," for example, or "women in the past" (Taha 2017: 198). These oftentimes collective shadow subjects feature prominently in everyday interaction, as well as in written/digital discourse.

In elitist stancetaking, stance is specifically implicated in the discursive construction of superiority vis-à-vis real and imagined others. In considering how travelogue writers perform social evaluations in texts by commenting on what is desirable – and more often, what is undesirable – Jaworski and Thurlow (2009) find that the evaluations expressed in stance acts are not easily identifiable, but rather are generally presented as neutral observations. It is these disguised judgements of superiority and taste that are oftentimes more powerful than overt elitism. And, as Jaworski and Thurlow point out, multiple re-enactments of stancetaking behaviors contribute to a normalizing and solidifying of ideologies, including those pertinent to class, gender, race and sexual politics. To this point, Jaffe (2009: 9) notes how "speakers engage in both explicit and implicit forms of social categorization and evaluation, attribute intentionality, affect, knowledge, agency to themselves and others, and lay claim to particular social and/or moral identities." Thus, as the aforementioned works also establish, stancetaking is a dynamic process that is inherent to the production and maintenance of social status, and is always in relation to other participants (including past selves). Martín Rojo and Molina (2017: 673) consider how this sort of behavior unfolds in a conversation among students and lecturers, who can be seen constructing various "cosmopolitan" identities based on issues pertaining to travel and politics. Importantly, their paper "explores the extent to which sociocultural and ideological factors underlie stance alignment" (Martín Rojo and Molina 2017: 673); like Jaworski and Thurlow, they conclude that the reinforcing of ideologies should be of particular relevance to any contemporary study of stance. In this regard, I argue here that the ideological force of elitist stancetaking in @nytfood #tbt posts hinges on a contrasting of contemporary and historical consumerist beliefs and practices. Furthermore, it is via the institutional legacy of the NYT that we see an instructing in, and enforcing of, particular alignments in the discourse of its audience. In this way, I demonstrate how @nytfood and its followers perform superior, moral identities relative to the "shadow subjects" featured in #tbt posts. It is in this way that classist ideologies are (re)produced and disseminated.

3 Data and methodology

3.1 Instagram

Instagram is a mobile-based application for sharing edited/filtered photographs and videos within one's (customizable) public or private network – users are then able to "follow" other users, "like" their images, and comment on their posts. The social media platform has been widely documented in recent years across various disciplines, including sociolinguistics and discourse analysis (e.g., Zappavigna 2016 on "mommy bloggers"; Zhao & Zappavigna 2017 on selfies; Tiidenberg & Baym 2017 on "performing pregnancy"; and Portmann 2020 on Swiss grocery store marketing). My particular orientation to Instagram necessitates an understanding of how it is used as a tool for "pseudo-sociality" (see Thurlow 2013); this ties into what some have called "ambient affiliation" (Zappavigna

2011) or "ambient sociability" (Gillen & Merchant 2013). Squires (2016: 372) applies this concept to her analysis of Twitter use, writing that its "network creates connections and collective content that are felt to exist but are not necessarily individually articulable: it constitutes a form of distributed knowledge and sociality." This is particularly true in the context of celebrity users, or "elite" institutions like the NYT; in these cases, social media like Instagram operate under the guise of erasing social boundaries, while simultaneously (re)producing them.[1] Thus, in becoming supposedly more open and inclusive via Instagram, the famed distinction or status associated with @nytfood is effectively downplayed, but nonetheless (re)inscribed, or, alternatively, made "palatable" for the masses. This juxtaposition of concerns surfaces in unique ways throughout their #tbt posts.

3.2 What is "#tbt" or "#throwbackthursday"?

Despite the ubiquitous presence of the hash symbol (#) in contemporary society, so-called hashtags are still a relatively understudied phenomenon in sociolinguistic literature, especially with regards to Instagram (see Zappavigna 2011, 2015 and Page 2012 for analyses of hashtags on Twitter; and Heyd & Puschmann's 2017 examination of their use outside social media). While hashtags were originally intended to serve as topic-markers on Twitter, Zappavigna (2015) observes additional functions such as conveying experiential and interpersonal meanings (by expressing evaluative stance, for example). Hashtags are searchable across multiple social media platforms, allowing users to find content in which they are interested. This categorical (and coordinating) function is used especially for commercial accounts, which largely rely on hashtags to attract followers and in so doing promote their business. However, for personal accounts especially, hashtags frequently serve as a kind of linguistic play – they often signal a humorous or sarcastic evaluation of the content, a function which I elaborate in a later section.

It is difficult to pinpoint the popularization of #tbt and/or #throwbackthursday on social media; the phrase itself is thought to originate from earlier references by basketball jersey and sneaker enthusiasts who collected "throwback" basketball paraphernalia, and followed a blog that featured a pair of vintage sneakers every Thursday.[2] According to the Digital Trends website, however, it seems that the first mention of #tbt on Instagram was in 2011, and people started searching the hashtag on Google more regularly in February 2012.[3] It has since increased significantly in popularity; at the time of writing, approximately 503 million posts have been tagged with #tbt on Instagram, and over 48 million with #throwbackthursday. Oftentimes these posts feature photos of the user as a child, but they also might tag images of their parents, or even objects that are somehow old-fashioned or historical looking. Some posts simply feature past experiences or memories (e.g., it's not uncommon to see a #tbt photo of a party, vacation, or dinner from several weeks before). The significance of the hashtag for the current study is best expressed by the fact that the very first image posted by @nytfood on Instagram is tagged #tbt. At the time of the post, 16 September 2014, "throwback Thursday" had become a cultural phenomenon.

3.3 Data selection and analytical process

I began following @nytfood from my personal Instagram account in September 2015. I was quickly struck by the #tbt posts, as their monochromatic color scheme (they appear in black and white) is particularly noticeable in comparison to the rest of the photos that @nytfood posts. Out of intellectual curiosity I decided to incorporate a dataset comprised solely of these posts into a larger project, which included various other genres of food discourse. I expected to comment mostly on the construction of institutional authority or legitimation by reference to historical tradition – however, I ultimately found the rhetorical work of these posts to be much more complex. I archived #tbt data between 15 June and 15 August 2016.[4] I cataloged each singular #tbt post on the @nytfood account up until the last day of the collection period, resulting in a corpus of 83 posts, all of which are old photographs from previous issues of the NYT food section. The majority (over 80 percent) feature photos from the 1940s and 1950s, with just sixteen images from the 1960s, 1970s, and 1980s combined.

My analytical process largely follows the steps outlined in Thurlow and Aiello (2007), moving from broader description using content analysis, to more finegrained, interpretive discourse analysis, and then onto critique. I began with an initial close reading, during which time I recorded salient themes and patterns. I continued this descriptive phase in subsequent readings, coding these posts according to observed similarities. Because an Instagram post is comprised of three general parts, or semiotic genres (photograph, written caption, and user comments), I itemized patterns accordingly. For this reason, I address images, written captions, and user comments separately in my analysis, focusing on patterns within the bounds of each genre. Of course, while I use these distinct semiotic genres as analytical devices, they are certainly co-constitutive, coproduced and indeed, dialogical in the Bakhtinian (1981) sense. The photograph,

Table 3.1 Characteristics of @nytfood #tbt posts

Semiotic Genre	Common characteristics
1. photograph	a) black and white b) neat/orderly c) laboring women's hands (most of which feature polished nails)
2. caption	a) sardonic/humorous statement b) detail (using detailed description) c) direct quotation d) additional hashtags
3. user comments	a) sardonic/humorous statement b) emoji[5] c) tagging d) general comment concerning progress e) direct negative evaluation

caption, and user comments are all in conversation with each other, so to speak. However, for the purposes of this chapter, I consider the work they accomplish separately as a means of understanding how elitist stancetaking occurs multimodally across the entirety of each post. In Table 3.1 I list the main characteristics I identified within these semiotic genres (in no particular order). Although not every characteristic is present in each #tbt post, they are generally representative of the majority of my dataset. In coding the data I noticed overlap across some of the characteristics: In the user comments, for example, some sardonic and/or humorous statements might also be considered negative evaluation (depending on their perceived level of contempt). As such, I do not count how often each of the characteristics occurs in the data, but rather use them to provide a general description of the dataset. It is therefore not my intent to offer a quantitative, statistically-significant analysis of @nytfood #tbt posts; instead, I seek to qualitatively illuminate how these particular posts are set apart from standard @nytfood posts (i.e., those that are not tagged with the "throwback Thursday" hashtag).

4 Case study analysis: Orders of elitist stancetaking

In this analysis, I suggest that @nytfood #tbt Instagram posts demonstrate three distinct orders of elitist stancetaking. My use of "order" here follows Silverstein's (2003) discussion of "indexical order," in the sense that the meanings associated with particular sociolinguistic phenomena are conveyed with varying degrees of social salience. In Silverstein's schemata, so-called "first order" signifiers demonstrate the highest level of indexical agency. So for example, the first order of elitist stancetaking in @nytfood posts is enacted by the institution itself, the NYT. In posting old, black and white photos from previous issues of their food section, the NYT establishes its historical authority, credibility, and superiority – all via the modern medium of Instagram. In this way, these #tbt posts in their entirety serve as stance acts that "legitimize" (van Leeuwen 2007) the historicity of @nytfood, and consequently remind users of the longevity and tradition associated with this elite publication. These posts serve as tangible evidence of the public's historical trust in the NYT for guidance concerning appropriate eating habits. The second order of elitist stancetaking, also institutionally-produced, is represented by @nytfood's particular choice of image and accompanying caption, which paint these historical food trends as derisible and inferior – in direct contrast with "progress"-oriented rhetorics of simplicity, and locality/sustainability, for example. Lastly, @nytfood followers produce the third order of elitist stancetaking: Throughout their various comments we see participants constructing particular "self-and other-identities" (see Jaworski & Coupland 2005). In mocking antiquated food practices, @nytfood followers align to assert their own fashionable modernity-cum-superiority, demonstrating once again how supposedly egalitarian digital platforms are also spaces of/for social hierarchy. My analysis centers on a representative post from the dataset, which will serve as a case study (see Figure 3.1), and is organized by attending, in turn, to the aforementioned semiotic genres: photograph, caption, and user comments. Across each section of analysis I elaborate on common characteristics, arguing that these are instrumental to participants' stance acts across genres, and are central to the production of privileged standards of good taste (Bourdieu 1984) and contemporary, fashionable eating.

4.1 Semiotic genre 1: Photograph

Admittedly, the image is probably the most important semiotic feature of an Instagram post, due perhaps to its size in comparison to the other modes (cf. Ross & Zappavigna 2020). Based on my own experience as a frequent Instagrammer, the image might be the only component of a post that users notice as they habitually check the app on their mobile phones. For this reason, the information conveyed by @nytfood's images is essential both to the user experience, and to the institution's particular, constructed identity as an

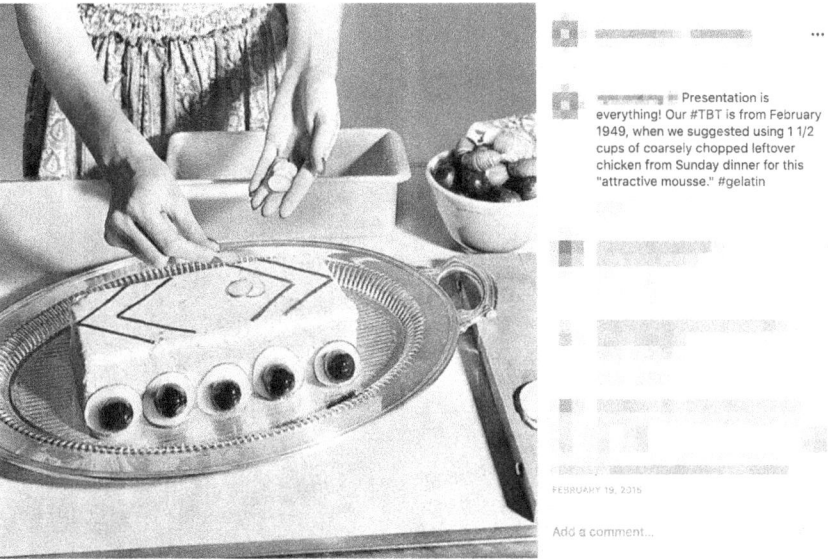

Figure 3.1 @nytfood post from 19 Feb. 2015 (their fourteenth #tbt post). The featured image was originally printed in 1949; it pictures a chopped chicken mousse. User comments have been blurred to preserve anonymity.

historically relevant source. In this vein, what is most striking about the images used in #tbt posts is that they all feature a black and white photograph, marking them not only as antiquated and historical, but more importantly, as particularly deficient in comparison to contemporary food photography. The aestheticized portrayals of food for modern consumption are notoriously colorful, and heavily saturated. The post shown in Figure 3.2, for example is, in its original color format, characterized by vivid, purple-red berry compote, which, in places, is swirled with stark white cream or staining the edges of a golden-yellow cornmeal biscuit. Followers of food-focused Instagram accounts are inundated with these artful, vibrant depictions that are likewise perceived (for better or worse) as *real* – as possessing a high level of modality, in Kress and van Leeuwen's (2006) terms (cf. Machin 2007). Thus, the use of black and white in this context indexes a clear absence. Because these images blatantly contrast the performed verisimilitude of contemporary food photography, users become immediately aware that #tbt posts serve a different semiotic purpose than contemporary posts. These images are not meant to transmit modern values concerning food and eating, but rather, as I argue later, to educate users about the past practices that stand in opposition to contemporary ideals.

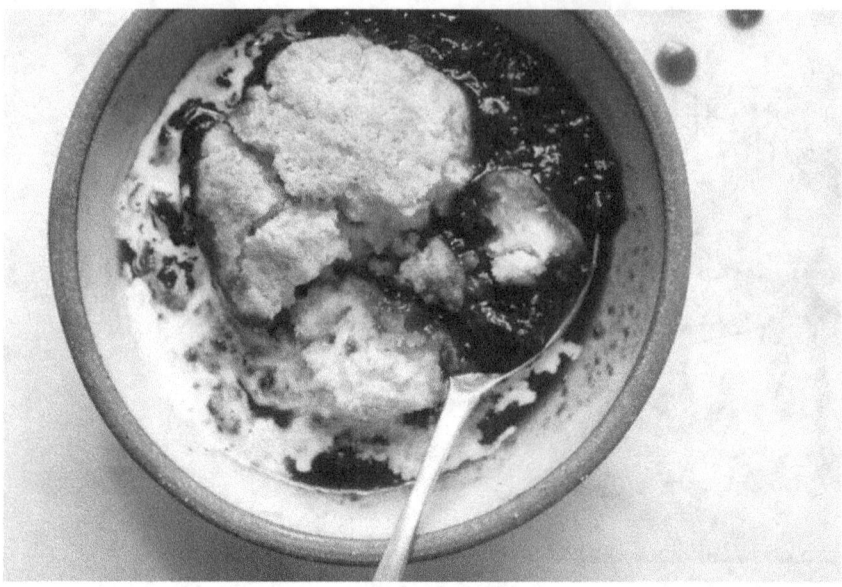

Figure 3.2 Contemporary photo (@nytfood). Craig Lee © 2020 The New York Times Company.

In addition to their black and white color scheme, 99 percent of the #tbt images in my dataset can be classified as "neat" and "orderly" – by this I mean there is a notable absence of smears, crumbs, crumpling of table linen, and residue on hands or serving utensils. Again, this neatness is striking in comparison to modern standards for food photography, which tend to favor (stylized) performances of natural-looking and "authentic" scenes – Figure 3.2 is one such example, but peruse @nytfood's feed to see multiple others. By contrast, Figure 3.1 features a polished silver tray and a countertop that is wiped clean. The baking dish in between the woman's body and the tray is presumably meant to be the same dish that was used to bake/mold the chicken mousse; however, if it did actually serve this purpose, any trace has been removed from its sides. In this sense, it has been placed in the photograph purely to add interest to the scene, which adds to the overall fabricated and false (i.e., inauthentic) nature of the image. Another striking detail is the bowl in the upper-right corner. The contents of the bowl are difficult to discern, especially for users viewing this image on their smartphones. Nonetheless, having enlarged the photo, I was able to conclude that the bowl is partially filled with black olives, which also dot the side of the mousse, as well as with sliced radishes – which are being placed on the top of the mousse in the full photograph. Thus, the bowl contains ingredients essential to preparation. However, curiously, the radishes seem to be sliced partially through, so that they retain their round shape and green sprigs. This is perhaps the ultimate example of exaggerated orderliness and staging in the image. Instead of featuring the vegetables in their natural state, the food photographer arranges them into faux-sliced, neat piles. The labor involved in such an impractical task has been effectively erased from view. Rather, it is an implausibly tidy aesthetic that remains. Thurlow and Jaworski (2014) delve into what they call "visible-invisible labor," arguing that certain details (like perfectly cut vegetables) serve as subtle markers of the work required for performing privilege – whereas the actual evidence of that work has been removed. The significance of visible-invisible labor lies in the overtness with which it conveys eliteness, and conspicuous consumption. As others have pointed out (e.g., Khan 2014) this sort of traditional display of privilege is not valued in contemporary society but rather looked down upon as too snobbish. The neat and orderly nature of the #tbt images directly opposes that which is valued in other @nytfood posts, featuring explicitly messy, partially-eaten or splattered scenes (such as Figure 3.2). It is the artful performance of *un*-styled that defines fashionable food photography.[6] In this way, these contrasting images represent chronotopically different notions of "good" food; by posting an image that is easily identifiable as suspect, and as "other," @nytfood thus takes an elitist stance towards the food trends of the past.

This sort of stancetaking is enhanced by the very particular sort of labor which is distinctively present in Figure 3.1, revealed by the woman's manicured hands, which are actively adding decorative detail to the chicken mousse. Over a quarter (26.5 percent) of the dataset features women's laboring hands, and 98 percent of these images include polished nails (only one photograph depicts noticeably masculine hands). Figures 3.3–3.5 demonstrate other examples of these laboring, manicured women's hands. In each instance, the action is centered in the photograph and thus marked as key (Kress & van Leeuwen 2006). In Figure 3.1 viewers' eyes are drawn to the center, and to the hands carefully placing sliced radishes on top of the chicken mousse. We are led to assume that these same hands added the ornamental diagonal lines on top, as well as the black olives and cucumber disks along the side – despite the fact that they appear to be clean, and dry. In fact, all the women's hands in the dataset are immaculate, and stereotypically feminine; their wrists are slender; their skin is also lily-white.

Every performed action seems almost gentle and careful: Spoons are held (unreasonably) gracefully, and a glass pot is poised mid-action, with painted nails noticeably on display. Thus, the sort of visible, performed labor in these images reflects what Bourdieu (1984: 190) identified as the gentleness, refinement, and restraint associated with women's eating and food preparation habits – in direct contrast, of course, to those of men. The #tbt photographs present normatively gendered, classed, and raced depictions of cooking in the mid-1900s. This is only reinforced by the interpersonal function of these "offer" images. The participants serve as objects "of contemplation, impersonally, as though [they] were [specimens] in a display case" (Kress & van Leeuwen 2006: 124). Not only because no subjects are shown gazing back at the camera, but also because their choice to gaze at the camera has been explicitly removed by the photographer, or by the editor. These shadow subjects lack faces, heads, and oftentimes, bodies. They are dehumanized, aside from their distinctly feminized labor. In this sense, it seems that the women's perfect hands serve as objects of desire and consumption, along with the food items they are preparing for their midcentury readership.

What becomes apparent from the three notable characteristics of these #tbt images is that in choosing to feature photographs of this kind, @nytfood demonstrates elitist stancetaking. Specifically, the striking way in which their black and white color scheme contrasts the verisimilitude of contemporary food images; the excessive, staged orderliness of the featured foods and preparation surfaces; and the normative depiction of women's labor and associated place in the home – all serve to mark midcentury food trends as particularly derisible (at least in the context of its relatively youthful audience).[7] And importantly, these chronotopic #tbt posts are highly communicative representations of specific times, places, and most noticeably, *personhoods*. As Agha (2007: 321–322) discusses, figures or "sketches" of personhood allow participants to more fully experience the conveyed spatio-temporal meanings. Thus, the "other" identities displayed by these women, and by the foods and dishes they prepare, are visceral depictions of opposition to the institutional persona @nytfood portrays in its contemporary posts. The #tbt posts are not representative of the "progressive" (but, elite) authenticity that is characteristic of modern food trends (see Mapes 2018), and that is practiced by fashionable, knowledgeable consumers. By highlighting those things that differentiate our modern age from the past, @nytfood takes an elitist stance towards the traditional performance of status and privileged eating in their #tbt images.

Mediatizing the Fashionable Eater in @nytfood #tbt Posts 71

Figures 3.3, 3.4, and 3.5 Posts featuring women's hands with polished nails. © 2020 The New York Times Company.

4.2 Semiotic genre 2: Written caption

Figure 3.6 is typical of most written captions in the dataset. It includes the required hashtag (#tbt), original year of publication, information about what is pictured in the photograph, direct quotation from the accompanying article, as well as a final hashtag. Additionally, it begins with what I have classified as a sardonic/humorous statement: "Presentation is everything!"[8] This phrase assumingly evokes a metaphorical eye roll from @nytfood followers, who not only prioritize *taste* above all else (see Johnston & Baumann 2010), but who also prefer a markedly different sort of presentation. Sarcastic statements like these abound in the dataset. Generally speaking, the information they convey is superfluous to any detail concerning the featured photograph and recipe. Instead, these statements tend to represent the @nytfood writer's humorous (and oftentimes biting) evaluation of the content of the post. In this particular example, @nytfood emphasizes the presentation of the chicken mousse, thus acknowledging the negative reaction they expect from their followers. The mocking tone behind this sardonic statement is fueled by two factors: 1) the seemingly preposterous undertaking of making chicken mousse presentable or appealing; and 2) the painstaking care and labor displayed by the tiny details in the image – as I have already pointed out, it is not fashionable to cook and present something that can be so easily identified as "styled." Furthermore, contemporary trends favor "natural" foods, and most certainly not those that have been blended and supplemented with questionable ingredients (like gelatin). Rather, it is effortlessness and unpretentious simplicity that are valued in contemporary cooking – or the appearance thereof. Once again, the NYT food section Instagram account illustrates how elitist stancetaking effectively divides fashionable, modern eaters from derisible, old-fashioned culinary practices.

The use of detail by @nytfood is another mechanism for these sorts of stance acts. Concerning detail in face-to-face conversation, Tannen (2007: 134) writes

> **nytfood** Presentation is everything! Our #TBT is from February 1949, when we suggested using 1 1/2 cups of coarsely chopped leftover chicken from Sunday dinner for this "attractive mousse." #gelatin

Figure 3.6 Case study written caption (as seen in Fig. 3.1)

that its role is to create scenes, which in turn "spark emotions, making possible both understanding and involvement." Van Dijk (2012: 600) reiterates these ideas, noting that detail establishes credibility, and is consequently an effective means of persuasion. With these things in mind, the detail in Figure 3.6 is all the more interesting, as it acts as a noticeable parody. While the caption mentions a 1949 NYT article which advised readers to use "1 ½ cups of coarsely chopped chicken from Sunday dinner," this detail is not to make the recipe more credible, nor to persuade readers to make the chicken mousse. Rather, this comment accomplishes the exact opposite. It is a parodic use of detail, meant to mock the various components of the message. First, @nytfood provides an exact measurement, "1½ cups" – pretending, of course, that their Instagram followers are actually interested in preparing this dated recipe. Furthermore, it alludes to the traditional, and normative practice of preparing roast chicken for Sunday dinner (after church, one would assume, and surely by the matriarch of the family in question). This additional detail thus indexes a practice that is contrary to modern (secular, feminist) ideals, and accentuates the old-fashioned nature of the "throwback" recipe. Details such as these serve as anachronistic, elitist stance acts that signal to @nytfood followers what not to value, and explicitly what not to cook. Similarly, direct quotation typically heightens the more ridiculous (according to contemporary trends) aspects of the featured recipes. This is also apparent in the case study caption: Highlighting how the NYT article described this chicken gelatin loaf as an "attractive mousse" reinforces the hilarity, disdain, and overall elitist stance towards the product, and the practice. First, because the lexical item "mousse" is a clearly euphemized – not to mention upscale – way of naming the featured item. As Jurafsky (2014) points out, French is often used in restaurant menus to convey high status. Hence, "chicken gelatin" becomes "mousse." As such, @nytfood is mocking the apparent need to inflate or even disguise the recipe's contents, as well as the choice to use a term that seems obviously "upper class" – for that particular time period, at least. Second, the appearance of the mousse (refer again to Figure 3.1) is certainly not "attractive" for modern, fashionable consumers of food and food imagery. In this way we see how the different Instagram genres work in tandem to successfully employ elitist stance acts in these #tbt posts.

Lastly, additional hashtags are also seen contributing to @nytfood's elitist stancetaking. Of course, all posts in the current dataset are traceable via #tbt, and also because of the hashtag "#NYTcooking," which appears on every post. However, many of these posts also include other hashtags – either within the body of the caption, or more typically at the very end. Some of these serve an informational function, and contain unremarkable details concerning the featured recipe or item (#dessert, for instance). The ones of interest to me are those that are part of elitist stance acts; the use of #gelatin in the case study is one such example, because of the unlikelihood that anyone interested in contemporary eating or in contemporary food photography would search for posts that include it. Gelatin is certainly not a popular ingredient for savory foods nowadays, nor one that is associated with elite or authentic good taste. In this sense, @nytfood knows users most certainly will not find this particular post because of the hashtag. It is inserted purely for its humorous value. As I alluded earlier, this linguistic play is not an uncommon use of hashtags, especially in posts by personal Instagram accounts. Thus, #gelatin serves as a way for @nytfood to mock an ingredient routinely used by midcentury housewives (with manicured hands), and to simultaneously perform "ambient sociability" – providing the illusion of collective engagement and access (Gillen & Merchant 2013). However, this sort of mocking is perhaps best encapsulated by the "#<nail painting emoji>" (Figure 3.7), which accompanies another post in the dataset that features a woman's hand spooning chopped mushrooms into veal chops. Once again, the polished nails of the protagonists (pictured or unpictured) in these #tbt posts are explicitly tagged as objects of our modern mockery and scorn. And likewise, across all these instances of elitist stancetaking in the written captions there seems to be an

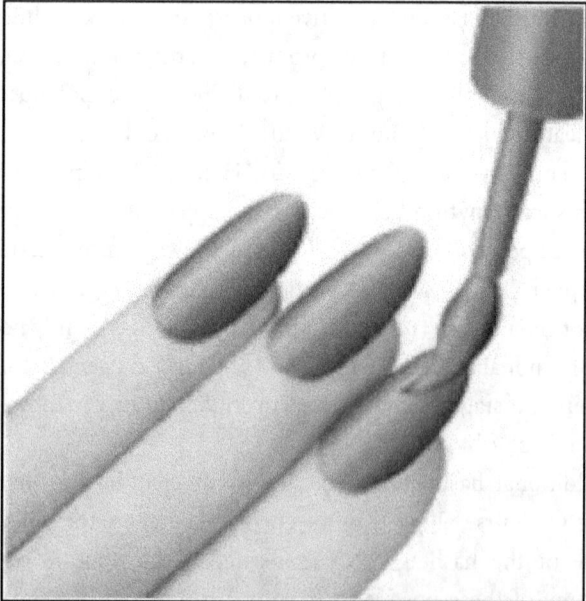

Figure 3.7 Nail painting emoji with hashtag

explicit attempt by @nytfood to maintain "ironic distance" (Žižek 1989) from the ignorant and normative tastes of the past, and more specifically, *their* past. They thereby position themselves, and their followers, as relatively sophisticated and superior. It is this subtle positioning which exemplifies the teaching and disciplining of consumers into acceptable, modern ways of being elite.

4.4 Semiotic genre 3: User comments

I now turn to the user comments from Figure 3.1, reproduced below. In general, I understand user comments on Instagram functioning as conversational turns, helping to reinforce the meanings cued in posts' photographs and captions. The number of user comments on each #tbt post varies significantly – there are ten comments included in the case study post (see Figure 3.8), but most posts from 2016 tend to have hundreds. No matter how many user comments, however, they

> **Comment 1** @username
> **Comment 2** Oh how times have changed!
> **Comment 3** @username @username
> 😊
> **Comment 4** This is SO good!!
> **Comment 5** If attractive = strange-looking.
> **Comment 6** @username recipe idea?
> **Comment 7** Ewww
> **Comment 8** @username @username lol! Throwback all right... 1949, 2014, whatevs!
> **Comment 9** We have progressed since then
> **Comment 10** These weird, twisted, sick recipes were probably the designs of bored stay at home 1950's wives strung out on Valium.

Figure 3.8 User comments (reproduced from Fig. 3.1)

all generally include the characteristics outlined in Table 3.1. One might occasionally see comments concerning nostalgia, or even positive evaluation if the post pictures a recipe or practice that is more in line with contemporary food trends, but because these are not typical, and are not related to elitist stance acts, I do not include them in my analysis. More commonly, sardonic and humorous statements make up the bulk of user comments on #tbt posts, and resemble those that appear in the written captions. However, because they are not institutionally-produced by professional writers, they are visibly less crafted, and less witty. They also generally occur in tandem with tagging other users, and emoji – characteristics I return to in a moment. But first consider Comment 4: "This is SO good!!" (referring, I presume, to the post, and not to the chicken mousse itself). This user is signifying their reception of and alignment with the sarcasm with which @nytfood posted the photo of the chicken mousse, acknowledging that they get the joke. Potentially one could argue that the user might actually be positively evaluating the dish, but their use of "is" rather than "looks" suggests that this is meant to signal appreciation for the hilarity of the photo rather than a serious consideration of its value as a consumable product. And furthermore, the general elitist stancetaking exhibited by @nytfood, and other users, has instructed this user into the appropriate reception of the post. It is similar in tone to Comment 3 with the <laughing face emoji>, which simply expresses laughter and humor – in both cases these users are signaling their general understanding of the #tbt post as comedic.

In tagging other users, @nytfood followers explicitly position their friends into agreement. This, of course, is the essence of Du Bois's (2007) stance triangle in which stance subjects align in their evaluation of the stance object. These "mass mediated personal encounter[s]" (Agha 2007: 325) are key to the co-construction of elitist stancetaking behaviors: A tagged user either "follows" the original stance act, or risks ridicule for not being "in the know." For example, Commenter 8 responds to being tagged in Comment 3, writing "lol! Throwback alright … 1949, 2014, whatevs!," effectively reiterating the humorous and ridiculous nature of the post. Consider also Comment 6: "@username recipe idea?" We can assume that the poster is joking, and is not actually suggesting they make the chicken mousse. Again, we are cued to this interpretation because of the orders of elitist stancetaking – we know the NYT intends for this recipe to be interpreted as humorous, and not as a practical cooking idea. Likewise, we can even assume Comment 1, which simply tags another user without emoji or additional evaluation, is probably also somewhat sarcastic. Whereas users might tag friends on @nytfood's contemporary posts as a means of suggesting they go out to eat at a particular restaurant, or make a certain recipe, in the case of #tbt posts, tagging is generally meant for aligning together in mutually mocking outdated food practices. In essence, these user comments succeed in delineating the self/other identity distinctions required for ingroup status (cf. Jaworski & Coupland 2005). Thus, it is partly in their sardonic/humorous othering of historical food practices that users' uptake of elitist stancetaking becomes particularly noticeable.

It is also typical for users to comment explicitly on the general progress of food culture on #tbt images. There are two examples of this sort of assessment in Figure 3.8: "Oh how times have changed!" and "we have progressed since then," both of which express users' knowledge concerning food trends and what is currently of value (i.e., not chicken mousse), as well as the marked difference between the past and the present. Another common expression of this idea is seen in comments like "We've come a long way, baby" (from a post on 4 August 2016), presumably an intertextual reference to the Virginia Slims cigarette company slogan which associated smoking with the "Women's Lib" movement and social equality.[9] In this sense, a narrative of progress – which permeates discourses of race, gender, sexuality, and class (see, for example, Thurlow 2016 on "post-class ideology") – is also present in food discourse. Of course, some contemporary trends really are less harmful than those of the past; after all, eating less-processed foods and using sustainable production methods is surely better than the alternative. However, the situation is definitively more complicated. By emphasizing progress in comments, users are burying a negative evaluation of historical practices within a positive evaluation of the present. As Thurlow (2017) notes, this "serves to elevate the status of modernity (and modern people) at the expense of the past ..." (14). However subtle, stance acts like these are key to constructing attitudes of superiority and privilege. And importantly, contemporary displays of status rely partly on the morality of modern ideals, and the belief that we've moved beyond certain societal problems (see Kenway & Lazarus 2017). Therefore, in focusing on progress and improvement in comparison to the past, @nytfood commenters positively stylize themselves as responsible, moral individuals with contemporary, good taste.

Whereas the former characteristic exemplifies more implicit elitist stancetaking, direct negative evaluation entails an explicit dislike of the featured #tbt post. It can be expressed simply, through the user's personal reaction (e.g., with emoji, or gustatory expressions) as well as more elaborately, by commenting on something specific related to the featured item; both types are demonstrated in the case study user comments. For example, one user simply comments "ewww" while another writes, "If attractive = strange-looking." The latter commenter demonstrates their uptake of the @nytfood's stance act using direct quotation, challenging the original writer's use of "attractive" to describe the chicken mousse. Most interesting, however, is Comment 10: "These weird, twisted sick recipes were probably the designs of bored stay at home 1950s wives strung out on Valium." It is particularly striking that this user relies on a markedly clichéd perception of the 1950s to critique an (obviously) fabricated image of an imagined housewife. And crucially, they not only negatively evaluate the chicken mousse recipe, but also all featured #tbt posts in their pluralizing of "these" and "recipes," thus collectively describing all food practices that don't follow contemporary trends as "twisted" and "sick." These lexemes do not just imply a dislike of the midcentury recipes, but rather exemplify a different sort of assessment – one that ludicrously seems to imply an intentional desire to produce "bad" food. Furthermore, it is also here that we begin to understand the complex gender politics of @nytfood's #tbt posts, and the true importance of the personhoods that are embedded within chronotopic representations. The accusation that "stay at home 1950s wives" were "bored" and addicted to prescription pain killers conveniently erases the fact that as far as gender inequality is concerned, these women were not the perpetrators, but the victims of a male-dominated society. However, this sort of misguided resentment is expected, on some level, because the user is simply demonstrating the elitist stancetaking behavior that has been touted by @nytfood in the photograph and caption. The reality is that our supposedly cosmopolitan, progressive society is also rife with inequality and normativity, but by emphasizing how far we have come, we mitigate and conceal how far we have *not* come. Thus, in voicing disdain for the supposed "bad taste" of previous generations, Instagram users take up @nytfood's instructional cues, asserting their status on the grounds of superior, modern virtues.

5 Conclusion: The "vengeful present tense"

> Every new Fashion is a refusal to inherit, a subversion against the oppression of the preceding Fashion; Fashion experiences itself as a Right, the natural right of the present over the past.
>
> Barthes [1967] 1990: 273

As with all ideological phenomena, the construction of modern, fashionable eating relies on its being perceived as naturalized and normalized in society. It is this process to which Barthes alludes in the quotation above; the orders of elitist stancetaking in @nytfood #tbt posts are beholden to a widespread acceptance of the present's "rightful" superiority over the past. And indeed, "fashion" is an inherently chronotopic concept, as it is patently seamed to the passage of time, and to the progress-oriented evolution of taste. In this chapter I have not only demonstrated how these issues manifest in an especially mediatized context, but also how they are inextricably linked to the performance of status – all of which hinges on the micro- to macro-sociological orders (to use Silverstein's 2003 terms) through which they are disseminated and interpreted. In the simple act of posting photographs from back issues of the NYT food section, for example, @nytfood asserts its institutional tradition of documenting and producing privileged food practices, effectively reinforcing its powerful reputation as an elite source for fashionable consumerist behavior. This is the first order of elitist stancetaking. As a second order, @nytfood seems to purposefully choose images and publish captions which highlight the historical food trends that are most derisible in comparison to contemporary food values – especially those concerned with progress and authenticity. The neat, black and white images featuring laboring women's hands, as well as the sardonic captions demonstrating unnecessary detail, direct quotation, and humorous hashtags together represent institutional elitist stancetaking toward past culinary practices. Furthermore, these posts are "grounded in large-scale cultural ideologies and sociopolitical formations" (Agha 2007: 324). Arguably, it is the recognizability of the inferior eating practices of the past that serves as motivation for @nytfood's posts. They strategically reclaim this narrative by mocking the recipes they previously endorsed, thus setting up their followers to be in-the-know and get the joke. In the third order, Instagram users follow the stance acts of @nytfood in their comments, co-constructing superiority and modernity in relation to the pictured food items via sardonic/humorous statements, emoji, tagging, focusing on "progress," and direct negative evaluation. Ultimately, the data demonstrate how elitist stancetaking can oftentimes be expressed through "the lens of the negative" (Jaworski & Thurlow 2009: 203); what is evaluated as good – contemporary eating – comes to be defined by what it is not – outdated, unfashionable eating. It is this sort of evaluative work that is key to "chronotopic contexts" (see Blommaert 2018).

In their paper concerning "mobile chronotopes" Lyons and Tagg (2019) consider how digital communication complicates configurations of time and space, especially for their migrant participants, who routinely engage in interactions with family and friends from their countries of origin. My discussion here, however, demonstrates a different sort of mobile chronotope – one that is less about the fluctuation of physical contexts and rather more about the legitimacy of action in particular spatiotemporal frames. In this regard, Blommaert (2015:

111) notes that "'how-it-was' can be invoked as relevant context in discourse and affect what can and does happen in discursive events." As a case in point, my data demonstrate how the "timespace constellation" can determine what sort of discourse unfolds (Blommaert 2018: 3). And importantly, the sort of sociocultural work being accomplished in these #tbt posts becomes integrally *moralized*; there are ways of participating which are deemed appropriate, or not. In sum, for all its claims of egalitarian participation, Instagram is certainly still a hierarchically-organized and charged space. Indeed, Marwick (2013: 14) contends that social media "intrinsically demonstrate how to be a proper modern person," and furthermore, because of their general alignment with the dominant ideologies, they "also function as a mode of governance, or governmentality." Therefore, Instagram is simply a different tool through which the powerful put forward particular views of self, disciplining users into social behaviors that are deemed valuable, and status-producing. However, these discourses are not straightforward or easily identifiable as elitist. Rather, they depend on what Kenway and Lazarus (2017) describe as an enticing display of modern "virtue." It is this attitude that conveys the right form of status – the quest to be elite but not elitist works as a mechanism for the ultimate disavowal of one's privileged position.

As the data also show, this struggle for status is not always in relation to other users of social media in real time, but sometimes relative to Taha's (2017) so-called shadow subjects; in this particular case, to past figures, trends, and practices, including one's own. And importantly, in posting these #tbt images, @nytfood is not only mocking the past, but also erasing the realities of the past. Instagram users are encouraged to be scornful of the practices these posts portray, but in so doing they forget and disregard the fact that these are photos of a war-time and post-war society. When people laugh at ingredients like gelatin and preservatives, they also mock their economic necessity in the 1940s and 1950s. As Barthes ([1967] 1990: 273) attests, this is the "absolute, dogmatic, vengeful present tense in which Fashion speaks." It is convenient for progressive, modern individuals to consider their own knowledge and practices superior to those of other historical periods. However, this serves as another example of the general denial of our relative privilege and elite status in Western contemporary society. Notably, the oftentimes subtle, naturalized, less-noticeable ways in which we assume and adopt an elitist stance towards an easily identifiable "other" reflects the powerful ideologies to which each of us is bound. It should be our goal as discourse analysts to interrogate the miniscule ways in which these small, everyday discursive acts contribute to (re)producing and normalizing moral superiority, and relatedly, social inequality.

Notes

1. In Mapes 2018 I explain the grounds for characterizing the NYT as elite. However, see also: <http://nytmediakit.com/newspaper> (click on 'Weekday/Sunday Audience' tab).
2. See *Sports Illustrated* article, "From Hardwood to Hashtag: How NBA Culture Gave Rise to Throwback Thursday" <https://www.si.com/extra-mustard/2013/08/22/from-hardwood-to-hashtag-how-nba-culture-gave-rise-to-throwback-thursday>.
3. Digital Trends Everything you need to know about your favorite day: Throwback Thursday (er, #tbt) <https://www.digitaltrends.com/social-media/where-did-throwbackthusday-come-from/>.
4. These dates were designed for analytical convenience, and correspond with my PhD research.
5. While I am including emoji as a characteristic in the user comments, I would like to also point out that emoji are frequently used in the captions of many @nytfood posts (including those that do not have the #tbt hashtag). I do not consider emoji as a common characteristic for the captions because they are not a key mechanism for separating these posts from standard posts – i.e., they are generally not used for elitist stance acts.
6. See, for example, the work required for contemporary food styling: "Lights, Camera, Food!" by Mark E. Trent, 2015. <https://well.blogs.nytimes.com/2015/03/13/lights-camera-food/>.
7. According to recent statistics, most (approximately 85 percent) Instagram users are under the age of 45. See <https://blog.hootsuite.com/instagram-demographics/>.
8. Please note that irony and/or humor are present across the various characteristics; however, examples that I placed in this category are those that are explicitly sardonic, and served only this purpose in the written caption.
9. See <https://flashbak.com/youve-come-a-long-way-baby-virginia-slims-advertising-year-by-year-365664/>.

References

Agha, Asif (2007), 'Recombinant Selves in Mass Mediated Spacetime', *Language & Communication*, 27: 320–335.

Agha, Asif (2011), 'Meet Mediatization', *Language & Communication*, 31(3): 163–170.

Althusser, Louis (1971), 'Ideology and Ideological State Apparatuses: Notes Towards an Investigation', in Ben Brewster (ed), *Lenin and Philosophy*, 85–126, New York: Monthly Review Press.

Androutsopoulos, Jannis (2014), 'Mediatization and Sociolinguistic Change. Key Concepts, Research Traditions, Open Issues', in Jannis Androutsopoulos (ed), *Mediatization and Sociolinguistic Change*, 3–48, Berlin: De Gruyter.

Bakhtin, Mikhail ([1975] 1981), *The Dialogic Imagination: Four Essays by M. M. Bakhtin*, ed. Michael Holquist, trans. Caryl Emerson and Michael Holquist, Austin, TX: University of Texas Press.

Barthes, Roland ([1967] 1990), 'Rhetorics of the Sign: The Reason of Fashion', in Roland Barthes, *The Fashion System*, 263–273, trans. Matthew Ward and Richard Howard, Berkeley, CA: University of California Press.

Blommaert, Jan (2015), 'Chronotopes, Scales, and Complexity in the Study of Language in Society', *Annual Review of Anthropology*, 44: 105–116.

Blommaert, Jan (2018), 'Are Chronotopes Helpful?', Working Papers in *Urban Language & Literacies*. Paper 243. Available online: https://www.academia.edu/36905272/WP243_Blommaert_2018._Are_chronotopes_helpful

Bourdieu, Pierre (1984), *Distinction: A Social Critique of the Judgment of Taste*, trans. Richard Nice, Cambridge, MA: Harvard University Press.

Cavanaugh, Jillian R. and Kathleen C. Riley, eds. (2017), 'The Semiotics of Food-and-Language', Special Issue, *Semiotic Review*, 5. Available online: https://www.semioticreview.com/ojs/index.php/sr/issue/view/1.

Damari, Rebecca Rubin (2010), 'Intertextual Stancetaking and the Local Negotiation of Cultural Identities by a Binational Couple', *Journal of Sociolinguistics*, 14(5): 609–629.

Du Bois, John (2007), 'The Stance Triangle', in Robert Englebretson (ed), *Stancetaking in Discourse*, 139–182, Amsterdam: John Benjamins.

Englebretson, Robert, ed. (2007), *Stancetaking in Discourse: Subjectivity, Evaluation, Interaction*, Amsterdam: John Benjamins.

Gillen, Julia and Guy Merchant (2013), 'Contact Calls: Twitter as a Dialogic Social and Linguistic Practice, *Language Sciences*, (35): 47–58.

Heyd, Theresa and Cornelius Puschmann (2017), 'Hashtagging and Functional Shift: Adaptation and Appropriation of the #', *Journal of Pragmatics*, 116: 51–63.

Jaffe, Alexandra (2009), 'Introduction: The Sociolinguistics of Stance,' in Alexandra Jaffe (ed), *Stance: Sociolinguistic Perspectives*, 3–28, New York: Oxford University Press.

Jaworski, Adam and Crispin Thurlow (2009), 'Taking an Elitist Stance: Ideology and Discursive Production of Social Distinction', in Alexandra Jaffe (ed), *Stance: Sociolinguistic Perspectives*, 195–226, New York: Oxford University Press.

Jaworski, Adam and Crispin Thurlow (2017), 'Mediatizing the "Super-Rich," Normalizing Privilege', *Social Semiotics*, 27(3): 276–287.

Jaworski, Adam and Justine Coupland (2005), 'Othering in Gossip: "You Go Out You Have a Laugh and You Can Pull Yeah Okay But Like...", *Language in Society*, 34: 667–694.

Johnston, Josée and Shyon Baumann (2010), *Foodies: Democracy and Distinction in the Gourmet Foodscape*, New York: Taylor & Francis.

Jones, Rodney H., Alice Chik and Christoph Hafner (2015), 'Introduction: Discourse Analysis and Digital Practices', in Rodney H. Jones, Alice Chik and Christoph Hafner (eds), *Discourse and Digital Practices: Doing Discourse Analysis in the Digital Age*, 1–17, Abingdon, UK and New York: Routledge.

Jurafsky, Dan (2014), *The Language of Food: A Linguist Reads the Menu*, New York: W.W. Norton & Company.

Kenway, Jane and Michael Lazarus (2017), 'Elite Schools, Class Disavowal and the Mystification of Virtues', *Social Semiotics*, 27(3): 265–275.

Khan, Shamus R. (2014), 'The Ease of Mobility' in Thomas Birtchnell and Javier Caletrío (eds), *Elite Mobilities*, 136–148, London: Routledge.

Kiesling, Scott (2018), 'YouTube Yinzers: Stancetaking and the Performance of 'Pittsburghese'', in Reem Bassiouney (ed), *Identity and Dialect Performance: A Study of Communities and Dialects*, 245–264, London and New York: Routledge.

Kress, Gunther and Theo van Leeuwen (2006), *Reading Images: The Grammar of Visual Design*, 2nd edn, New York: Routledge.

Krotz, Friedrich (2009), 'Mediatization: A Concept with Which to Grasp Media and Societal Change', in Knut Lundby (ed), *Mediatization: Concept, Changes, Consequences*, 19–38, New York: Peter Lang.

Lempert, Michael (2009), 'On "Flip-Flopping": Branded Stance-Taking in the U.S. Electoral Politics', *Journal of Sociolinguistics*, 13(2): 223–248.

Lyons, Agnieszka and Caroline Tagg (2019), 'The Discursive Construction of Mobile Chronotopes in Mobile-Phone Messaging', *Language in Society*, 48(5): 657–683.

Machin, David (2007), *Introduction to Multimodal Analysis*, London: Bloomsbury.

Mapes, Gwynne (2018), '(De)constructing Distinction: Class Inequality and Elite Authenticity in Mediatized Food Discourse', *Journal of Sociolinguistics*, 23(2): 265–287.

Martín Rojo, Luisa and Clara Molina (2017), 'Cosmopolitan Stance Negotiation in Multicultural Academic Settings', *Journal of Sociolinguistics*, 21(5): 672–695.

Marwick, Alice E. (2013), *Status Update: Celebrity, Publicity, and Branding in the Social Media Age*, New Haven, CT: Yale University Press.

Ochs, Elinor (1992), 'Indexing Gender', in Alessandro Duranti and Charles Goodwin (eds), *Rethinking Context: Language as an Interactive Phenomenon*, 335–358, Cambridge: Cambridge University Press.

Page, Ruth E. (2012), 'The Linguistics of Self-Branding and Micro-Celebrity in Twitter: The Role of Hashtags', *Discourse & Communication*, 6(2): 181–201.

Portmann, Lara (2020), 'Designing "Good Taste": A Social Semiotic Analysis of Corporate Instagram Practices', in Crispin Thurlow, Christa Dürscheid and Federica Diémoz (eds), *Visualizing Digital Discourse: Interactional, Institutional and Ideological Perspectives*, 203–225, Berlin: De Gruyter.

Rauniomaa, Mirka (2003), '*Stance Accretion: Some Initial Observations*', Unpublished manuscript, University of California, Santa Barbara.

Ross, Andrew S. and Michele Zappavigna (2020), 'My Sport, My Perspectives: Intersubjectivity in Cyclist Instagram Posts', *Discourse, Context & Media*, 34.

Silverstein, Michael (2003), 'Indexical Order and the Dialectics of Sociolinguistic Life', *Language & Communication*, 23(3-4): 193–229.

Squires, Lauren (2016), 'Twitter: Design, Discourse, and the Implications of Public Text', in Alexandra Georgakopoulou and Tereza Spilioti (eds), *Handbook of Language and Digital Communication*, 239–255, Abingdon, UK and New York: Routledge.

Taha, Maisa C. (2017), 'Shadow Subjects: A Category of Analysis for Empathic Stancetaking', *Journal of Linguistic Anthropology*, 27(2): 190–209.

Tannen, Deborah (2007) *Talking Voices: Repetition, Dialogue, and Imagery in Conversational Discourse*, 2nd edn, New York and Cambridge, UK: Cambridge University Press.

Thurlow, Crispin (2013), 'Fakebook: Synthetic Media, Pseudo-Sociality and the Rhetorics of Web 2.0', in Deborah Tannen and Anna Marie Trester (eds), *Discourse 2.0: Language and New Media*, 225–249, Washington, DC: Georgetown University Press.

Thurlow, Crispin (2016), 'Queering Critical Discourse Studies or/and Performing Post-class Ideologies', *Critical Discourse Studies*, 13(5): 485–514.

Thurlow, Crispin (2017), '"Forget about the Words"? Tracking the Language, Media and Semiotic Ideologies of Digital Discourse: The Case of Sexting', *Discourse, Context & Media*, 20: 10–19.

Thurlow, Crispin and Adam Jaworski (2014), 'Visible-Invisible: The Social Semiotics of Labour in Luxury Tourism', in Thomas Birtchnell and Javier Caletrío (eds), *Elite Mobilities*, 176–193. London: Routledge.

Thurlow, Crispin and Giorgia Aiello (2007), 'National Pride, Global Capital: A Social Semiotic Analysis of Transnational Visual Branding in the Airline Industry', *Visual Communication*, 6: 304–344.

Tiidenberg, Katrin and Nancy K. Baym (2017), 'Learn It, Buy It, Work It: Intensive Pregnancy on Instagram', *Social Media + Society*: 1–13.

van Dijk, Teun (2012), 'Discourse and Knowledge', in James Paul Gee and Michael Handford (eds), *Routledge Handbook of Discourse Analysis*, 587–603, London: Routledge.

van Leeuwen, Theo (2007), 'Legitimation in Discourse and Communication', *Discourse and Communication*, 1(1): 91–112.

Zappavigna, Michele (2011), 'Ambient Affiliation: A Linguistic Perspective on Twitter', *New Media & Society*, 13(5): 788–806.

Zappavigna, Michele (2015), 'Searchable Talk: The Linguistic Functions of Hashtags', *Social Semiotics*, 25(3): 274–291.

Zappavigna, Michele (2016), 'Social Media Photography: Construing Subjectivity in Instagram Images', *Visual Communication*, 15(3): 271–292.

Zhao, Sumin and Michele Zappavigna (2017), 'Beyond the Self: Intersubjectivity and the Social Semiotic Interpretation of the Selfie', *New Media & Society*, 20(5): 1735–1754.

Žižek, Slavoj (1989), *The Sublime Object of Ideology*, London and New York: Verso.

Part Two

(Re)constructing and (Re)imagining Existing Food-related Language, Practices, and Actions in Digital Environments

4

Constructing Veganism Against the Backdrop of Omnivore Cuisine: The Use of Adjectives and Modifiers in Vegan Food Blogs

Cornelia Gerhardt

1 Introduction

The proliferation of food as a resource for identity construction and distinction in industrialized countries seems to have coincided with the advent of the internet and the rise of new technologies for sharing information and for interacting across space. One such happy marriage of foodiness and computer- or technologically mediated communication (CMC or TMC) is instantiated by vegan food blogs. They allow the bloggers and their followers to construct and celebrate a certain food-based lifestyle, to create symbolic capital (Bourdieu 1984) and a virtual, but, nevertheless, meaningful and relevant community across the globe. In the context of culinary linguistics (Gerhardt, Frobenius & Ley 2013), food blogs are of interest since they are connected to the centuries-old genre of the recipe. In the linguistic study of CMC, blogs represent an essential area of inquiry because of their importance in terms of popularity, reach, and ubiquity. Still, there has been little work to date analyzing the construction of specific food lifestyles such as veganism in the new media, especially with regard to language use (but see Hart 2018, and Sneijder & te Molder e.g., 2009). This paper adds to our knowledge about CMC, uniting the internet genre "blog" with the discursive conveyance of a lifestyle choice. In the field of culinary linguistics, this paper meets the increasing interest in inquiries at the crossroads between language and food. The analysis also contributes to an understanding of pre- and post-modifications in nominal phrases/groups and adjectives following copular verbs in English, German, and French, and how these are mobilized in vegan blogs.

In this paper,[1] I will analyze adjectives and other modifiers used in vegan food blogs with a view to the collaborative TMC construction of the vegan lifestyle. The data consist of the most popular English-language vegan blog *Oh She Glows* along with one German and one French vegan blog for context and comparison. Concentrating on those words or phrases that are specific to vegan blogs (in contrast to food blogs in general), the paper analyzes two classes of adjectives: (1) *vegan* and *plant-based* (and their German and French equivalents) and (2) adjectives that are derived from animals products (e.g., *creamy/crémeux*). Starting with a closer look at (1), the use of the term *vegan*, it becomes apparent that the contextual synonym *plant-based* has to be taken into account when looking at the three different languages (and blogs). While all three blogs use the term *vegan*, in French *végétal* (plant-based) is also very common. Generally, the term *vegan* is more closely associated with a specific lifestyle and belief system, whereas *plant-based* is limited to descriptions of a type of cuisine. Both adjectives are used in the data to veganize a traditionally animal product-based (non-vegan) cuisine. In other words, vegan cuisine is constructed against the backdrop of known dishes and ingredients (e.g., *vegan pancakes* or *fromage végétal* (plant-based cheese)), which treats meat and other animal products as unmarked or expected. Similarly, (2) the use of terms such as *creamy* indicates that the culinary vocabularies of English, French, and German are deeply entrenched in an omnivore cuisine, representing a further challenge to the blog writers. Even though terms such as *meaty* or *milchig* (milky) are derivations of nouns denoting animal products, they seem unavoidable when describing the textures or flavors of food. While such terms are mostly used without any discomfort, at times the bloggers find it necessary to distance themselves from the meaning of the stem by using quotation marks (e.g., *"meaty"*).

In what follows, after introducing the rising interest in culinary linguistics and literature on (food) blogs, veganism will be presented as a lifestyle choice. In the main part of the paper, I will analyze adjectives and modifications in three vegan food blogs that are respectively written in Canadian English, German, and French. The (1) analysis of the omnipresent adjective *vegan* (and to a lesser degree its contextual synonym *plant-based*) will be complemented by (2) a look at adjectives like *creamy* that derive from animal products.

2 Language and food – food blogs

Against the backdrop of a general rise in interest in food and nutrition by the public and long-standing research traditions in neighboring fields like sociology, anthropology, and history (Gerhardt 2013), there has been a recent surge of linguistic studies in the domain of food. A number of book-length publications have made the many-sided intricate entangling between these two major semiotic systems visible (Lavric & Konzett 2009; Newman 2009; Pinnavaia 2010; Szatrowski 2014; Diederich 2015). *Culinary Linguistics: The Chef's Special* on discourse and culture (Gerhardt 2013) opens with a first attempt of delimiting the field. Recently, an AILA ReN (Research Network by the Association Internationale de Linguistique Appliquée) has formed under the heading the "Linguistics of food." In a way, linguistics is only following in the footsteps of philosophy, anthropology, and sociology by recognizing the centrality of food for humankind as a historic, social, cultural, and linguistic construct.

Of interest for the construction of veganism in food blogs is Bourdieu's (1984) classic idea of distinction: the idea that our position in society determines our taste. Interestingly, taste is defined *ex negativo*, as not being the taste of "others":

> Tastes (i.e., manifested preferences) are the practical affirmation of an inevitable difference. It is no accident that, when they have to be justified, they are asserted purely negatively, by the refusal of other tastes. In matters of taste, more than anywhere else, all determination is negation and tastes are perhaps first and foremost distastes, disgust provoked by horror or visceral intolerance ('sick-making') of the tastes of others.
>
> Bourdieu 1984: 56

Similarly, in a study on organic farming, Cook (2007: 19) writes: "Organic food and farming are often defined as what they are not [...] Exclusively organic producers compare their produce with non-organic equivalents; retailers of both organic and non-organic produce do not." While for Bourdieu lower classes represent the "others" from whom one wants to distinguish oneself, in this paper I show that in vegan blogs it is sometimes the non-vegan cuisine that is indexed as "other," even though the bloggers heavily rely on it in their posts.

To continue with the literature on blogs, according to Miller and Shepherd (2012: 269), blogs consist of "dated, time-stamped entries, organized in reverse chronological order; most also include a link for reader commentary and the author's name" (cf. also Herring et al. 2004; Myers 2010; for more recent overviews, see Frobenius & Gerhardt 2017; Heyd 2017). Myers (2010: 2–4) states that, "despite all the possibilities open to bloggers for inclusion of pictures, sound and video, written language still remains central to most blogs." Food blogs specifically constitute a new, but by now well-established, culinary genre (Lofgren 2013) or digital food culture (Lupton 2018). The popularity and ubiquity of food blogs can be seen from attempts to set up associations (e.g., the UK food bloggers association, cf. Cox & Blake 2011). Because of their importance as a social phenomenon, they have been studied from a number of perspectives: the construction of media or culinary personae such as "the online domestic goddess" (Rodney et al. 2017; cf. also Salvio 2012 for blogs and domesticity) or mother (Seddon 2011; Domingo et al. 2014), the function of food blogs in diaspora (for South Asia, cf. Hegde 2014, or, for Russia, cf. Holak 2014), popular topics such as food porn (Dejmanee 2016) or health-related themes (see below), and the discourse about food and exercise (Lynch 2012). The food portrayed in a given blog "plays a defining role in the medium through how it portrays the unique character and community of a food blog" (McGaughey 2010: 74). Besides the obvious impact that culinary lifestyles or cultures have on food blogs, including content and visuality, the opposite has also been observed: namely, that food blogs influence the evolution of food cultures (Lee, Samdanis & Gkiousou 2014). Similarly, Véron (2016) sees veganism as having been popularized in France with the help of food blogs. Of importance for the analysis below, Diemer and Frobenius's (2013) study of structural and lexical features finds that a special-purpose vocabulary is used in food blogs pertaining to "ingredients, food and recipe types" (Diemer & Frobenius 2013: 59). It is in this lexical field where differences between vegan food blogs and food blogs in general (non-vegan food blogs) can be predicted. Other typical genre features reflected in jargon use (kitchen utensils, measurements), but also blog-specific vocabulary, will probably not differ across types of food blogs (Diemer & Frobenius 2013: 58; Cesiri 2016: 56). For the same reason, other structural, lexical, or syntactic features like verb use (Diemer & Frobenius 2013: 60), sentence length (Cesiri 2016: 55), or visual aspects (Koh 2014/2015) will not be considered here. The analysis will instead focus on lexical phenomena, specifically uses of adjectives and modifiers that construct the recipes as vegan.

3 Veganism and vegan discourse

Veganism can be traced back to the 1940s, when Donald Watson founded *The Vegan Society*. Veganism is defined as "a way of living which seeks to exclude, as far as is possible and practicable, all forms of exploitation of, and cruelty to, animals for food, clothing or any other purpose" (Vegan Society 2017: n.p.).[2] One main pillar of veganism is a plant-based diet with no animal products, including eggs, fish, insects, dairy products, and honey. However, veganism not only represents a specific diet, but also a complex lifestyle choice:

Vegans are people who object to the use of nonhuman animal products for food, cosmetics, clothing, and vivisection – virtually all invasive activities involving nonhuman animals. In the United States adopting such a lifestyle is a major change from the normative practice and ideology of human dominance over nonhuman animals.

McDonald 2000: 2

Hence, people who identify as "ethical vegans" believe in the equality of humans and animals as a general worldview, for instance, by using the terms "human and nonhuman animals" (cf. also public debates under the heading "speciesism"). This ethical position stands in contrast to vegetarianism since the latter tends to be associated with a specific diet only. "Because veganism encompasses all aspects of daily living, not just diet, it is inaccurate for people to define themselves as [vegan] simply because they have adopted the vegan mode of eating" (Stepaniak 1998: 21). Vegans frame themselves as "Living with conscience, conviction and compassion" (Stepaniak 2000: front cover). They learn about the vegan lifestyle through reading organizational newsletters and brochures from animal rights and vegan organizations, as well as cookbooks and magazines (McDonald 2000: 13). I assume that with the proliferation of new media, online genres such as blogs, particularly vegan food blogs, also play a meaningful role in this learning process.

A differentiation should be made between "health" and "ethical" vegans (Dyett et al. 2013; Radnitz, Beezhold & DiMatteo 2015). While health vegans choose the lifestyle assuming that it is beneficial for themselves, ethical vegans are concerned about animal well-being. Both parties not only have different reasons for choosing veganism, but their compliance and nutrition also differ: Health vegans adhere to the diet for longer periods of time, and typically consume more high-sugar food, both fruit and sweets (Radnitz, Beezhold & DiMatteo 2015). However, the health advantages of veganism seem disputable. A publication by the Vegan Society states: "Sensible vegan diets provide ample amounts of all the essential nutrients, but established guidelines must be followed to ensure sound nutrition" (Langley 1995). Hence, as with any diet, the norms of veganism may not always be congruent with their everyday application. While ideal diets may cover all nutritional needs, how often vegans adhere to those guidelines in their everyday lives remains unclear.

To contextualize this study, especially with the proliferation of anti-science post-truth rhetoric online – including regarding dietary practices – I summarize some recent research about the healthfulness of veganism. The following studies are all concerned with the nutritional effects of veganism based on physiological studies (including blood or fecal tests, Body Mass Index, and cardiograms). In other words, they are not concerned with the ideals of vegan dietary guidelines, but with the actual health of practicing vegans.

A number of studies indicate that nutritional deficits are frequently diagnosed among practicing vegans. A major study based on German data recommends that vegans take "supplements containing riboflavin, cobalamin, calcium, and iodine. Intake of total energy and protein should also be improved" (Waldmann et al. 2003: 947). Overall, the study's "results confirm the notion that a vegan diet is deficient in vitamin B-12, which may have an unfavorable effect on CHD [coronary heart disease] risk" (Waldmann et al. 2005). It is also suggested that young women monitor their iron status (Waldmann et al. 2004). Studies from other countries confirm that "micronutrients of special concern for the vegan include vitamins B-12 and D, calcium, and long-chain n-3 (omega-3) fatty acids. Unless vegans regularly consume foods that are fortified with these nutrients, appropriate supplements should be consumed. In some cases, the iron and zinc status of vegans may also be of concern" (Craig 2009). Again, "vegans may be at increased risk for deficiencies in vitamin B-12, iron, calcium, vitamin D, omega-3 fatty acids, and protein" (Fields et al. 2016, cf. also Burkert et al. 2014 for nutritional deficits for Austrian vegans). With regard to children, Sanders and Manning (1992: 11) find that they "can be successfully reared on a vegan diet providing sufficient care is taken to avoid the known pitfalls of a bulky diet and vitamin B-12 deficiency."

A number of studies show the benefits of a vegan diet for specific groups of people, such as fibromyalgia (Kaartinen et al. 2000) and rheumatoid arthritis patients (Hänninen et al. 1999). Moreover, vegan diets have a positive effect on the prevention of specific diseases like cancer (Dinu et al. 2016), type 2 diabetes (Barnard et al. 2006), or obesity (Turner-McGrievy, Barnard & Scialli 2007). Goff et al. (2005; similarly, Craig 2009) observe that vegan diets are often good for the heart and cardiovascular health generally (but see Waldmann et al. 2005 who found an unfavorable effect).

Since I am not a physician or dietician, I do not want to venture to draw conclusions from this. However, importantly for this paper, the complexity of the question should have become clear: Veganism is not as easy to follow or self-evident as it is often portrayed to be on CMC sites for vegans (Sneijder & te Molder 2009). The question of whether or not veganism is healthy cannot be easily answered. However, existing research indicates that veganism for health reasons entails a number of complex nutritional choices for the individual. Conflicting results complicate the topic even further. In addition, in the framework of a book on social media and food, it is important to note that food blogs in general do not necessarily offer nutritionally balanced recipes (Lynch 2010; Schneider et al. 2013) and that consumers do not necessarily trust the information on food blogs (Ho & Chien 2010). Moreover, evidence has been found that the content of healthy living blogs, a related genre, is thematically consistent with dysfunctional eating attitudes (Boepple & Thompson 2014).

Studies pertaining to the language used in naturally occurring vegan discourse seem scarce: Hart (2018) shows that traditional gender norms are perpetuated in vegan food blogs. Sneijder and te Molder (2004, 2005, 2009) discuss vegan online forums from the perspective of discursive psychology. In their 2009 paper, they raise a point that is directly related to the section above: Users of the Dutch online forum for vegans that they examine construct vegan meal preparation as simple, ordinary practices (including the avoidance of monotony). Furthermore, methods for health control, i.e., taking pills, are portrayed as routine procedures. In earlier papers, they discuss script-formulations such as *if... then...*, e.g., *If you ensure that you get enough calcium... it's impossible for a problem to occur* (Sneijder & te Molder 2004: 605) or *if you eat a varied diet, then you don't have any problems* (Sneijder & te Molder 2005: 675) which attribute health problems to the behavior of individuals. Even though many vegans choose the lifestyle because of its supposed healthiness, it is often health problems caused by veganism such as vitamin deficiencies that are discussed in such forums (Sneijder & te Molder 2004).

4 Data and research methods

This study is based on the Canadian English-language blog *Oh She Glows* (Liddon 2016). The blog was chosen because it ranked first in a study on vegan food blogs by the Academy of Culinary Nutrition (ACN 2015), thus representing a ratified exemplar within the vegan community. The corpus, collected in January 2016, encompasses 10,631 words (1,841 types and 10,481 tokens)[3] consisting of all blog posts to date,[4] including titles, recipes, and all other text by the blogger. To provide an intercultural and cross-linguistic perspective, the results of this corpus-based research were compared to the language use in one German and one French vegan blog in October 2017. These two blogs were not analyzed quantitatively. Rather, all of their blog posts to date were searched for occurrences of the adjectives and pre-/post-modifiers that were found in the English language blog (for the exact list, see below in Section 5. Both were also chosen because of their popularity. *Nicole Just*, known as La Veganista (Just 2017), published a number of vegan cookery books and regularly appears on public national television (ARD). The French blog *100% Végétal - Cuisine Vegan* is also run by a woman (Laforêt 2017); it appears that the vegan world is one that is primarily populated by women. Since veganism is a global trend, a broadening of the database to non-English language data may help forestall a local (in this case, Canadian) bias. Even though I look at these three blogs cross-linguistically, they should be understood as three specimens of one global trend, which happen to be in different languages. Hence, differences found in these three blogs should not necessarily be seen as indications of different cultures, but rather as illustrating the scope of vegan food blogs.

5 A lexical analysis of vegan blogs: Adjectives and modifiers

As stated earlier, it is primarily with regard to the special-purpose vocabulary used in food blogs that vegan blogs differ from other food blogs in general. Examining the corpus with regard to technical terms pertaining to "ingredients, food and recipe types" (Diemer & Frobenius 2013: 59) it soon becomes apparent that "veganism" is semantically referred to and syntactically constructed with the help of pre-modification and adjectives as subject-complements. The following expressions were used in the English corpus to identify the special features of recipes (the numbers indicate the number of times each expression was used in the corpus):

> *vegan* (47), *gluten-free* (26), *raw* (21), *soy-free* (13), *refined sugar free* (10), *cashew cream* (9), *nut-free* (8), *creamy* (7), *almond milk* (6), *grain-free* (6), *coconut whipped cream* (4), *low-sodium* (4), *unflavoured* (2), *unsweetened* (2), *cashew sour cream* (3), *no bake/raw* (3), *coconut cream* (2), *non-dairy* (2), *oil-free* (2), *almond butter* (1), *animal-based* (1), *"cheesy"* (1), *"meaty"* (1), *meatloaf* (1), *meaty* (1), *nut and seed based parmesan cheese* (1), *nut and seed parmesan cheese* (1), *plant-based* (1), *soy milk* (1), *taco meat* (1), *veggie-centric* (1), *veggie-packed* (1)

As one can see, the recipes in the Canadian English-language vegan blog are not only qualified as *vegan*, they are also often attributed other qualities such as *gluten-free*. All of these concepts were searched in the French and the German blogs. Because of the grammatical differences between these three languages, syntactic differences must be expected. In German, besides phrasal pre-modifiers like adjectives, we may expect longer clausal pre-modification. One could imagine constructions such as *der in der Schüssel vorbereitete Teig* (the in-the-bowl prepared dough) or *der bereits abgekühlte Kuchen* (the already chilled cake). In French, on the other hand, most adjectives are post-modifiers such as *Terrine végétale* (plant-based pie). However, as stated earlier, despite these syntactic differences that are without any doubt linguistically relevant, the main interest of this paper lies in the use and the meaning of the terms referring to the vegan nature of the recipes in the blogs.

In the following, the adjectives and modifiers found in the three vegan food blogs will be analyzed in two groups. First, (1) the abundant use of *vegan* will be further scrutinized, also with regard to the contextual synonyms *plant-based/ végétal*. Then, (2) I will discuss *creamy/cremig/sahnig/crémeux* against the backdrop of traditional food and dishes in Western countries that often include animal products.

5.1 Veganizing omnivore cuisine: The adjectives vegan/plant-based and their German and French equivalents

V*egan* is by far the most frequently used adjective in the Canadian blog (47 times). This finding can be expected for a number of reasons: First, *vegan* represents the base from which *veganism* derived, and is itself a derivation of the clipping *veg* (from *vegetable*) and the suffix *-an* (according to the OED), although its etymology is lost in the pronunciation. It represents the obvious choice of an adjective to modify dishes and food items in vegan cuisine. In the context of CMC, it has the added value of making the recipes easily retrievable for search engines or tagging. The adjective *vegan* often modifies dishes or recipes that traditionally contain animal products.

(1) *Crowd-Pleasing Vegan Caesar Salad*
(2) *Easy Vegan and Gluten-Free Pancakes (Strawberry Shortcake w/Whipped Cream)*
(3) *My Favourite Vegan Chili with Homemade Sour Cream*
(4) *Cauli-power Fettuccine "Alfredo" (Vegan)*
(5) *Next Level Vegan Enchiladas*

For instance, *Caesar Salad* (1) traditionally contains parmesan cheese and a dressing made of egg yolks and anchovies (fish), *Pancakes* (2) are prepared with milk and eggs, and *Chili* (3) is usually *con carne*, i.e., "with meat" (Spanish). Similar constructions can be found in the German blog:

(6) *Veganer Linseneintopf wie bei Mama*
     (Vegan lentil stew like at mom's/like at home)
(7) *Veganer Käsekuchen*
     (Vegan cheesecake)
(8) *Vegane Piroggen mit dreierlei Füllung*
     (Vegan pierogi with three kinds of filling)

For instance, *Linseneintopf* (6)[5] traditionally contains sausages or speck, and *Käsekuchen* (7) is made with cheese and eggs. However, in the German blog, we do find examples of recipes that are unmodified with *vegan* (for instance, *Meine 3 Lieblings-Pancake-Rezepte* (my 3 favorite pancake recipes) or *Porridge mit Ananas-Minze-Salat* (porridge with pineapple-mint-salad) even though both contain animal products (eggs and milk, and milk, respectively) in their traditional forms. The German blogger seems to rely on the general multimodal framing of the website as a context for the narrowing of meaning to "vegan X."

While German borrowed the word *vegan* from English and the blogger uses it almost exclusively to describe her recipes, the French blog studied uses *végétal* much more frequently, an adjective that has been borrowed from Latin (a derivation of "vegetare") in the sixteenth century. Hence, its literal meaning in English is plant-based (for the use of the English borrowing *vegan* in French, though, see below). Note that vegetables in present day French are called légumes (not *végétal*). So, in the French blog, *végétal* is used like *vegan* in the English and German blogs:

(9) *Blinis de sarrasin et caviar végétale*
     (Buckwheat blinis and vegan caviar)
(10) *Terrine végétale aux noix*
     (Vegan terrine with walnuts)

In both dishes (9, 10), the dough or mixture presupposes the use of animal products like milk and eggs. Rather than using *vegan* though, a borrowing that can be found in French (see below), the blogger uses the term *végétal* (plant-based). Also, in contrast to the Canadian and German blogs, the French recipes or dishes are far less often described on that level (as vegan or plant-based). For instance, the blog contains 6 recipes for *Terrine* and only one (example 10 above) is modified with *végétale* (with the feminine gender inflection).[6]

The term *vegan* is also used, albeit much less frequently. It is marked as a foreign borrowing, not fully integrated into French syntax and phonology. For instance, in *cuisine vegan* (vegan cuisine) or *Makis vegan colorés* (colored vegan makis) the adjective *vegan* is not inflected (interestingly, in contrast to the

Constructing Veganism Against the Backdrop of Omnivore Cuisine 97

Japanese term *maki* that does get the French inflectional plural morpheme). In addition, the acute accent is missing that one would expect in this position for French phonology and spelling (végan).

Apart from dishes or recipes, it is often specific food items which semantically presuppose an animal product that are modified by the adjective *vegan*.

(11) *I recommend serving this casserole with a pat of vegan butter or coconut oil to really take it over the top.*

(12) *This time I served the chili with a homemade vegan sour cream and now I can't believe that I've been eating my chili without it for all this time.*

Both *butter* (11) and *sour cream* (12) are typically dairy products. By adding *vegan*, the blogger clarifies that it is actually an entirely different substance that is used in these recipes. Such substances are often necessary for the texture (e.g., to replace eggs or cream), or they have to be added to bulk up the recipe (e.g., to replace the meat in chili con carne). The example in (13) involves cheese: *fromage végétal*.

(13) *Tartelettes aux figues et fromage végétal aux noix*
(Fig tarts and vegan walnut cheese)

The exact nature of this vegan cheese (13) is left open. It may be made out of nut milk or the walnuts may represent extra ingredients, like in non-vegan walnut cheeses. Even classic meat products can be veganized in this way:

(14) *Veganes Mett – Das muss mett dabei sein!*
(Vegan ground meat – This must be part (of this blog))[7]

(15) *Lentil loaf : le pain de viande vegan*
(Lentil loaf: the vegan meatloaf (syntactically: the loaf of meat vegan))

In the German example (14), the nature of the whole dish "vegan ground meat" is opaque. One cannot know what it is actually made of and what type of dish this recipe title advertises until one reads the list of ingredients. In the French example (15) the blogger first uses the borrowing *lentil loaf* which may be unclear to French speakers (even though *lentil* might be close enough to its origin, which happens to be French, i.e., *lentille*). The following explication though *le pain de viande vegan* (the vegan meatloaf) is, again, nontransparent regarding the actual nature of the dish. In other words, if one wanted to know what kind of dish (15) represented or what the main ingredient was, one would have to gather that from the English *lentil*. Hence, with regard to recipes that consist entirely of meat in traditional cuisine, the modification with *vegan* raises the question of what dish one would actually prepare. So regarding recipes that one could label as surrogates or substitutes (for animal products) e.g., *fromage végétal* (vegan cheese), it seems that it is often taken to be more important to frame them in terms of an omnivore cuisine than to inform the readers about the nature of the actual dish, i.e., its main ingredients. The synonym *plant-based* is used only once in the Canadian corpus. This may partly be an effect of CMC, since *vegan* will be the more common search term. However, it is also connected to the discourse about veganism being a lifestyle. The adjective *plant-based* applies to a certain kind of diet with no or little animal products. While it may be a contextual synonym in the data, elsewhere it might be more ambiguous. *Vegan*, in contrast, indexes a whole worldview which gives animals the same status as humans, e.g., through the use of terms such as "nonhuman animal" (McDonald 2000). Hence, the use of *vegan* positions the blog within the vegan movement, indicating that it is not just a website listing plant-based recipes.

To sum up, the English blog uses *vegan* more consistently than the German one and even more than the French one, though this could be idiosyncratic for this blogger (this exploratory study does not allow a generalization because of its limited scope and should not be taken as indicative of the three different languages). In the context of CMC, with respect to search engine optimization, the Canadian blogger's frequent use of *vegan* seems an effective strategy to increase the likelihood of having her recipes found and featured prominently. While *vegan* can be understood as representing a lifestyle choice, the contextual synonym *plant-based* functions as a descriptor of a type of recipe. This section has illustrated that vegan bloggers predominantly use omnivore cuisine as a backdrop for their vegan recipes, in this manner referencing the known and traditional culinary culture. This strategy is all-prevalent with regard to classic dishes containing animal products such as pancakes or lentil stew, and for a number of animal products that are frequently used in omnivore cuisine such as cream or milk. While this practice allows the readers to rely on their existing knowledge both about a cuisine that has been passed down through generations (e.g., cheesecake) or about recent global trends (e.g., chili or blini), concurrently, this may entail a lack of information about the exact nature of the dish (e.g., a mixture of crumbled rice cakes with tomato paste as vegan ground meat). While in such cases, the terms *vegan/végétal* index the replacement of animal-based products with plant-based substitutes, the following section concentrates on adjectives that derive from animal products.

5.2 The use of adjectival derivations from animal products (e.g., creamy and meaty)

This section will examine the adjective *creamy* – for the German blog *cremig/sahnig* and for French *crémeux* – as well as *meaty* and *cheesy*, all derivations of nouns denoting animal products. Since there are hardly any "native" vegans in the sense that such vegans would have only tasted vegan food throughout their lives, the bloggers can typically rely on their readers' knowledge of the taste and texture of animal products and meat. Furthermore, it seems that the languages studied here – all historically representing cultures that have no long-standing vegan tradition – make the use of animal-based concepts unavoidable. So the affordances or deficiencies of English, German, and French may force the bloggers to use such words. As we can see in the following examples from the Canadian blog, the derivations *meaty* and *cheesy*, which can be used to refer to specific tastes or textures, are clearly "othered" (Bourdieu 1984) or flagged as being out-of-place through the use of quotation marks.

(16) *Browned, almost caramelized bottoms, crispy, blackened leaves, and a tender yet "meaty" texture. Yes, I just said meaty texture.*

(17) *The nutritional yeast gives this sauce a lovely "cheesy" flavour while the blended cauliflower creates a luxurious (but light) creamy base.*

By using quotation marks, the blogger distances herself from the meaning of the stem of the word that refers to an animal product. In addition, the repetition, an indirect self-quotation, *Yes, I just said meaty texture* (16), together with the quasi-interaction with the blog users indicates that the blogger is well aware that her choice of words may seem out of place in the context of a vegan food blog. In (17), *cheesy* might potentially also be used with quotation marks because of its polysemy, with the figurative meaning being much more common. In German, too, the uncommon use of *käsig* (cheesy) is marked with quotation marks in *käsig-würzig* (cheesy-aromatic) (18), potentially because of the uncommon ad hoc compounding. *Fleischig* (meaty), however, can only be found in *rotfleischig* (red-fleshed) as a denomination for a certain type of melon.[8]

(18) *Nährhefeflocken*: Auch als Würzhefeflocken im Handel. Schmecken ganz leicht „käsig-würzig". Ich mache daraus veganen Parmesan,*
(Nutritional yeast flakes*: Also available as seasoned yeast flakes. Taste slightly "cheesy-aromatic". I make vegan parmesan out of them,)

In French, these derivations could not be found: Neither *fromageux* nor *viandeux* were used in the blog. The reason may be that both adjectives are used in vegan contexts to refer to people who eat cheese or meat.⁹

Of further interest is the adjective *creamy*, derived from *cream*, an early borrowing from Old French to Middle English, which also denotes an animal product.

(19) *For a creamy twist, try subbing some of the butter/oil in the sweet potato mash for full-fat canned coconut cream.*
(20) *A delicious, creamy vegan Caesar salad that will please a crowd!*
(21) *Eric is in love with this creamy cauliflower pasta dish.*

As one can see in these examples (19–21), they all mean creamy in texture. Moreover, *creamy* is used unapologetically; it seems that no reference to the animal origin remains. Apparently, the "beastly nature" of the term is not transparent in the usage of the blogger.¹⁰

The linguistic forms used in German and French are different. German uses another word, *Sahne*, for the animal product (its adjectival derivation being *sahnig*); the noun *Creme* is reserved for cosmetic or medical creams (the adjectival derivation being *cremig*). So in German *cremig* is not a derivation from a word denoting an animal-product word. Its use is similar to the use of *creamy* though, in the context of food.

(22) *Cremiges Kokoseis mit Vanille: Nur 5 Zutaten, ohne Kochen*
(Creamy coconut ice cream with vanilla: only 5 ingredients, no cooking)
(23) *Buntes Gemüse, zu Rosen gedreht und in einer cremig-herzhaften Quiche mit Mürbeteigboden verpackt.*
(Vegetables with different colors, rolled up into roses and boxed in a creamy, savory quiche with a short pastry base.)

As these examples indicate (22–23), *cremig* is used in the same way as in English, to indicate texture. Likewise, the same seems to hold for *sahnig*, even though it represents a derivation from the animal product Sahne (cream):

(24) *Aus den Resten im Mixbehälter mache ich schnelle „Cashewmilch" oder „-sahne"… Nun solange Wasser zugießen, bis die gewünschte Konsistenz (von sahnig bis milchig) erreicht ist.*
(Out of the residues in the blender I make fast "cashew milk" or "cream" … Now add water until the desired texture (from creamy to milky) is achieved.)
(25) *Die eingeweichten Cashewkerne mit 300 ml Wasser sehr fein pürieren, so dass eine sahnige Flüssigkeit entsteht.*

(Blend the soaked cashew nuts very fine with 300 ml water to produce a creamy liquid.)

In example (24), it is the nouns „*Cashewmilch*" *oder* „*-sahne*" ("cashew milk" or "cream") that are marked as non-standard usages with the use of quotation marks. However, again the adjective *sahnig* indicates the texture and is not understood as referring to an animal product. So even though German offers the alternative *cremig* (a derivation of medical cream) for *sahnig*, the blogger does not seem to mind using a derivation which is based on the animal product. The blogger uses both alternatives without any quotation marks or other means of signaling distancing from the term(s).

In French, the cognate *crémeux*, on the other hand, is not a borrowing and may for this reason be potentially semantically more transparent. However, in the French blog, too, *crémeux* is used without any signs of distancing:

(26) *Le mélange va devenir plus épais, bien crémeux et une partie de l'alcool du vin va s'évaporer à la cuisson.*
(The mixture will become thicker, quite creamy, and some of the alcohol in the wine will evaporate during cooking.)

(27) *Fondante, crémeuse (un poil plus que la féta d'origine animale pour être exacte, mais personnellement je ne suis pas dérangée par un peu plus de crémeux !) incroyablement parfumée,*
(Melty, creamy (a little more than feta of animal origin to be exact, but personally I'm not bothered by a little more creamy [texture]!), incredibly fragrant,)

Interestingly, the French blogger distances herself from the use of *simili carné* (meat surrogates or substitutes) though:

(28) *Pour un projet ... on m'a demandé de créer quelques recettes autour des fameux "simili carnés". Ces deux mots ont tendance à me faire grimacer*
(For a project ... I was asked to create some recipes for those famous "meat substitutes". Those two words tend to make me make faces)

So surrogates for dairy products, hence, words for dairy products (e.g., in the German blog „*Cashewmilch*" *oder* „*-sahne*" ("cashew milk" or "cream") (24) or in the English blog *vegan butter* (11)) are used very frequently and often without any distancing, whereas meat-related products and words (*meaty* or *carné* (out of meat)) are projected as "the other" (Bourdieu 1984).

In sum, while *meaty* and *cheesy* are only used carefully by the English blogger, the derivations of *cream* do not seem reminiscent of their etymology as an animal product, but rather are used to describe texture throughout. Even though German offers a contextual synonym (*cremig*) that is not based on an animal product, one still finds the derivation *sahnig*, which in turn does derive from an animal product, *Sahne* (cream). In French, *crémeux* might be more transparent, since *crème* is not a borrowing. However, both the German and the French blogs use terms derived from animal products without any signs of discomfort. While the use of *creamy* and *crémeux* may seem to a certain extent unavoidable in English and French, the German example indicates that the blogger does not seem to be as aware of such issues of word use or does not seem to mind. The abundance of dairy surrogates and relative scarcity of meat surrogates indicates that meat is considered more problematic than other animal products.

6 Discussion and conclusion

The present analysis of adjectives and modifiers in three food blogs in different languages represents an inquiry into the construction of veganism as found in a CMC context. By far the most frequently used adjectives are *vegan* (English), *vegan* (German), and *végétal* (French) to modify dishes and ingredients. While *vegan* may represent the most obvious word choice, in a CMC context, this also represents a good strategy since it allows the recipes to be more easily found with the help of search engines; put differently, they become "searchable talk" (Zappavigna 2018). Different patterns emerged for modifications of dishes compared to those of ingredients. With regard to dishes, *vegan* usually not only represents a syntactic, but also a semantic modification in that the core of the dish seems preserved. Examples include *Fettuccine* (4), *Pancakes* (2) or *Linseneintopf* (lentil stew) (6), all of which continue to remain fettucine, pancakes, and lentil stew after being modified as/with *vegan*. In contrast, this is not the case for ingredients modified with *vegan*. By adding *vegan* to some animal product, the nature of the ingredient becomes unclear and the question arises as to how transparent these designations are. The actual ingredients, for instance, of *fromage végétale* (vegan cheese) (13) are unclear. This holds even more for dishes that are made almost entirely of meat: *Veganes Mett* (vegan ground meat) (14) frames the recipe in a traditional context, with *Veganes Mett* as a replacement for *Mett* (ground meat). However, the actual ingredients, the taste and texture cannot be inferred from the name of the recipe. Moreover, the functions that *Mett* may have as an ingredient for other dishes is not fulfilled since this *Vegane Mett* consists of crumbled rice cakes with tomato paste.[11] Nominal compounds (here for dairy products) uniting the surrogate (as modifier) with the original dairy (as head) such as *full-fat canned coconut cream* (19) or „*Cashewmilch*" *oder "-sahne"* ("cashew milk" or "cream") (24) are semantically more transparent. These constructions also function as nominalized teaching sequences: The blog readers learn which vegan ingredients they can use as surrogates, e.g., for dairy products with regard to texture, function, or, potentially, taste. In this way, the readers of these blogs can develop their vegan competencies as they learn about vegan cooking and nutrition, and the vegan lifestyle. The lack of meat surrogates indicates a more pronounced distancing from meat than other animal products (cf. The French blogger's disdainful comments about *simili carnés* (meat surrogates)). While the adjectives *meaty* (and, potentially *cheesy*) seem to require distancing, *creamy*, *sahnig*, and *crémeux* are used unapologetically, seemingly without the realization that they too derive from animal products.

The data suggest that veganism is a global trend (illustrated by e.g., the use of borrowings) which may instantiate in digital media in slightly different fashions, because of the affordances of different languages, both syntactically (e.g., French post-modification) and lexically (e.g., German choice between *sahnig* and *cremig*). Overwhelmingly, though, the three blogs from different cultures, different languages, and different parts of the world underline that veganism is a global phenomenon that faces the difficulty of having to be constructed against the background of omnivore cuisine. This holds for all of these three different data sets. It would be interesting to compare these findings to blogs from a culture where vegetarianism and veganism are much more traditional (e.g., the Jainist culture in India). Another aspect that is beyond the scope of this study, but deserves further exploration, is the interactional features of blogs. Because of the nature of the data (online blogs rather than, for instance, recipes from cookbooks), it is possible to see how the bloggers' constructions of veganism are taken up by the readers of the blogs (Gerhardt 2020). In other words, studying the comments section of vegan blogs would allow for an exploration of whether the readers may protest against the use of e.g., *creamy* or *sahnig*. This co-construction of discourse represents one of the affordances of digital media and differentiates it from the appropriation of classic media, e.g., television discourse and its reception (Ayass & Gerhardt 2012).

Notes

1 Parts of this research have been published in German (Gerhardt 2019).
2 Note that in this definition, too, veganism is framed as *not* something (as the lack of something), namely cruelty to and exploitation of animals.

3 To explain the type-token difference with the help of an example: V*egan* occurs 47 times as a token, but it only represents one type.
4 I would like to thank Isabel Schul for allowing me to use her corpus and examples from her Bachelor's dissertation for this paper.
5 Interestingly, the lentil stew is described as *wie bei Mama*, i.e., "as at mom's" or "like at home," even though one can probably assume that mom was not a vegan herself. Instead, we can see that veganism is constructed against the known, in this case the food that we are used to eating at home when we were kids. Thus, it is the whole phrase *Linseneintopf wie bei Mama* including the post-modification that is pre-modified here with *veganer*. As we will see elsewhere in this paper, usually it is omnivore cuisine that is used as a point of reference, that is, as the known.
6 The blogger also refers to *la newsletter végétale* on her site, again with the feminine ending. Apparently, the French *lettre*, a feminine noun, has returned (from English) to French in the borrowed compound *newsletter*.
7 This is a very free translation since blog is not mentioned. Literally it means, "this must with along be" *mit* (with) being replaced by *mett* (ground meat) as a word play. The sentence could also be translated as "it must be taken along," e.g., for a picnic.
8 The compound *fleischartig* (meat-like), which could also be used as a synonym for *meaty*, did not occur in the data.
9 There is one comment by a blog reader, though, mentioning *un goût de fromage "Classique"* (a classic taste of cheese). This represents the only case where the prepositional phrase *de X* (*de fromage* or *de viande*) is used in the same sense as the derivations *fromageux* or *viandeux*.
10 For the ingredient cream, surrogates are used: *full-fat canned coconut cream* (19). In those cases, the stem *cream* is used as nominal head in compound constructions.
11 The blogger herself writes: "Schon erstaunlich, mit welch einfachen Mittel man tierische Produkte veganisieren kann!" (It's amazing how easy it is to veganize animal products). Note the neologism *veganisieren*, which also exists in English *veganize* and French *veganiser* (25).

Acknowledgments

I would like to thank the editors of this volume for their helpful comments and also my students Michelle Castor, Rebecca Rück, and Maren Luthringshauser for their help with this article. I am also indebted to the audiences of the panel "Food for thought and social action: Constructing ideologies in food-related communication across digital and cultural contexts" organized by Cynthia Gordon for the Conference of the International Pragmatics Association in Belfast, Ireland, July 16–21, 2017 and participants in the conference "Talking about food: Local and global contexts" organized by Sofia Rüdiger and Susanne Mühleisen in Bayreuth, Germany, April 27–28, 2018 for their many helpful suggestions.

References

ACN Academy of Culinary Nutrition (2019), 'Top 50 Vegan Foodblogs'. Available online: http://www.culinarynutrition.com/top-50-vegan-blogs/

Ayass, Ruth and Cornelia Gerhardt, eds. (2012), *The Appropriation of Media in Everyday Life*, Amsterdam and Philadelphia: John Benjamins.

Barnard, Neal D., Joshua Cohen, David J. A. Jenkins, Gabrielle M. Turner-McGrievy, Lise Gloede, Brent Jaster, Kim Seidl, Amber A. Green and Stanley Talpers (2006), 'A Low-Fat Vegan Diet Improves Glycemic Control and Cardiovascular Risk Factors in a Randomized Clinical Trial in Individuals with Type 2 Diabetes', *Diabetes Care*, 29(8): 1777–1783.

Boepple, Leah and Joel Kevin Thompson (2014), 'A Content Analysis of Healthy Living Blogs: Evidence of Content Thematically Consistent with Dysfunctional Eating Attitudes and Behaviors', *International Journal of Eating Disorders*, 47(4): 362–367.

Bourdieu, Pierre (1984), *Distinction: A Social Critique of the Judgement of Taste*, Cambridge: Harvard University Press.

Burkert, Nathalie Tatjana, Wolfgang Freidl, Franziska Großschädel, Johanna Muckenhuber, Willibald J. Stronegger and Éva Rásky (2014), 'Nutrition and Health: Different Forms of Diet and Their Relationship with Various Health Parameters among Austrian Adults', *Wiener Klinische Wochenschrift*, 126(3-4): 113–118.

Cesiri, Daniela (2016), 'The Blog is Served: Crossing the 'Expert/Non-Expert' Border in a Corpus of Food Blogs', *Colloquium: New Philologies*, 1(1): 47–62.

Cook, Guy (2007), *The Discourse of Organic Food Promotion: Language, Intentions, and Effects: Full Research Report*. ESRC End of Award Report, RES-000-22-1626. Swindon: ESRC.

Cox, Andrew M. and Megan K. Blake (2011), 'Information and Food Blogging as Serious Leisure', *ASLIB Proceedings*, 63(2/3): 204–220.

Craig, Winston J. (2009), 'Health Effects of Vegan Diets', *The American Journal of Clinical Nutrition*, 89(5): 1627–1633.

Dejmanee, Tisha (2016), '"Food Porn" as Postfeminist Play: Digital Femininity and the Female Body on Food Blogs', *Television & New Media*, 17(5): 429–448.

Diederich, Catherine (2015), *Sensory Adjectives in the Discourse of Food: A Frame-Semantic Approach to Language and Perception*, Amsterdam and Philadelphia: John Benjamins.

Diemer, Stefan and Maximiliane Frobenius (2013), 'When Making Pie, All Ingredients Must Be Chilled. Including You: Lexical, Syntactic and Interactive Features in

Online Discourse – A Synchronic Study of Food Blogs', in Cornelia Gerhardt, Maximiliane Frobenius and Susanne Ley (eds), *Culinary Linguistics: The Chef's Special*, 53–82, Amsterdam and Philadelphia: John Benjamins.

Dinu, Monica, Rosanna Abbate, Gian Franco Gensini, Alessandro Casini and Francesco Sofi (2016), 'Vegetarian, Vegan Diets and Multiple Health Outcomes: A Systematic Review with Meta-Analysis of Observational Studies', *Critical Reviews in Food Science and Nutrition*, 57(17): 3640–3649.

Domingo, Myrrh, Gunther Kress, Rebecca O'Connell, Heather Elliott, Corinne Squire, Carey Jewitt and Elisabetta Adami (2014), 'Development of Methodologies for Researching Online: The Case of Food Blogs', *NCRM Working Paper*.

Dyett, Patricia A., Joan Sabaté, Ella Haddad, Sujatha Rajaram and David Shavlik (2013), 'Vegan Lifestyle Behaviors: An Exploration of Congruence with Health-Related Beliefs and Assessed Health Indices', *Appetite*, 67: 119–124.

Fields, Heather, Barbara Ruddy, Mark R. Wallace, Amit Shah, Denise Millstine and Lisa Marks (2016), 'How to Monitor and Advise Vegans to Ensure Adequate Nutrient Intake', *The Journal of American Osteopathic Association*, 116(2): 96–99.

Frobenius, Maximiliane and Cornelia Gerhardt (2017), 'Discourse and Organisation', in Wolfram Bublitz and Christian Hoffmann (eds), *Handbook of Pragmatics 11: Pragmatics of Social Media*, 245–274, Berlin: de Gruyter Mouton.

Gerhardt, Cornelia (2013), 'Food and Language – Language and Food', in Cornelia Gerhardt, Maximiliane Frobenius and Susanne Ley (eds), *Culinary Linguistics: The Chef's Special*, 3–50, Amsterdam and Philadelphia: John Benjamins.

Gerhardt, Cornelia (2019), 'Vegane Foodblogs: Fachsprachliche Adjektive und Modifikationen', in Calderón, Marietta and Carmen Konzett-Firth (eds), *Dynamische Approximationen. Festschriftliches pünktlichst zu Eva Lavrics 62,5. Geburtstag* (= *Kontrastes/Kontraste* 3), Berlin: Peter Lang.

Gerhardt, Cornelia (2020), 'How Less Means More in the Comments Section of Vegan Food Blogs: Exgredients Such as *Gluten-Free* and Extreme Case Formulations', *Talking about Food: The Social and the Global in Eating Communities* (= *IMPACT Studies in Language, Culture and Society* 47), 15–34, Amsterdam and Philadelphia: John Benjamins.

Gerhardt, Cornelia, Maximiliane Frobenius and Susanne Ley, eds. (2013), *Culinary Linguistics: The Chef's Special*, Amsterdam and Philadelphia: John Benjamins.

Goff, Louise M., Jimmy David Bell, Po-Wah So, Anne Dornhorst and Gary S. Frost (2005), 'Veganism and Its Relationship with Insulin Resistance and Intramyocellular Lipid', *European Journal of Clinical Nutrition*, 59: 291–298.

Hänninen, Otto, Anna-Liisa Rauma, Kati Kaartinen and Matti Nenonen (1999), 'Vegan Diet in Physiological Health Promotion', *Acta Physiologica Hungarica*, 86(3-4):171–180.

Hart, Dana (2018), 'Faux-Meat and Masculinity: The Gendering of Food on Three Vegan Blogs', *Canadian Food Studies / La Revue Canadienne des Etudes sur l'Alimentation*, 5(1): 133–155.

Hegde, Radha S. (2014), 'Food Blogs and the Digital Reimagination of South Asian Diasporic Publics', *South Asian Diaspora*, 6(1): 89–103.

Herring, Susan C., Lois Ann Scheidt, Sabrina Bonus and Elijah Wright (2004), 'Bridging the Gap: A Genre Analysis of Weblogs' *Proceedings of the 37th Annual Hawaii International Conference on System Sciences* (= *HICSS-37*). Los Alamitos, CA: IEEE Computer Society: 1–11.

Heyd, Theresa (2017), 'Blogs', in Wolfram Bublitz and Christian Hoffmann (eds), *Handbook of Pragmatics 11: Pragmatics of Social Media*, 151–172, Berlin: de Gruyter Mouton.

Ho, Hui-Yi and Pi-Hsuan Chang Chien (2010), 'Influence of Message Trust in Online Word-of-Mouth on Consumer Behavior – By the Example of Food Blog', *2010 International Conference on Electronics and Information Engineering*, 1: 395–399.

Holak, Susan L. (2014), 'From Brighton Beach to Blogs: Exploring Food-Related Nostalgia in the Russian diaspora', *Consumption Markets & Culture*, 17(2): 185–207.

Just, Nicole (2017), '*Nicole Just*'. Available online: www.nicole-just.de

Kaartinen, K., K. Lammi, M. Hypen, M. Nenonen, O. Hanninen and A.L. Rauma (2000), 'Vegan Diet Alleviates Fibromyalgia Symptoms', *Scandinavian Journal of Rheumatology*, 29(5): 308–313.

Koh, Gladys (2014/2015), 'Food Porn as Visual Narrative: Food Blogging and Identity Construction,' *Southeast Asian Review of English*, 52(1): 122–142.

Laforêt, Marie (2017), '*100% Végétal – Cuisine Vegan*'. Available online: www.100-vegetal.com

Langley, Gill (1995), *Vegan Nutrition*, St. Leonards-on-Sea: Vegan Society.

Lavric, Eva and Carmen Konzett, eds. (2009), *Food and Language – Sprache und Essen*, Frankfurt am Main: Peter Lang.

Lee, Soo Hee, Marios Samdanis and Sofia Gkiousou (2014), 'Hybridizing Food Cultures in Computer-Mediated Environments: Creativity and Improvisation in Greek Food Blogs', *International Journal of Human-Computer Studies*, 72(2): 224–238.

Liddon, Angela (2015–2016), '*Oh She Glows*'. Available online: www.ohsheglows.com

Lofgren, Jennifer (2013), 'Food Blogging and Food-Related Media Convergence', *M/C Journal: A Journal of Media and Culture*, 16(3). Available online: http://journal.media-culture.org.au/index.php/mcjournal/article/view/638

Lupton, Deborah (2018), 'Cooking, Eating, Uploading: Digital Food Cultures', in Kathleen LeBesco and Peter Naccarato (eds), *The Bloomsbury Handbook of Food and Popular Culture*, 66–79, London and New York: Bloomsbury.

Lynch, Meghan (2010), 'Healthy Habits or Damaging Diets: An Exploratory Study of a Food Blogging Community', *Ecology of Food and Nutrition*, 49(4): 316–335.

Lynch, Meghan (2012), 'From Food to Fuel: Perceptions of Exercise and Food in a Community of Food Bloggers', *Health Education*, 71(1): 72–79.

McDonald, Barbara (2000), 'Once You Know Something, You Can't not Know It: An Empirical Look at Becoming Vegan,' *Society & Animals*, 8(1): 1–23.

McGaughey, Kerstin (2010), 'Food in Binary: Identity and Interaction in Two German Food Blogs', *Cultural Analysis*, 9: 69–98.

Miller, Carolyn R. and Dawn Shepherd (2012), 'Questions for genre theory from the blogosphere', in Janet Giltrow and Dieter Stein (eds), *Genres in the Internet: Issues in the Theory of Genre*, 263-290, Amsterdam and Philadelphia: John Benjamins.

Myers, Greg (2010), *The Discourse of Blogs and Wikis*, London: Continuum.

Newman, John, ed. (2009), *The Linguistics of Eating and Drinking*, Amsterdam and Philadelphia: John Benjamins.

Pinnavaia, Laura (2010), *Sugar and Spice: Exploring Food and Drink Idioms in English*, Milan: Polimetrica.

Radnitz, Cynthia, Bonnie Beezhold and Julie DiMatteo (2015), 'Investigation of Lifestyle Choices of Individuals Following a Vegan Diet for Health and Ethical Reasons', *Appetite*, 90: 31-36.

Rodney, Alexandra, Sarah Cappeliez, Merin Oleschuk and Josée Jonhston (2017), 'The Online Domestic Goddess: An Analysis of Food Blog Femininities', *Food, Culture & Society*, 20(4): 685-707.

Salvio, Paula M. (2012), 'Dishing It Out: Food Blogs and Post-Feminist Domesticity', *Gastronomica*, 12(3): 31-39.

Sanders, Thomas A. B. and Joan Manning (1992), 'The Growth and Development of Vegan Children', *Journal of Human Nutrition and Dietetics*, 5(1): 11-21.

Schneider, Elizabeth P., Emily E. McGovern, Colleen L. Lynch and Lisa S. Brown (2013), 'Do Food Blogs Serve as a Source of Nutritionally Balanced Recipes? An Analysis of 6 Popular Food Blogs', *Journal of Nutrition Education and Behavior*, 45(6): 696-700.

Seddon, Klara (2011), 'Bento Blogs: Japanese Women's Expression in Digital Food Culture', *Women and Performance*, 21(3): 301-319.

Sneijder, Petra and Hedwig te Molder (2004), 'Health Should not Have to Be a Problem: Talking Health and Accountability in an Internet Forum on Veganism', *Journal of Health Psychology*, 9(4): 599-616.

Sneijder, Petra and Hedwig te Molder (2005), 'Moral Logic and Logical Morality: Attributions of Responsibility and Blame in Online Discourse on Veganism', *Discourse & Society*, 16(5): 675-696.

Sneijder, Petra and Hedwig te Molder (2009), 'Normalizing Ideological Food Choice and Eating Practices: Identity Work in Online Discussions on Veganism', *Appetite*, 52(3): 621-630.

Stepaniak, Joanne (1998), *The Vegan Sourcebook*, Los Angeles: Lowell House.

Stepaniak, Joanne (2000), *Being Vegan: Living with Conscience, Conviction and Compassion*, Lincolnwood: Lowell House.

Szatrowski, Polly E., ed. (2014), *Language and Food: Verbal and Nonverbal Experiences*, Amsterdam and Philadelphia: John Benjamins.

Turner-McGrievy, Gabrielle M., Neal D. Barnard and Anthony R. Scialli (2007), 'A Two-Year Randomized Weight Loss Trial Comparing a Vegan Diet to a More Moderate Low-Fat Diet', *Obesity*, 15(9): 2276-2281.

Vegan Society, The (2017), *The Vegan Society: One World, Many Lives, Our Choice: Definition of Veganism*. Available online: https://www.vegansociety.com/go-vegan/definition-veganism

Véron, Ophélie (2016), 'From Seitan Bourguignon to Tofu Blanquette: Popularizing Veganism in France with Food Blogs', in Jodey Castricano and Rasmus R. Simonsen (eds), *Critical Perspectives on Veganism*, 287–305, Basingstoke: Palgrave Macmillan.

Waldmann, Anika, Jochen W. Koschizke, Claus Leitzmann and Andreas Hahn (2003), 'Dietary Intakes and Lifestyle Factors of a Vegan Population in Germany: Results from the German Vegan Study', *European Journal of Clinical Nutrition*, 57: 947–955.

Waldmann, Anika, Jochen W. Koschizke, Claus Leitzmann and Andreas Hahn (2004), 'Dietary Iron Intake and Iron Status of German Female Vegans: Results of the German Vegan Study', *Annals of Nutrition and Metabolism*, 48(2): 103–108.

Waldmann, Anika, Jochen W. Koschizke, Claus Leitzmann and Andreas Hahn (2005), 'German Vegan Study: Diet, Life-Style Factors, and Cardiovascular Risk Profile', *Annals of Nutrition and Metabolism*, 49(6): 366–372.

Zappavigna, Michele (2018), *Searchable Talk: Hashtags and Social Media Metadiscourse*, London: Bloomsbury.

What if the Customer is Wrong?: Debates About Food on Yelp and TripAdvisor

Camilla Vásquez

1 Introduction

Contemporary technologies offer spaces for new forms of communication. Among these spaces are consumer review sites, where individuals can share their positive or negative experiences with products and services online, and in doing so, reach a potentially vast audience. In the past, many of us relied on word of mouth (WOM) recommendations from family and friends, and until relatively recently, this type of communication was restricted to our immediate social networks. Today, however, sites which feature user-generated "electronic word of mouth" (or eWOM, a term coined by marketing scholars) may be read by dozens, if not hundreds or even thousands, of consumers. Economists have demonstrated the measurable positive impact of these forms of digital communication on product sales (Chevalier & Mayzlin 2006) as well as on restaurant sales, more specifically (Luca 2011).

Although eWOM can be beneficial for businesses, its negative effects have also been documented (e.g., Park & Lee 2009). Negative comments can be threatening to a business, which is why some businesses engage in online reputation management. Responding to consumer comments online may be viewed as a type of professional impression management (Goffman 1959). Many consumer review sites offer businesses a "right of reply" space (Heyes & Kapur 2012) in which businesses can respond publicly to user-generated reviews. The number of businesses that have taken advantage of this affordance, by responding publicly to reviews, has increased over the last several years (O'Connor 2010; Vásquez 2014). In order to gain insight into contemporary businesses' discourse practices related to managing their online reputations, I examine the ways in which businesses respond to negative reviews on two popular reviewing sites. Specifically, I focus on how restaurants respond to food-related complaints posted on *Yelp* and *TripAdvisor*.

In the past, a consumer-to-business complaint about a negative service experience was normally a restricted form of communication, taking place privately between the consumer and a business representative – instantiated as either a face-to-face complaint, a private letter, or a completed customer satisfaction survey. However, online review sites have enabled consumers to not only make a complaint publicly, but also to address multiple audiences simultaneously – i.e., both the businesses itself, as well as other consumers (Vásquez 2011) – thereby shifting the participation structure from a private one-to-one interaction, to a public one-to-many form of communication. In the same fashion, when businesses choose to respond to consumer reviews in online fora, although their comments may be directed to one specific aggrieved consumer, the audience for these texts actually extends to all other current and future readers of the site. Consequently, such responses have the potential of influencing current and future customers. Building on prior research which has examined the discursive practices of different types of businesses responding to consumer complaints online (e.g., Page 2014; Zhang & Vásquez 2014; Creelman 2015) – a genre of business communication referred to by marketing scholars as "webcare" (van Noort & Willemsen 2011) – the present study examined 96 public responses from businesses to negative restaurant reviews posted on *Yelp* and *TripAdvisor*.

As will be discussed in more detail, businesses use multiple strategies for attending to food-related complaints online, including avoiding reference to food-related issues altogether, and/or concentrating instead on other aspects of the dining "experience"; asking reviewers to provide more details about the meal via a private channel; addressing some (or all) of the food-related complaints specifically; or "educating" reviewers about some aspect(s) of the restaurant's practices. Businesses also vary in terms of whether they adopt a relatively impersonal approach to responding to specific complaints, or whether they personalize their responses in a number of possible ways.

2 Research on restaurant reviews

Although research examining various aspects of online reviews has been carried out from a range of disciplines (e.g., economics, computer science, marketing, information systems), studies investigating the language of reviews, in particular, have tended to focus on reviews of products (e.g., Pollach 2006; Mackiewicz 2008, 2010a, b; Skalicky 2013) and reviews of hotels (e.g., Vásquez 2011, 2012; Tian 2013; Goethals 2016; Cenni & Goethals 2017). Fewer studies have concentrated specifically on restaurant reviews. Among those that have, Jurafsky et al. (2014), in their analysis of over 800,000 *Yelp* restaurant reviews, found that class-based differences are often realized at the level of linguistic expression: Reviewers of more expensive restaurants write longer reviews and use more complex words than reviewers of less expensive restaurants. Similarly, Vásquez and Chik (2015) also considered issues of class – particularly with respect to how reviewers position themselves – in their analysis of reviews of Michelin-rated restaurants in both New York and Hong Kong. And, in Chik and Vásquez (2017), the same authors offer a comparative analysis of reviews from online reviewing sites associated with the two locations: *Yelp* and *Open Rice*, finding that Hong Kong *Open Rice* restaurant reviewers were much more likely to mention specific dishes in their reviews, and also tended to be more detailed in describing food taste, smell, and appearance than their New York counterparts. In fact, many English-language *Yelp* restaurant reviewers provided only general overall evaluations of the food as (i.e., as *good, ok, not bad*), instead of going into details about its taste, texture, appearance, and so on.

In addition, research comparing the language features of restaurant reviews with other types of reviews has found many similarities in the way that reviewers position themselves, evaluate their consumer experiences, and structure their texts, regardless of the specific products being evaluated (Vásquez 2014). Moreover, in terms of their temporal references, restaurant reviews pattern quite similarly to hotel reviews, since both are consumer experiences that unfold over time (Vásquez 2015). By concentrating only on restaurant reviews, the present study extends the line of inquiry into this genre, by taking as its starting point the various ways that restaurant reviewers formulate their food-related complaints. In the U.S. alone, the restaurant industry currently generates nearly 800 billion dollars in sales (National Restaurant Association 2017), so it comes as no surprise that many restaurants take online reviewing activities very seriously. For this reason, the present study further explores the relationship between food-related complaints in online reviews, and how businesses respond to those complaints.

3 Discourse features of businesses' responses to negative online reviews

Prior research examining the responses of businesses to negative online reviews has identified a number of rhetorical moves that appear in these types of texts (Zhang & Vásquez 2014). In addition to apologies, these include other involvement strategies (Tannen 1984, 1989), such as addressing the customer by their first name (or user ID), thanking the customer for their feedback, and inviting the customer back for a repeat visit. Table 5.1, below, illustrates these moves (originally identified in hotel responses to online reviews by Zhang & Vásquez 2014), featuring examples taken from restaurant response data gathered for the present study. It should be noted that these moves account for a major proportion – though not all – of the restaurants' responses in the data set. As will become evident, where food-related complaints are concerned, many restaurants, in fact, use other moves, such as providing various "counter-claims" in their online responses to reviewers' negative statements about food.

In general, businesses' public responses on review sites such as *Yelp* and *TripAdvisor* tend to be relatively formal and "letter-like," often exploiting epistolary conventions such as openings (e.g., *Hello Jennifer*, *Hi Katie*) which address the author by name, as well as complimentary closings (e.g., *Best Regards*, [name], *General Manager*).

Not surprisingly, in their responses to consumer complaints in online reviews, most businesses include an apology, which addresses the consumer's disappointment or displeasure. In the digital era, it is not unusual for businesses to refer to these activities as doing "online reputation management," and even predating the internet, apologies were identified as a set of interactional strategies referred to by sociologist Goffman as "impression management." In addition to apologizing, businesses engage in other forms of impression management, such as thanking reviewers for their comments, or acknowledging the importance of customer feedback. Several businesses stress their openness to receiving both positive as well as negative feedback (e.g., "*We learn from each experience, positive and negative*", "*It means a lot to us when people take the time to really spell out the good AND the bad*", "*We take customer reviews very seriously and appreciate all feedback*."). This projects an image of a business that is interested in, and responsive to, a wide range of customer reviews. Additionally, businesses may indicate some evidence of action they have taken to address the problem, or a promise that the problem identified in the review will not happen in the future. Businesses may also include in their response some type of call to action: either inviting the consumer for another visit, or soliciting further (usually private) communication.

In terms of audience design, some of these moves are more oriented to the aggrieved customer specifically (e.g., openings which address the reviewer by name, or an invitation for a free meal), while others are equally relevant to both the aggrieved consumer as well as to a broader audience of potential

Table 5.1 Typical moves in businesses' responses to complaints in online consumer reviews

	Move	Examples
1	Use opening pleasantries	*Greetings Terry* *Hey there Ellen!*
2	Express gratitude	<u>*Thanks*</u> *for taking the time to comment about your recent experience at [restaurant name].* <u>*Thank you*</u> *once again for giving us your feedback.*
3	Refer to customer reviews	*I wanted to address a few points in* <u>*your review*</u> … *Truly, our attitude toward those with a camera is not* <u>*as you've described*</u>.
4	Apologize for sources of trouble	<u>*Sorry*</u> *for the misunderstanding!* <u>*I am terribly sorry*</u> *to learn that twice we have fallen short of both your expectations and ours.*
5	Proof of action	<u>*All of the staff who was involved is being counseled.*</u> *I want to tell you again that I'm glad we were able to get in touch and* <u>*resolve the issue*</u>! <u>*I'll be using your review in our upcoming all hands meeting*</u> *as an example of how things can be perceived and the importance of attentive service.*
6	Avoidance of reoccurring problems	*You can be assured that your comments have been reviewed with the appropriate staff members* <u>*to prevent a reoccurance in the future*</u>. <u>*I assure you this will not happen again.*</u>
7	Acknowledge complaints/feedback	<u>*We take customer reviews very seriously*</u> *and appreciate all feedback.* *In order to grow and better understand our restaurant and staff* <u>*we must learn from our mistakes and it's reviews like yours that allow us to do so.*</u>
8	Solicit response	*Would you* <u>*please email us*</u> *at [email address] so that a member of Management may contact you?* *I'd like to know more about your time here. If you're interested in discussing it further,* <u>*please email me privately*</u>.
9	Invite for a second visit	*I hope that you will* <u>*come back and give us another try*</u> *and we can show you the quality of our food.* *I'm sorry that you feel that you won't return, but if that should change,* <u>*we would much appreciate your business*</u>.
10	Closing pleasantries	*Sincerely, [name], Director of PR* *Best Regards [name], General Manager*

consumers – especially those communicative moves that project an image of a concerned, responsive business who reads and considers feedback, not only responding to, but also acting on suggestions, and in some cases, by fixing problems once they are brought to their attention. These types of moves may be also considered impression management strategies, which function to cast the business in a favorable light – especially important in the digital era, where customer service interactions such as these have become, in the words of one popular author, a "spectator sport" (Baer 2016: xii).

One area in which there is a wide range of variability is the extent to which businesses address specific points made in the review, compared to adopting a more "generic" approach – for instance, by repeating the same (or similar) type of message in response to very different types of complaints. Indeed, reviewers can address many different aspects of their restaurant experience (e.g., service, location, wait time, ambiance, cost). However, because food is arguably one of the defining features of the restaurant experience, I now turn to a closer examination of food-related complaints in restaurant reviews – as well as how restaurants address those complaints that are specifically about food quality. As I will show, the original review text may shape, influence or constrain the subsequent business response.

4 Methods

To better understand how restaurants respond to food-related complaints online, this analysis focuses on restaurants in one metropolitan area in the Southeast United States. Using a local newspaper's recent list of "Top 50 Restaurants in the Area" to define the sample, I considered all of the negative (1-star and 2-star) reviews that appeared on two popular reviewing sites, *TripAdvisor* and *Yelp*,[1] for these 50 restaurants. All of the 50 businesses had received some negative reviews on either one or both of the sites, with an average of six 1-star and nine 2-star reviews per business.

Of the total 1,539 negative reviews in the sample, only 6 percent (N=96) were followed by public responses from businesses on the review site where they were posted. Interestingly, only 16 out of the 50 restaurants responded publicly to one or more negative reviews on either *Yelp* or *TripAdvisor*. In spite of the conventional expression "the customer is always right," the majority (68 percent) of the restaurant businesses in the data set posted no public responses to negative online reviews. It should be noted, however, that both review sites allow businesses to send private messages to individual reviewers, and as I later learned (during a series of follow-up interviews with several of the businesses who were willing to speak with me), many businesses prefer this private, one-to-one mode for communicating about complaints or problems with aggrieved customers. While this may seem counterintuitive – and even goes against recommendations from popular sources of advice for successful customer service in the digital age (e.g., Baer 2016) – this preference for private communication seemed driven by a concern or fear over differences of opinion eventually escalating to a larger conflict played out in a public forum. As one business representative succinctly explained: "[I respond in private because] I don't want to add fuel to the fire."

In general, the restaurants that did respond to complaints publicly on review sites tended to respond to one out of every three negative reviews. Most restaurants had only one or two individuals (e.g., owner, business manager, general manager, public relations manager, social media manager) who responded to reviews. Businesses' responses to negative reviews in this data set average around 115 words, and range in length from 18 words to 908 words.

In the analysis below, I start by providing an overview of general trends found in the data, and I illustrate some of the most typical findings with a selection of representative examples. I offer specific interpretations of how both customers as well as businesses address food-related issues in their texts, and I consider the interactions between the two texts, by discussing them in relation to each other.

As noted earlier, restaurant reviews are multifaceted, in that they can – and often do – address a wide range of phenomena relevant to the overall dining experience, including ambiance, service, wait, price/value, and of course, food quality. It this discussion, I focus only on the latter: matters of food quality. More specifically, I present the results of an analysis, which considered: first, the type of food-related complaints that tend to appear in online restaurant reviews; and second, the interaction between the nature of the complaint and type of response.

5 Findings

Of the 96 sets of negative reviews and business responses that comprise the sample, approximately two-thirds (N=67) of the negative reviews included at least one food-related complaint. The remaining 29 reviews in the sample focused on other issues, such as service, ambiance, value per cost, noise, seating, wait time, valet parking, reservation policy, and cleanliness, but did not mention anything at all related to food. For those reviews that did include food-related issues, comments centered either on general food quality, or addressed more specific issues related to the taste, appearance, temperature, texture or smell of a particular dish(es). In a few other cases, food-related issues had to do with items on the menu which were unavailable, receiving the wrong food, or a perceived lack of authenticity of the dishes. The latter only applied to restaurants featuring a specific type of cuisine (e.g., BBQ, Italian, New Orleans Creole).

The remainder of this discussion is divided into two main sections. The first focuses on general food complaints, and in it, I identify four main strategies that businesses use to respond to such unspecified complaints: 1) ignore, 2) provide a counter-claim, 3) invite the reviewer to provide more information, and 4) educate the reviewer. In particular, I highlight the discursive strategies of apologies and counter-claims, as well as more micro-level linguistic features such as pronoun choice. I addition, I note the interrelatedness between the intensity of the negative food evaluation in the review and the restaurant response.

5.1 General food complaints and responses

Looking closely at food-related complaints, it is possible to classify them into two broad categories: general and specific. General complaints are those which offer some vague, and usually underspecified, assessment of the restaurant's food, without mentioning any specific dish or item: e.g., *the food was very disappointing*. Only 17 of the 67 food-related complaints in the dataset were classified as general; the remaining 50 mentioned one or more specific dish(es), or menu item(s).[2] Most of the time, general food-related complaints appeared in reviews in which reviewers concentrated on other issues, and where the reviewer's main concerns had to do with some non-food related aspect of the restaurant experience (e.g., service, wait time, noise, value). Moreover, there was very little syntactic variation found in general food complaints: The typical formulation of this was "*The food was/is X*" or "*X food*," with *X* representing an adjective or adjectival phrase of non-positive evaluation. I have organized these non-positive lexical and phrasal evaluations from lowest intensity (*mediocre*) to highest intensity (*terrible*) in Table 5.2.

Not surprisingly, when the food-related complaint is both general as well as mild in intensity (e.g., *mediocre*), some restaurant representatives choose to ignore it in their response, focusing instead on the other aspects of experience mentioned in the review. For instance, one negative customer review mentioned three separate issues: long wait time to be seated, the small size of wine pours,

Table 5.2 Examples of evaluative adjectival phrases occurring in general food complaints

mediocre, just average, meh, ordinary, just ok, nothing special
below average, lacking, less than impressed
very poor, very disappointing, dull and dreary like the interior décor
atrocious, terrible

and the following vaguely formulated complaint about food. Example 1 shows a brief excerpt of the longer review.

Example 1
  The food is meh.

In his response, the restaurant's business manager provided an account for the unusual wait time that evening (i.e., weather conditions), and an explanation of the restaurant's two sizes of wine pours along with their respective pricing, yet he did not address anything related to the reviewer's general food-related comment – choosing instead to ignore that aspect of the review. So, not addressing generally-formulated food-related complaints at all is one strategy used by businesses.

It is much more common, however, for general food-related complaints to be "matched" by an equally general food-related response by the restaurant's management. For instance, in Example 2a, another customer makes a general type of food-related comment, which is very similar to, and no different in intensity from, the previous example. This food-related comment occurs in a longer review that also mentions wait time to be seated, as well as the unenthusiastic host staff.

Example 2a
  The food was just average.

After providing an account for the unusual delay in seating and apologizing for the staff's demeanor, in this instance, the manager's[3] response in 2b *does* address the food quality issue, in contrast to the case of Example 1. Although there is no specific dish, or aspect of the food provided by the reviewer in 2a for management to address, the restaurant's representative nevertheless responds to this customer's claim, by providing an alternative portrayal: a counter-claim about the restaurant's food, told from the perspective of the business.

Example 2b
   ... *We take great pride in our food, service and guest experience. I do apologize if anyone on the* [restaurant name] *team was less than pleasant during your dining experience. We take great care in preparing our food and ensuring an exceptional dining experience for each guest. Thank you.*

While "taking pride" and "taking great care" in food preparation does not directly contradict or challenge the reviewer's evaluation of "just average" food quality, it does send a message that indirectly counters the reviewer's claimed experience, by stressing that food quality and preparation does matter a great deal to the restaurant. Other restaurants in this dataset also adopt this strategy in responding to issues of food quality, by providing their own food-related counter-claims, which stress/highlight a positive perspective with respect to food quality. This type of communicative move may actually accomplish multiple goals. By overtly stating that the restaurant values food quality, they implicitly position the complaining customer's review as an outlier, because either: 1) taste is subjective, so it could be that this particular customer just happens to have bad taste (i.e., the restaurant puts the same care into every dish, so the customer could be the problem in this rare instance), or 2) perhaps the restaurant failed on this one occasion, and thus by extension, this customer's experience was an exceptional occurrence and should not be taken as representative of the restaurant's food more generally. Regardless of the impression readers have after reading such a response, this move of insisting on the restaurant's strong commitment to food quality is clearly a reputation management strategy on the part of the business. Providing some sort counter-claim, therefore represents a second possible discourse strategy that businesses can adopt, when responding to a customer's general food-related complaint.

It is also worth pointing out the pronoun alternation in the excerpt of the restaurant response in Example 2b. The use of the first-person plural pronoun, *we*, emphasizes the restaurant staff as a collective, or a team that works together in the preparation of food, whereas the first-person singular pronoun, *I*, helps to personalize the apology, and indicates that there is a single individual representing the restaurant who is willing to take responsibility for customer service missteps.

On other occasions, general food-related critiques are responded to by the restaurant representative with a request for further, private communication. For instance, in Example 3a, the reviewer (who, earlier in the review, had complained more specifically about the pricing of the food) also mentions being dissatisfied with the overall quality of the food. Once again, this complaint is formulated in general terms, referring only to *food*, but not mentioning any specific menu items.[4]

Example 3a
  ... I was less than impressed with the flavor of the food. [...] Tldr: over priced, food sucks, portion sizes small, looks good from afar but far from good ...

In this case, the restaurant's business manager uses the review site's public response function to elicit further information from this aggrieved customer, as seen in the excerpt in Example 3b. Although the business manager begins by apologizing for the customer's experience, the way that she formulates the problem is from the guest's perspective (*We are sorry* [...] *you were not pleased with your experience*), rather than from the restaurant's perspective (e.g., *We are very sorry we disappointed you*). In addition, in discussing the guest's complaint, she uses the general noun, *experience*, which does not specify which aspects of the restaurant visit were problematic, and thus avoids the repetition of *food*. Indeed, this general noun, *experience*, is used frequently by representatives of several different restaurants when responding to general, as well as to specific, complaints about food. No doubt that *experience* is a very useful general noun in this context, because it can encompass multiple issues (e.g., food, service) simultaneously. Further, it accomplishes impression management in the sense of not revitalizing, for readers of the restaurant response, specific negative comments about the food, while still engaging in apologetic discourse.

Example 3b
  Greetings! We are very sorry to see that you were not pleased with your first experience at [restaurant name] [...] *it is commentary such as this which allows us to see areas of opportunity from a guests perspective and seek improvement in whichever ways are necessary. The voice of our visitors is incredibly valuable, and if you're willing to discuss this further, please feel free to send a private message. Thank you for your time. Sincerely,* [first name]

In 3b, the business manager avoids specificity once again at the end of her message, by using demonstrative pronoun, *this* (which refers anaphorically back to *experience*) and which, again, leaves the issue of food unstated. Similar to the restaurant manager in 2b, this manager uses repeated first-person plural references (e.g., *we, us*) in order to portray the restaurant staff as a team. However, by choosing to sign off on this message with her first name and last initial, she simultaneously highlights her own identity as an individual, and the person who is responsible for addressing complaints. Closing a message with a personal signature is an optional feature of restaurant responses and, strictly speaking, a redundant one, since the review site's interface requires business representatives to provide their names and/or position titles, and automatically displays this information along with the business's response. Signing one's name to a message thus represents a form of relational work (Locher & Watts 2008) and functions to further personalize this instance of public business communication. This particular business manager performs other types of relational work as well: for instance, by emphasizing repeatedly that her business values customer feedback (e.g., *guests perspective, voice of our visitors*). Therefore, inviting further communication is a third way that businesses can address a general, food-related customer complaint.

In addition, a fourth approach was found in restaurants' responses to general complaints about food quality. In these more unusual instances, restaurant representatives use the review space to "educate" the reviewer about the underspecified nature of their food-related complaint. This usually happens with complaints that convey a stronger evaluative stance than some of the earlier, more moderate, examples discussed (e.g., 1 and 2a). For instance, the customer in Example 4a complains that the *food was very poor*, and this intensified negative evaluation is underscored by the following three clauses, which express general, yet unambiguously negative, sentiments about the restaurant's food quality. Example 4a shows the negative review text in its entirety.

> Example 4a
> *Whole Family five of us had a booth in the back, really loud you could not have a conversation, food was very poor, I can make better at home, was highly disappointed, would not recommend. Outdoor seating may have been a better choice but the place is overrated! After 7 pm still had a wait but the staff are accommodating.*

In his response, the restaurant owner begins by apologizing for the noise, offering an explanation for it (i.e., *on a busy night, the noise level is in line with other busy restaurants. Noise is incredibly difficult to control*), and indicating that the restaurant has taken measures to reduce the noise. The rest of his response addresses the reviewer's assessment of the restaurant's food as "[very] poor" – by taking the reviewer to task for writing such an underspecified review!

> Example 4b
> *To say the food was "poor" and give no examples is unjustified and gives me absolutely nothing to respond to or to address with our team. I look at reviews as a way to improve our service and quality, and I take every review seriously and discuss with our staff. Unfortunately, your review gives me nothing to go on except that our restaurant is noisy. Perhaps you could be more specific, since I find it hard to believe that all our "food was poor."*

Responding to a review that he perceives as unfair (*unjustified*) and unhelpful (*no examples ... gives me absolutely nothing to respond to*), this owner's response is understandably a bit exasperated in tone, as he closes by challenging the veracity of the reviewer's assessment (*I find it hard to believe*). Several examples similar to this one (i.e., restaurant representatives questioning, or even directly challenging, the reviewer's comments, as a form of impression management) were found in the data (Vásquez 2018). From a linguistic perspective, it is interesting to note the metadiscursive content of this restaurant response, in that it provides a metacommentary on the review itself (i.e., what items the reviewer did, and did not, include in the original review). This response also demonstrates the business owner's awareness of the interdependent nature of this particular type of intertextual chain (Fairclough 1995) by making explicit reference to the fact that responses are reliant upon the information provided in the original reviews (i.e., incomplete information in the review results in an inability to respond specifically, or to act in order to effect change). It is easy to see how vague or incomplete information represents an obstacle to effective communication in this online environment. Nevertheless, when faced with the identical challenge of addressing reviews with unspecified, yet clearly negative, food-related evaluation, it is worth pointing out that the restaurant representatives in Examples 3b and 4b chose to adopt very different approaches in their responses.

In summary, I identified the following four strategies that were used by restaurants choosing to respond to general, underspecified food-related complaints: 1) ignore the food-related comment and instead address the other (non-food) issues mentioned in the review; 2) provide a general counter-claim that somehow portrays the restaurant's food quality in a more favorable light; 3) invite the reviewer to provide more specific information via some private, one-to-one mode of communication (e.g., private message, email, phone call); or 4) "educate" that reviewer, by explaining that unspecified complaints are not helpful from the business's perspective for making improvements. In many cases, the level of intensity was reciprocal between consumer complaints and businesses' responses.

5.2 Specific food complaints and responses

As mentioned in the previous section, the majority of food-related reviews were specific in mentioning at least one particular dish or item that was not satisfactory (N=50). Most of these mentioned one dish (N=19), however some reviewers complained about two or more dishes, and the greatest number of

Table 5.3 Evaluative adjectival phrases occurring in complaints about specific dishes or food items[5]

Taste	bitter, **bland**, fake (from a box), fishy, **flavorless**, frozen, not fresh, muddled, extremely **salty**, tasteless, under seasoned, **weak**
Texture	chewy, dried out, **dry**, **greasy**, gristly, hard, **soggy**, stale, tough
Temperature	burnt, cold, frozen, lukewarm, **raw**, undercooked, barely warm
Appearance	brown (as in rotten), gray
Other/General	**awful**, **bad**, didn't taste good, inedible, unappetizing, underwhelming, weird and not good

complained-about dishes in a single review was seven. Table 5.3 shows typical kinds of descriptors used to complain about food – the items in bold appeared in more than one review.

Unlike the previous category of general food complaints, by making a complaint about a specific dish and linking it to a particular unfavorable characteristic, a reviewer provides the business with something concrete to respond to. However, this does not mean that all restaurant representatives will choose to respond with a corresponding level of specificity. In fact, as the discussion below illustrates, when confronted with a specific food-related complaint, restaurant representatives can: 1) take a relatively generic approach, by referring more generally to customers' *expectations* or their *experience*; 2) state that restaurant management will follow up privately to obtain more details about the complaint, or invite the customer to do so; 3) directly address the food-related issue(s), and therefore contradict (either implicitly, or explicitly) the customer's claim.

For example, as Example 5b shows, many restaurants still opt to take a generic approach in their responses, even after being presented with a specific food-related complaint. While the main complaint of the reviewer in 5a is the perceived value per cost of the restaurant's menu (i.e., *overpriced*), she also mentions disappointment with the service – and she includes a specific food-related complaint about the temperature of one of the dishes (i.e., *undercooked scallops*).

Example 5a
 . . . Undercooked scallops and an inattentive server makes this place easy to bypass . . .

Rather than addressing this specific food-related issue, the restaurant's general manager takes more of a generic approach (5b), by apologizing for not meeting the customer's "expectations." Expectations could refer to any aspect of the restaurant experience, and there is no mention of food at all in this restaurant response. Example 5b shows the complete response text.

Example 5b
   We are deeply apologetic that we did not live up to your expectations. Please come back and try us again.

This mismatch between a very specific food-related complaint, and a very generic business response was not unusual in the dataset. In fact, similar to the what Zhang and Vásquez (2014) found with hotels' responses to reviews, a few of the restaurants in the sample even posted an identical message in response to several very different reviews, such as the following text used by one restaurant to respond to three different negative food-related reviews (one was general, one addressed the temperature of a specific dish, and the other addressed the texture of a specific dish).

Example 6
   Thank you very much for giving us your feedback. Please know that we take concerns such as yours very seriously. It is our goal to offer every one of our guests personalized service and the excellent food for which we are known. The General Manager from our location/restaurant will be contacting you directly to discuss your dining experience.

This response suggests a "copy and paste" approach – or perhaps the business's policy of publicly responding to any negative review in exactly the same fashion. Rather ironically, in spite of the mention of offering their customers *personalized service*, this is the most impersonal response type possible. This particular text includes some of the strategies identified in the previous section, such as providing a counter-claim (i.e., *the excellent food for which we are known*), as well as soliciting additional information from the customer. As mentioned earlier, this type of counter-claim may suggest to readers that a bad experience mentioned by an individual reviewer should be considered anomalous, or to stress that the reviewer's subjective experience differs from the evaluations of numerous other diners. Unlike the approach taken in Example 3b, where the manager invited the customer to follow up by contacting the business, in Example 6, the public relations manager for the restaurant indicates that the restaurant's general manager will be contacting the customer. Besides posting the identical response to several different reviews, as well as including no first-person singular references within the response itself, this response is made even more impersonal in the construction, *The General Manager from our location/restaurant*. This suggests that the individual writing the response (i.e., the public relations manager) is responding on behalf of a number of different locations and restaurants, rather than representing one specific team of individuals. Very likely, this public relations manager works for a group of restaurants, and is responsible for responding online on behalf of several businesses.

In the previous section, we saw that some restaurant representatives responded by soliciting more details when reviewers failed to specify what exactly the food-related issue(s) consisted of. In some cases, restaurants take this same approach even when reviewers are extremely specific about matters of food quality. For instance, in spite of the very specific complaints about four different food items (steak, fries, bread, butter) in Example 7a, the business owner responds (7b) by asking the customer to provide their email address, so that a staff member can follow up.

Example 7a
... The steak was overdone & had to be sent back, my water glass came dirty, the truffle fries were greasy & swimming in some kind of melted cheese, the one slice of bread (from France) was dry and the recycled butter with honey & sea salt was unappetizing. The presentation of the food on the prison plate was underwhelming...

Example 7b
Hi [firstname], Thank you for sharing your feedback. We aim for 100% guest satisfaction. A member of management would like to speak to you to gather more details about your experience. Would you please email us your contact information at [email address]?

Although the reviewer's food-related complaints are clearly spelled out, the request for a follow-up in this case may involve asking the reviewer for more details about the date and circumstances of their visit. As in several of the above examples, the restaurant owner's use of the generic noun, *experience*, does not specify food-related issues. Furthermore, there is no apology in this response (shown above it is entirety).

However, not all restaurant personnel responding to specific complaints evaded issues of food quality in their responses. The excerpt shown in 8b represents an exemplary text in this regard. As seen in Example 8a, the reviewer names a specific dish and complains that it tasted *fishy*, contrasting it with the server's description of the same item as *fresh*.

Example 8a
... I had ordered the baby spinach salad with salmon. The server said it was 'fresh' but it tasted 'fishy.' ...

In Example 8b, the manager repeats the offending item, *salmon*, rather than using a general noun, or some other vague formulation (e.g., *dish, meal, experience, expectations*).

Example 8b
... Thank you for sharing honestly the highs and lows of your most recent experience. Although I'm certain that the salmon was fresh, as Chef [first name] operates with very high standards in her kitchen, you're always welcome to return any items that appear sub par or are simply displeasing to you. We want every customer to walk away happy, healthy and satisfied! ...

By insisting that the salmon was fresh, the business manager manages to underscore her own certainty, and at the same time, implicitly contradict the customer's claim, without using any negative constructions. Later in the same sentence, she simultaneously acknowledges the subjectivity of food tastes across individuals (i.e., *you're always welcome to return any <u>items that appear sub par</u> or <u>are simply displeasing to you</u>*). In this manner, the manager acknowledges that individual tastes differ, while conveying the message that satisfying the customer matters more to her than whether the customer is right or wrong.

One challenge facing many restaurant representatives is how to address a review in which multiple dishes are referenced and evaluated negatively. One possibility – as was observed in Example 7b – is simply to provide a generic response. However, other restaurant representatives do respond to every single food-related complaint. For instance, in example 9a, the reviewer complained about the size and texture of the steak, being charged for each dish, and that fact that the dessert was not made in-house.

Example 9a
... we had grisly strip steak which was small. Everything was ala carte [...] The cake was good but that was gotten from an outside vendor ...

In his response, the restaurant owner chooses to tackle each of these assessments, one at a time. After indicating that if the customer would have said something during their visit, the owner could have rectified the situation, the owner then proceeds to address each of these individual complaints, as shown in Example 9b. In a stronger variant of the "provide a counter-claim" response strategy, this owner challenges each one of the reviewer's individual claims.

Example 9b

...The steaks that you mention are Meyer Prime grade strip steaks and are, at a minimum, of 8 ounces each. They are not a la carte, and come with potato dauphinoise and fresh sauteed vegetables. [...] Entrees are followed by dessert which is ALWAYS made in house [...] Everything that we serve is always made from scratch in our kitchen, from local sources...

In his response (9b), the restaurant owner provides a detailed explanation of the quality of the steak, the types of accompaniments that come with the main course, as well as an explanation that the desserts they serve are made by the restaurant. The owner's use of repeated extreme case formulations (Pomerantz 1986), such as *always, everything* – in one instance, even emphasized with all caps (*ALWAYS*) – directly contradicts the assertions made by the reviewer, and thereby indirectly challenges the reviewer's credibility. It is worth pointing out that this was not an isolated instance in the set of restaurant responses: 18 of the 50 reviews that included some type of specific food-related complaint actually received responses in which the restaurant representative directly questioned, challenged, or contradicted the reviewer's account of their experience. In several of these cases, the responding individual self-identified as the owner of the business.

A somewhat similar situation can be observed in Examples 10a and 10b, in which the customer complains about several menu items, and the restaurant owner responds to some (though not all) of these specific food-related complaints. The reviewer complains about the temperature of the meat, the taste of one of the desserts, and describes two additional dishes (i.e., macaroni and cheese, apple crisp) as *okay*.

Example 10a

...The actual bbq meat may have been good but it was kinda hard to tell because it was cold when the server handed it to us. Really?! It didn't seem like it was horrible but it definitely was not tasty. The mac&chz were okay, the sweet potato soufflé was waaaaaayyy too sweet, and the apple crisp was okay. Everything was mediocre. I won't go back.

In his response (10b), the restaurant's owner first apologizes, and similar to the approach taken by the manager in 3b, frames the apology from the perspective from the customer, not from the perspective of the business (i.e., *you didn't enjoy your experience with us*). By placing the emphasis on the individual reviewer, the owner may be indirectly alluding to the subjectivity of taste (i.e., by implying that *other consumers* enjoy *their* experience with us).

Example 10b
> Hello [username]. *First of all I'm sorry you didn't enjoy your experience with us. I am the owner and I assure that cold food is never our standard. I was hoping to find out more information about your visit? The apple crisp hasn't been on the menu for well over a month so I'm wondering was this a recent visit? I hope that you will come back and give us another try and we can show you the quality of our food.*

After stating his professional role (i.e., *I am the owner*),[6] he then provides an alternative account about the food temperature: *cold food is never our standard*. This strategy does not directly contradict the customer's claim (i.e., it does not engage with whether the meat was cold or not), instead it frames this issue in terms of what is "standard" at the restaurant. In this way, the owner's statement leaves some room for interpretation. The restaurant owner also indirectly invites the reviewer to provide more information. However, the construction he chooses (*I was hoping to find out more information about your visit?*) does not specify whether the customer should get in touch with the business (as in Example 3b), or if the business will get in touch with the customer (as in Example 6). In his next sentence, the restaurant owner addresses the second of the four items mentioned by the reviewer (i.e., the apple crisp): First, he indicates that this item has not been on the restaurant's menu for over a month, which he then follows with an embedded question (*so I'm wondering was this a recent visit?*), possibly casting aspersions on the relevance of this review – or perhaps even on the veracity of the claims made by the reviewer. For some unknown reason, the owner does not address the remaining two items discussed by the reviewer: the sweet potato soufflé and the macaroni and cheese.

The review in the final example is exceptional in terms of the amount of detail provided. In this 557-word review, the reviewer complains (among other things) about various elements of four different dishes. Example 11a presents an excerpt of this much longer review.

Example 11a
> *The Redfish dish as a whole was under seasoned, especially the fish. I could not make out any discernible flavors of bourbon sweetness within the sauce, which was rather bland. The amount of sauce on the plate caused the brabant sweet potatoes, which were swimming within it, to loose their crispiness and become soggy. Additionally, despite the description, my dish lacked any pralines. The Etouffee also disappointed. The sauce was muddled, it had a very strong flavor yet lacked complexity and distinction. The strength of the sauce easily overpowered the crawfish, which I was hoping to be the center of the dish. I nearly forgot we ordered*

a side of smoked mac and cheese, which is suiting since it lacked any said smokiness and was rather dry. [...] For dessert we ordered the Vintage Baked Alaska and Pecan Bread Pudding. I was looking forward to the Baked Alaska after hearing several positive reviews, however again this was a disappointment. The gelato was nearly frozen solid, and the banana fosters completely frozen solid. It took a bit of elbow just to cut through it with a spoon. It tasted ok, but at these temperature you clearly can't taste it as it was intended.

Although the owner provides a relatively lengthy response (220 words), which addresses a number of issues raised by the reviewer (both food-related and non-food-related), she does not address any of the specific food-related complaints produced by the author of 11a. Instead, she refers to them generally (i.e., *the meal*). However, she does provide some metadiscursive commentary on the extraordinarily comprehensive nature of the review text (i.e., *thorough comments* and *take the time to really spell out*), as seen in Example 11b.

> Example 11b
> Thank you for your business and your thorough comments – we really appreciate both. It means a lot to us when people take the time to really spell out the good AND the bad. We learn from both. First things first: I am so sorry you had such a bad experience. I dine out frequently and I know it's really frustrating when the meal and service fall extremely short of my expectations. We are brand new and will be constantly tweaking menu items until we hit strike the balance that makes our customers happy and showcases the talents of our kitchen team . . .

The restaurant owner here apologizes, again framing the complaint from the perspective of the customer: *you had such a bad experience*. Unlike 9b, this restaurant owner addresses the complaints in terms of customer expectations rather presenting an alternative version of an objective reality; however, she also empathizes with the customer by identifying as a fellow diner, *I dine out frequently and I know it's really frustrating when the meal and service fall extremely short of my expectations*. Interestingly, although some of the reviewer's complaints in 11a were presented as unqualified facts, many of his evaluative statements were also framed in terms of his own expectations (e.g., *disappointed, which I was hoping to be, I was looking forward to*). In addition, this restaurant owner, in her response, shifts several times in her choice of personal pronouns: from second person (*you*) when referring to the customer's review; to first person plural (*we, us*) when representing the perspective of the business as a collective; to first person singular (*I, my*), as she not only apologizes but also empathizes with the reviewer, and in doing so, she emphasizes multiple aspects of her own identity (i.e., business owner, fellow diner); to finally, returning again to first person plural (*we*), in order to conclude the response by speaking on behalf of the (new) restaurant establishment as a whole.

In sum, in responding to specific food-related complaints, restaurant representatives used a number of strategies. In some cases, managers or owners responded with a very general message, in spite of having been given detailed information about food-related issues. In other cases, in spite of getting detailed descriptions of complained-about dishes, restaurant representatives requested further communication, presumably in order to gather more information about the circumstances of the customer's visit. In addition, a number of restaurant representatives responded with a degree of specificity that matched the review, by addressing some – if not all – of the food-related complaints, one by one. Examples 8, 9, and 10 illustrate this last strategy, although they also represent rather different stances taken up by restaurant representatives. Some of the variation found in restaurants' responses to specific food-related issues may be due to nature of the complaint itself, to the professional role of the person responding (i.e., PR manager for multiple businesses vs. individual owner of a small business), or even to the restaurant policy about how to deal with this type of communication. The analysis also highlighted the ways in which different micro-strategies (e.g., personal pronouns, extreme case formulations) contributed to the overall stance constructed by the business in their response.

6 Conclusions

Responding publicly to online consumer complaints about food poses a complex communicative challenge for many restaurants. As this chapter has pointed out, this may be due to the general, underspecified nature of some reviewers' complaints, which provide restaurant representatives nothing specific to respond to. As a result, they are left with the options of either responding in an equally vague manner – or they can solicit further information from the reviewer, usually opting to do so using a private mode of communication. However, even when customer complaints about food *are* formulated in very specific terms, it is obviously never in the restaurant's best interest to agree that the quality of their food was somehow not good. Consequently, restaurant representatives must manage the public's impression of their business, while engaging in the interactionally tricky task of challenging or disagreeing with the customer's claim and instead offering some type of a counter-claim: in essence, stating directly, or implying more indirectly, that the customer is wrong. In some instances, these disagreements are explicitly formulated, but – more often than not – restaurant representatives use a range of alternative discursive strategies to remind readers about the subjectivity of taste in food; to imply that a negative food experience is not the norm and was thus likely anomalous; or to suggest that a reviewer's expectations about the food may have been unrealistic. At the same time, restaurant representatives must engage in relational work as they formulate their responses, by recognizing and attending to the interpersonal nature of this type of online business communication. As one restaurant owner explained, "The guest is not always right, but [s]/he has to gain the impression that one takes him/[her] seriously" (Lane 2014: 142).

From the perspective of some businesses, online consumer reviews – especially negative ones – may represent an uninvited additional encroachment of technology into their professional activities. In other words, restaurant owners do not get to decide whether they would like to opt in, or opt out of, review sites: Their businesses are rated and reviewed on sites such as these whether they like it or not. However, where they *do* get to exercise some control is whether or not, when, and how, they choose to react and respond to online reviews. Some restaurants (and, in fact, the majority, 68 percent, in this study) do not respond publicly to online reviews. Other restaurants, who view this as an opportunity for "service recovery" – or a chance to "turn around" a specific aggrieved customer – may choose to communicate privately about a negative dining experience. And still other restaurants, who recognize the one-to-many communicative potential of fora such as *TripAdvisor* and *Yelp*, treat them as arenas where they can engage in webcare (van Noort & Willemsen 2011), as they nurture customer relationships while simultaneously monitoring and managing their online reputations. This chapter has highlighted some of the possible interactions between the review text and the response text where food-related matters are concerned, and has also illustrated the wide range of variability in businesses' responses. What remains underexamined is the effectiveness of such responses in these particular contexts. Nevertheless, it could be argued that even when customers are "wrong," responding publicly to a negative review is one way of indicating – perhaps more importantly, to *other*, potential customers – that the business does indeed take their customers seriously.

Notes

1 Both platforms use a 5-star rating system.

2   In Chik and Vásquez (2017), we examined a different set of *Yelp* reviews and found that just around 60 percent of *Yelp* reviewers mentioned at least one specific dish, 27 percent only made a general reference to food, and 13 percent included no mention of food at all in their restaurant reviews. These proportions are not dissimilar to the findings reported here.
3   The position titles that I use when discussing restaurant representatives – e.g., business manager, manager, owner – are the ones that appeared on the review sites along with their responses. Both *Yelp* and *TripAdvisor* require businesses responding to customer reviews to identify themselves either by name, position title, or both.
4   This example contains a common internet acronym for presenting a summary statement: *Tldr*, which stands for "too long didn't read."
5   Of course, some examples could potentially refer to more than one category. For instance, in a statement such as *the toast was burnt*, this could be addressing appearance, smell, texture, etc. However, when there was no further specification from the reviewer, I selected the category that I deemed to be the most basic one. (In this case, it is unclear if the reviewer tasted/smelled etc. the toast; and burnt toast is the result of over-exposure to heat, and is thus a matter of temperature.)
6   In this particular instance, I noticed a discrepancy between the name and position title that was indicated by the review site's autofill slot (i.e., [first name last initial], *Business Manager*), and how the author self-identified in the body response text (i.e., *I am the owner*). It was the only such instance that I observed.

Acknowledgments

I thank Alla and Cynthia for their constructive comments on an earlier draft of this chapter. The usual disclaimers apply.

References

Baer, Jay (2016), *Hug Your Haters: How to Embrace Complaints and Keep Your Customers*, New York: Penguin.
Cenni, Irene and Patrick Goethals (2017), 'Negative Hotel Reviews on *TripAdvisor*: A Cross-linguistic Analysis', *Discourse, Context & Media*, 16: 22–30.
Chevalier, Judith A. and Dina Mayzlin (2006), 'The Effect of Word of Mouth on Sales: Online Book Reviews', *Journal of Marketing Research*, 43: 345–354.
Chik, Alice and Camilla Vásquez (2017), 'A Comparative Multimodal Discourse Analysis of Restaurant Reviews from Two Geographical Contexts', *Visual Communication*, 16(1): 3–26.

Creelman, Valerie (2015), 'Sheer Outrage: Negotiating Customer Dissatisfaction and Interaction in the Blogosphere', in Erika Darics (ed), *Digital Business Discourse*, 160–185, London: Palgrave Macmillan.

Fairclough, Norman (1995), *Critical Discourse Analysis*, London: Longman.

Goethals, Patrick (2016), 'Language and International Tourism: A Content- and Discourse-Based Approach to Language-Related Judgments in Web 2.0 Hotel Reviews', *Language and Intercultural Communication*, 2: 235–253.

Goffman, Erving (1959), *The Presentation of Self in Everyday Life*, New York: Anchor.

Heyes, Anthony and Sandeep Kapur (2012), 'Angry Customers, E-Word-of-Mouth and Incentives Provision', *Journal of Economic Behavior & Organization*, 84: 813–828.

Jurafsky, Dan, Victor Chahuneau, Brian R. Routledge and Noah A. Smith (2014), 'Narrative Framing of Consumer Sentiment in Online Restaurant Reviews', *First Monday* 19. Available online: http://firstmonday.org/ojs/index.php/fm/article/view/4944

Lane, Christel (2014), *The Cultivation of Taste*, Oxford: Oxford University Press.

Locher, Miriam and Richard Watts (2008), 'Relational Work and Impoliteness: Negotiating Norms of Linguistic Behavior', In Derek Bousfield and Miriam Locher (eds), *Impoliteness in Language: Studies on its Interplay with Power in Theory and Practice*, 77–99, Berlin: Mouton de Gruyter.

Luca, Michael (2011), 'Reviews, Reputation, and Revenue: The Case of *Yelp*.com', *Harvard Business School Working Paper 12-016*. Available online: http://go.mainstreethub.com/rs/mainstreethub/images/Yelp%20Study.pdf

Mackiewicz, Jo (2008), 'Reviewer Motivations, Bias, and Credibility in Online Reviews', in Sigrid Kelsey and Kirk St. Amant (eds), *Handbook of Research on Computer Mediated Communication*, 252–266, Hershey, PA: The Idea Group Publishers.

Mackiewicz, Jo (2010a), 'Assertions of Expertise in Online Product Reviews', *Journal of Business and Technical Communication*, 24(1): 3–28.

Mackiewicz, Jo (2010b), 'The Co-construction of Credibility in Online Product Reviews', *Technical Communication Quarterly*, 19(4): 403–426.

National Restaurant Association (2017), *State of the Industry Report*. Available online: http://www.restaurant.org/News-Research/Research/soi

O'Connor, Peter (2010), 'Managing a Hotel's Image on *TripAdvisor*', *Journal of Hospitality Marketing and Management*, 19(7): 754–772.

Page, Ruth (2014), 'Saying 'Sorry': Corporate Apologies Posted on Twitter', *Journal of Pragmatics*, 62: 30–45.

Park, Cheol and Thae Min Lee (2009), 'Information Direction, Website Reputation and eWOM Effect: A Moderating Role of Product Type', *Journal of Business Research*, 62(1): 61–67.

Pollach, Irene (2006), 'Electronic Word of Mouth: A Genre Analysis of Product Reviews on Consumer Opinion Web Sites', In *Proceedings of the 39th Hawaii International Conference on System Sciences*. IEEE Computer Society.

Pomerantz, Anita (1986), 'Extreme Case Formulations: A Way of Legitimizing Claims,' *Human Studies*, 9(2–3): 219–229.

Skalicky, Stephen (2013), 'Was This Analysis Helpful? A Genre Analysis of the Amazon.com Discourse Community and Its "Most helpful" Product Reviews', *Discourse, Context & Media*, 2(2): 84–93.

Tannen, Deborah (1984), *Conversational Style: Analyzing Talk among Friends*, Norwood, NJ: Ablex.

Tannen, Deborah (1989), *Talking Voices: Repetition, Dialogue, and Imagery in Conversational Discourse*, Cambridge: Cambridge University Press.

Tian, Youfei (2013), 'Engagement in Online Hotel reviews: A Comparative Study', *Discourse, Context & Media*, 2(3): 184–191.

van Noort, Guda and Lotte Willemsen (2011), 'Online Damage Control: The Effects of Proactive Versus Reactive Webcare Interventions in Consumer-Generated and Web-Generated Platforms', *Journal of Interactive Marketing*, 26: 131–140.

Vásquez, Camilla (2011), 'Complaints Online: The Case of *TripAdvisor*', *Journal of Pragmatics*, 43: 1707–1717.

Vásquez, Camilla (2012), 'Narrativity and Involvement in Online Consumer Reviews: The Case of *TripAdvisor*', *Narrative Inquiry*, 22(1): 105–121.

Vásquez, Camilla (2014), *The Discourse of Online Consumer Reviews*, London: Bloomsbury.

Vásquez, Camilla (2015), 'Right Now Versus Back Then: Recency and Remoteness as Discursive Resources in Online Reviews', *Discourse, Context & Media*, 9: 5–13.

Vásquez, Camilla (2018), '"*Nonsense. Very suspicious. Are you serious?*" Linguistic impoliteness in restaurants' responses to online reviews', Paper presented at the annual American Association of Applied Linguistics (AAAL) conference, March 25, Chicago, IL.

Vásquez, Camilla and Alice Chik (2015), '"I am not a foodie…": Culinary Capital in Online Reviews of Michelin Restaurants', *Food & Foodways*, 23(4): 231–250.

Zhang, Yi and Camilla Vásquez (2014), 'Hotels' Responses to Online Reviews: Managing Consumer Dissatisfaction', *Discourse, Context & Media*, 6: 54–64.

6

Mukbang as Your Digital Tablemate: Creating Commensality Online

Hanwool Choe

1 Introduction

Eating is not only an opportunity for nourishment, but also for sociability. Many cultures value commensality, or the practice of eating together, since it is a basic human social act, deeply linked to sociality (see Beeman 2014; Kerner, Chou & Warmind 2015). In Korea, the practice of common eating is especially important and recognized as a cultural hallmark: People eat together and share food while doing so. In fact, eating alone can be viewed as socially unacceptable (Bruno 2016) because Korean eating culture traditionally values togetherness. "Solo-eating" is often associated with "loneliness" (see Cho et al. 2015; Kim 2018).

In recent years, as noted in Steger and Jung (2017) and Pyun (2017), individualistic practices and values have been creeping into the everyday lives of Korea's millennials, against the more traditional collectivist social pressures. This rise of individualism has led to significant lifestyle changes and one of them is regarding the practice of eating together. While many young adult Koreans now live on their own (see Kim & Lee 2014), they are mobilizing technology to "eat together" in a somewhat innovative way: They watch "mukbang," a Korean livestream of eating, via a livestreaming website (see de Solier 2018; Kim 2018; Choe 2019).

Mukbang is a digital dinner table where an individual known as a "broadcast jockey" (BJ) displays an array of mouthwatering dishes (often with beverages) and enjoys eating them as hundreds of viewers watch. While it might seem like this is merely an opportunity for voyeurism, in fact it is a virtual way of eating together. Specifically, the broadcaster and viewers continually multimodally communicate with each other to co-create eating actions: The eater speaks to the viewers through the livestream camera while eating, and the viewers type real-time comments to each other and to the eater through a live chat room (see

Choe 2019). Thus, mukbang provides a virtual platform for sociable eating where participants are expected to work together.

The discourse(s) surrounding food and eating have received a great deal of research attention from various perspectives. Studies of social interaction have long focused on the context of mealtime (e.g., Erickson 1981 on topical cohesion, Tannen 2005 on conversational style, and Blum-Kulka 1993 on storytelling). More recently, scholars have begun to consider how the act of eating itself constructs, and is constructed in, interaction. In her analyses of video- and audio-recorded mealtime conversations, Wiggins (2002, 2013, 2014) shows how gustatory expressions like "yuck," "mmm," or "eugh" are embodied actions that construct and display tastes and preferences. Mandelbaum (2014) demonstrates how family members use requests to perform eating-related actions through questions ("can I have some jello"), statements ("I would like some [stuffing]"), and object names ("salt"). Digital contexts are also sites for food-related communication; existing studies have focused on restaurant reviews (e.g., Vásquez & Chik 2015), discussion threads about picky eating (Gordon & İkizoğlu 2017), and tweets about coffee (Zappavigna 2014), among others (see, for example, others mentioned in this volume's introduction).

In this study, I bridge these research areas by investigating multimodally coordinated eating as it occurs online in mukbang. Specifically, I bring together Goffman's (1974, 1981) notions of frame (a definition of a situation) and footing (alignment) and Tannen's (2007) sense of involvement to identify and explicate the linguistic, discursive, and multimodal resources – which include an exhortative form ("let's"), we-related Korean words such as "kathi" (together) and "wuli" (we), gestures, emojis, and pretend play – that participants use to achieve a sort of eating together that functions as a kind of commensality. The chapter lends insight into the joint construction of social practices that bridge online and offline, while also showing how Korea's cultural ideology of eating together is transferred to, and reconfigured for, an online space. It therefore contributes to a better understanding of the coordinated multimodal involvement that creates a digital social practice that revolves around food and eating. In addition, it adds to the growing literature on livestream discourse where people video-stream while communicating through a chat box, which occurs not only in mukbang (Choe 2019), but also in online gaming (e.g., Recktenwald 2017; Graham & Dutt 2019). My focus here, however, is on how the joint activity of sociable eating in mukbang is multimodally achieved, establishes involvement among participants, and thereby reproduces commensality online.

In what follows, I first describe in more detail what mukbang is. After introducing the theoretical background of the current chapter, which includes prior studies of mealtime discourse, framing and footing, and involvement and joint action, I introduce mukbang participants appearing in my data. I then analyze four examples of mukbang interaction. My analysis demonstrates how the participants make use of a variety of resources and strategies to create a context of virtually shared mealtime in mukbang. Finally, I discuss how mukbang has become an interactional place that enacts Korea's sociocultural ideologies of eating together and bridges online and offline.

2 Background

2.1 What is mukbang?

먹방 (*mukbang*) is short for 먹는방송 (*muknunbangsong*): 먹는 (*muknun*) combines the verb, 먹다 (*mukda*), "to eat," with a relativizer suffix, -는 (*-un*), and thus characterizes 방송 (*bangsong*), "broadcast." Thus, mukbang means, roughly, "a broadcast where people eat." Note that when it comes to "eating" in mukbang, it also involves drinking beverages. Mukbang broadcasts typically feature a solo eater, who consumes a large meal consisting of several dishes and speaks to (and through) a camera while viewers watch online and type comments using real-time chat. Sometimes the broadcast also includes cooking and cleaning up, but the primary focus of mukbang is the eating experience, including the visual display of plates or bites of food, the amplification of eating sounds, the use of gustatory expressions (see Wiggins 2002, 2013, 2014), and sometimes additional production resources such as music, costumes, and lighting effects.

Mukbang broadcasts are produced and watched live on livestreaming platforms like Afreeca TV (http://www.afreecatv.com) and YouTube (http://www.youtube.com). My data were excerpted from YouTube where mukbang broadcaster jockeys had uploaded their recorded mukbang clips after having livestreamed them on Afreeca TV. The livestreaming websites allow anyone to stream or watch livestreams on a variety of topics. These include gaming, singing, offering makeup tutorials, and cooking – and mukbang is among the most popular broadcast offerings in the websites. The terms I use to discuss mukbang here, and in the analysis, include technical terms like "BJs" to mean broadcaster jockeys and "star balloons" to refer to digital money; these are used in the Afreeca TV community. During live broadcasts, viewers can reward BJs with star balloons, a form of internet currency that can be converted into real cash (one star balloon was worth approximately eight U.S. cents at the time the initial data collection was conducted in 2015). The monetary benefits for popular BJs can be significant, and for some, livestreaming can become a main or sole source of income. Thus, BJs are often motivated to create fun, compelling content to attract more viewers.

Mukbang has been popular in Korea since the early 2000s. News articles (AFP/Relaxnews 2013; Choi 2015; Hu 2015) posit various reasons for the popularity of mukbang among young Koreans. First, mukbang may be seen as similar to what Western audiences know as "food porn" – it gives viewers vicarious satisfaction, especially through the sensory stimulation provided by visual and audio representations of eating. Care is given to the display of food, and mukbang BJs may intentionally eat loudly, sometimes increasing their microphone volume to dramatize their eating sounds. In the YouTube comments section of mukbang clips, viewers often express appreciation or gratitude to mukbang BJs. Some excerpted comments in English and Korean include "omggg so excited!! my fav foods," "love the slurping sound he makes," and "다이어트하는데 대리만족 되네요" ("It vicariously satisfies me while I am currently on a diet"). Comments like these suggest that mukbang BJs may help to sate the food cravings of those who cannot or do not eat such elaborate meals.

Second, and the focus of my analysis, mukbang is also a new way to be with other people and fulfills a desire not to eat alone. As mentioned earlier, eating alone is somewhat culturally stigmatized in Korea because eating together lies at the heart of traditional Korean dining culture that features communal dishes to share (see Cho et al. 2015; Hakimey & Yazdanifard 2015). However, as an interviewee from AFP/Relaxnews (2013) remarks, watching mukbang makes viewers feel emotionally connected as if they were having dinner with someone. As single-person households in Korea are gradually increasing (Kim & Lee 2014), people use mukbang as their new eating companion, enabling a feeling of virtual togetherness while physically eating alone. Even when viewers are not eating while watching, they still achieve commensality by co-constructing the BJ's eating action. In other words, through mukbang, technology makes possible online what is traditionally considered to be possible only offline, and this reality has social and emotional meaning for participants.

3 Theoretical framework

3.1 Mealtimes

Mealtimes are often used as a research site, as it is a site of everyday naturally occurring interaction. For example, Erickson (1981) investigates how one Italian

American family manages topical coherence and conversational floors in their video-recorded dinner table talk; Tannen (2005) demonstrates how friends use different conversational styles during a Thanksgiving dinner she audio-recorded and in which she participated; and Blum-Kulka (1993, 1997) compares the storytelling and other discursive means of socialization and sociability among members of American families and Israeli families at dinner. A series of studies by Ochs and her colleagues (e.g., Ochs, Smith & Taylor 1989; Ochs & Taylor 1995) focuses on dinnertime as a primary site for family narration, problem solving, and child socialization, while Bova and Arcidiacono (e.g., 2013, 2014) focus on authority and argumentative strategies in Italian and Swiss family dinner talk, including pertaining to food-related issues such as which foods, and how much, children are expected to eat.

Other studies have also highlighted the centrality of food and eating as part of mealtime interaction. People evaluate prepared dishes during mealtime (e.g., Wiggins 2002, 2013; Mondada 2009) and influence what and how others eat through monitoring, evaluating, and teaching (e.g., Ochs, Pontecorvo & Fasulo 1996; Tulviste et al. 2002; Kim 2006; Aronsson & Gottzén 2011). Participants also use other participants as resources to accomplish mealtime-related actions, including distributing food and eating (e.g., Mandelbaum 2014; Galatolo & Caronia 2018; Sicoli in press). In other words, mutual participation during mealtimes is constructed around and through food. Scholars have also examined how cultural and social factors such as gender, age, and family roles come into play in the context of food talk and consumption. For instance, Bova and Arcidianco (2014) demonstrate how parents do not simply feed children, but that feeding and eating are bidirectional and mutually achieved processes. In Sicoli (in press), the father of a Lachixío family complains about over-cooked tortillas and indirectly requests a drink of water (i.e., "a little water will help one get it down"). Making eye contact with one another, family members pass around the father's water request: The mother says to the son, "go get water for your father to drink." Then, the son passes the obligation to his sister: "now it's you because you're a woman." While they jointly work to resolve getting someone to do something, the participants' verbal and non-verbal actions both construct and display a series of hierarchical obligations.

These existing studies of mealtime talk typically involve family and friends eating together in person. We know little about how and why people who do not know each other in person gather together and accomplish eating together, especially in technology-mediated environments. Broadening the context of mealtime through the analysis of mukbang, the current chapter thus examines how anonymous strangers collaborate to enjoy a virtually shared mealtime that bridges online and offline, while also creating togetherness. To do this, I draw on the concepts of framing and footing, and conversational involvement, considered next.

3.2 Framing and footing

Building upon Bateson's (1972) psychological concept of a frame, Goffman (1974: 8) defines it as "what it is that's going on here" and examines how social activities and interaction are perceived and thus framed in certain ways. Goffman (1981) also proposes the notion of footing, or alignment that displays situational orientations of participations toward what is happening in the current interaction. He remarks that when we change footing, "it implies a change in the alignment we take up to ourselves and the others present as expressed in the way we manage the production or reception of an utterance" (Goffman 1981: 128). Footing changes show how interactional dynamics are ever-changing and they are usually accomplished through what Gumperz (1982) calls "contextualization cues" that signal how speakers mean what they say and do, and which include lexical items, syntactic structures, paralinguistic features (e.g., tone, pitch, laughter), and non-verbal actions (e.g., gesture, motion, and gaze). For example, Tannen and Wallat (1993) and Gordon (2009) demonstrate how frames and footings are created in the context of a pediatric encounter and family interaction, respectively. The notions of framing and footing help us understand how people use language to make meanings and interpret what is presently happening in interaction in these and many other contexts, including online (see e.g., Georgakopoulou 2011; Choe 2019).

3.3 Involvement and joint action

As people co-construct meaning, they also co-construct what Tannen (2007) calls "involvement"; this is the connection that binds speakers and listeners (or writers and readers) together. Involvement presupposes mutual understanding built upon shared background knowledge.

Although Tannen's discussion of involvement is primarily based on spoken and literary discourse, the concept also applies to multimodal aspects of social interaction and types of discourse. As scholars point out (e.g., Kress & van Leeuwen 2001; LeVine & Scollon 2004; Erickson 2015), different semiotic modes alongside language are used to formulate interaction; where interaction takes place, participants are expected to "work together" multimodally to create involvement. Scholars examine how people use bodily resources and collaboratively organize their bodily conduct to create joint courses of action during strips of talk in different kinds of contexts (e.g., Goodwin & Goodwin 2004; Streeck, Goodwin & LeBaron 2011). For example, in Wiggins (2015), when parents feed their infants, they use the babies' facial expressions, vocalizations, and bodily moments as cues of what foods they like or dislike. Also, infants use nonverbal means to signal when and how much more food should be offered during feeding. The mutual and reciprocal creation of eating-related action, as well as involvement through multimodal resources, is especially relevant to the context of Korean eating culture that values "togetherness" in terms of eating together and sharing dishes. Next, I introduce the mukbang participants as well as the methods for data collection and display that facilitate my analysis of commensality online.

4 Mukbang participants

4.1 Mukbang BJs

The two BJs whose livestreams I examine, BJ ChangHyun and BJ Haetnim, have both regularly livestreamed their mukbang via Afreeca TV. BJ ChangHyun started his mukbang around 2014; whereas Haetnim started roughly in 2015. Like many other BJs, they recorded their livestreams and then uploaded them to YouTube for others to watch later. I collected extracts from multiple videos that each BJ uploaded. ChangHyun's mukbang clips were livestreamed between September and October 2015 and Haetnim's were between May and July 2017.[1] Each of the mukbang clips I collected lasted between one hour and a half and two hours. I first collected ChangHyun's in 2015, and at that time, ChangHyun seemed to be the only BJ to consistently archive his mukbang broadcasts on YouTube, including the chat messages exchanged and contributed by his viewers during his livestreaming. Around this time, many mukbang broadcasters uploaded their mukbang clips only, without chat messages, to their YouTube channel; Haetnim started adding chat messages to her recorded mukbang clips in April 2016, and I collected her video clips in 2019.

Figure 6.1 shows the layout of a mukbang livestream. The chat messages appear in a chat screen in the upper right corner of the viewer's screen. ChangHyun's and Haetnim's extensive mukbang archives with real-time chat messages preserve the complexity of the livestream (where speaking, typing, and

Figure 6.1 BJ Haetnim reading chat messages during mukbang

making bodily actions occur simultaneously in interaction), as it unfolded in real time and is thus an ideal data set for analyzing eating as a collaborative practice and means of online commensality.

During the time the livestreams were collected in 2015 and 2019, ChangHyun and Haetnim hosted mukbang every night. Both eaters usually ate carry-out or had food delivered for each segment; they also cooked, but very occasionally.

4.2 Viewers

It is hard to know exactly how many viewers participated in chatting while watching the two BJs' livestreams because the Afreeca TV website does not count viewers and chat participants separately. Given the average number of viewers and the fast pace of chat messages visible onscreen, it is estimated that there were hundreds of participating viewers. In mukbang, there are two types of mukbang viewers: visible and invisible. Visible viewers are those who participate in chat messaging, so their presence is apparent through the chat messaging screen. Invisible viewers are those who watch without chatting at all, including potential viewers who watch the recorded clips on YouTube. There is no way to count invisible viewers.

5 Methods for data collection and display

BJs may broadcast and respond to viewers' chat messages during three phases of mukbang: preparing, eating, and cleaning up. The eating parts are usually referred to as what we know as "mukbang" and most hosts only record and upload those parts on YouTube. Examples considered here are thus excerpted from when both BJs eat and interact with their viewers.

With one exception (Example 2), I have transcribed the mukbang interactions as follows: There are two parties: 1) mukbang BJ and 2) viewers. I categorize mukbang participation into three parts: First, I include screen captures of the BJs' visible bodily actions. Second, I describe, in English, their bodily actions including facial expressions and gaze. Third, the BJs' spoken speech and the typed comments of their viewers are displayed in Korean, followed by idiomatic English translation in single quotation marks. Each chat message is shown with a participant's pseudo ID. Where speech and actions are simultaneous, they appear on the same row in the transcript. The mukbang BJs' actions are numbered by Arabic numerals, whereas viewers' actions are denoted by Roman alphabet letters. I do not translate some aspects of Korean online language to keep the sense of how it looks. Laughter is one such aspect; it is conventionally produced through repetition of the Korean consonant ㅋ (*kieuk*), equivalent to the English letter *k*. Another form I do not translate is the Korean vowel ㅠ (*yu*), which is used to represent an eye from which two tears are flowing (i.e., crying). I also do not translate the tilde (~), which is used in Korean discourse online to indicate sound lengthening (similar to how repeated letters are used in English, e.g., "hiiii"). Also, original chat messages are offered with Romanized Korean and/or linguistic glossary translation,[2] if necessary.

6 Mukbang interaction

I identify and present two types of mukbang interaction jointly undertaken by mukbang BJs and their visible viewers. First, I show how virtual togetherness between the hosts and their viewers is constructed. Second, I show how "eating for another" is achieved. My analysis illustrates how mukbang features and fulfills commensality, in ways both similar and different to how people physically eat together. These are not the only interactional patterns that contribute to digital commensality in mukbang, but they are the ones that I repeatedly encountered, and they additionally highlight key aspects of eating together through mukbang. I argue that they are the primary ways that hosts (BJs) and their viewers connect with each other and create involvement.

6.1 Virtual togetherness over physical remoteness

The following two examples demonstrate how each party (mukbang BJ and viewers) contributes to realizing virtual commensality. In Example 1, BJ Haetnim suggests drinking together and makes spoken and bodily actions to make a toast before drinking. Her viewers join the drinking activity by sending beer emojis and making other toast expressions in response, accomplishing a shared toast virtually. Example 2 is a list of collected chat messages from mukbang clips of ChangHyun and Haetnim. In chat messages, viewers integrate their ongoing offline eating moments with watching mukbang or bring up table manners, which, I note, signals a frame of the social situation: eating together.

Example 1 Virtual cheers

While waiting for fried chicken to be delivered, Haetnim prepares a cold beer to cool herself down because it was very hot earlier. Before drinking, she suggests drinking together and gives a toast. In aligning with her toast, her viewers virtually join the drinking activity. Not to overcrowd the transcript, I include only relevant chat messages to the current mukbang situation. Also, different Korean toast expressions are transcribed in Romanized English, with an explanation in italics, to display the variety of the expressions. (See transcript.)

Haetnim and her viewers jointly reproduce drinking together in a virtual context. Haetnim's spoken and bodily actions are powerful contextualization cues that frame the current mukbang as a shared mealtime started by a shared toast. For example, in line 5, her right hand moves the beer closer to the screen and in line 6, her eyes directly look at the screen as if she were making eye-contact with her viewers behind the screen. In line 6, through "Geonbae" ("cheers" in English), she now verbally invites her viewers to join her drinking action. These collective actions, made by Haetnim, construct mutual participation in the sense that mukbang performance is not simply a solo-eating show but rather a shared mealtime for all. By using an exhortative form ("Let's first have a beer to cool down") in line 2, she creates togetherness in her mukbang performance. Mentioning the hot weather in lines 3 and 4 ("Oh it was so hot today Right?"), Haetnim also produces the mutual need of drinking a cold beer, which is also supported by a viewer's chat message in line A ("It was so hot this afternoon and it made me think about chicken and beer!! Now you're having it for me").

In response to Haetnim's toast, viewers type a series of beer emojis (🍺) in lines B, C, and E, as if they were also holding a glass of beer. In lines C, D, E, and F, viewers also type different toast expressions such as "Jjan" (clinking glasses) and

IMAGE	BJ HAETNIM			VIEWERS		
	LINE	SPOKEN ACTION	BODILY ACTION	LINE	TYPED ACTION	ID
	1	아 시원하게 한잔 "Ah one beer to cool down"	Right hand holding the canned beer			
	2	일단 시원하게 한잔 합시다 iltan siwenha-key han-can ha-psita first cool-ly one-NC do-EXH.DEF "Let's first have a beer to cool down"		A	오늘 낮에 너무더워서 저도 치맥생각 엄청났는데!! 안니가 딱 드셔주시네요 "It was so hot this afternoon and it made me think about chicken and beer!! Now you're having it for me"	choco9907
	3	아우 오늘 너무 더웠어요 "Oh it was so hot today"				
	4	그죠? "Right?"				
	5	자 건배 Okay Geonbae *Geonbae is a Korean expression that is equivalent to cheers in English	Right hand bringing the beer closer to the screen Eyes looking at the screen			

IMAGE	BJ HAETNIM			VIEWERS		
	LINE	SPOKEN ACTION	BODILY ACTION	LINE	TYPED ACTION	ID
	6		Right hand holding the beer close to the screen			
	7	오 손시려 "Oh my hand is freezing"	Right hand bringing the beer back to her chest and her eyes frowning for a second	B	😂😂😂	lucky113
				C	😂😂😂 짠! "😂😂😂 Jjan!" *Jjan is a Korean sound word that describes clinking glasses and is also used as a toast expression.	dkssud
			Her mouth drinking the beer and her head orienting upward	D	짠! "Jjan!"	kmc275000
				E	위하여🍻 "Wihayeo 🍻" *Wihayeo is a toast expression in Korean and its direct English translation is "for." The expression can be equivalent to "here's to" in English. The object of wihayeo is often omitted.	poppyland
				F	짠 "Jjan"	hyuk2013

"Wihayeo" ("here's to" in English). Those chat messages with the beer emojis, also serving as contextualization cues, are in line with Haetnim's prior spoken and bodily actions that accompany drinking together virtually: They too are in the "drinking together" frame.

This (virtually) collaborative drinking between Haetnim and her viewers frames mukbang as a shared mealtime, rather than solo-eating show, which expects reciprocity and involvement through mutual participation. It also illuminates how mukbang is used as a virtual place where people come together and accomplish togetherness through food and eating (drinking in this context).

Example 2 What we talk about when we talk about mukbang: How viewers demonstrate and encourage involvement via chat messages

In chat messages occurring during mukbang, viewers often incorporate their (current) offline eating moments with the present activity of watching mukbang, thus creating the frame of the shared mealtime and bridging online and offline via food and eating. Below are five chat messages that, I note, represent mealtime-related interaction about food, eating, and table manners. Lines 1 and 5 are excerpted from BJ ChangHyun's livestream while the others from BJ Haetnim's. For the purpose of analysis, I provide a four-layer translation: Original messages (typed in Korean) are followed by Romanized Korean, linguistic glossary translation, and English idiomatic translation.

LINE	CHAT MESSAGES				
1	"아놔 a-nwa oh my god	저도 ce-to I-also	방금 pangkum just now	시킴 sikhi-m order-END		
	같이 kathi together	먹어요~" mek-eyo~ eat-EXH.POL~				
	"Oh my god I just ordered food as well Let's eat together~"					
2	"피자 phica pizza	식기전에 sik-kiceney cool down-before	얼른 ellun immediately	먹어요 mek-eyo eat-EXH.POL	우리" wuli we	
	"Let's eat pizza right now before it gets cold"					

LINE	CHAT MESSAGES		
3	"난 순살먹고 있는데 na-n swunsal-mek-ko iss-nuntey I-TOP boneless chicken-eat-and exist-CIRCUM 언니꺼가 넘나 맛나보입니다ㅠ enni-kke-ka nemna masna-poi-pnita ㅠ BJ Haetnim-thing-NOM very delicious-look-DEC.DEF ㅠ "I am eating boneless chicken and yours [your chicken] looks very delicious ㅠ."		
4	먹방에 집중해주세열 mekpang-ey cipcwungha-ycwu-se-yye-l mukbang-at focus on-do something for someone-SH-IMV.POL-CUTE "Please focus on mukbang"		
5	젓가락질을 왜 그렇게 하세요? ceskalak-cil-ul way kulehkey ha-sey-yo? chopsticks-the act of doing-ACC why like that do-SH-INT.POL? 눈에 거슬려요 nwun-ey kesully-eyo eye-to bother-DEC.POL "Why are you using chopsticks like that? It really bothers me"		

Lines 1 ("Oh my god I just ordered food as well Let's eat together") and 2 ("Let's eat pizza right now before it gets cold") signal how doing mukbang is not a BJ's solo task, but "our" joint activity because "we" share food or (and) eat together. In particular, lexical items such as "kathi" (together) and "wuli" (we) enhance the frame of the shared mealtime with an exhortative form ("let's"). In line 3 ("I am eating boneless chicken but yours looks much better"), a viewer creates the sense of sameness as the viewer is also eating the same kind of food as the BJ, and eating is the communal activity that "we" are presently doing. These three chat messages demonstrate how mukbang is used as a digital eating companion while each individual eats alone offline.

In line 4 ("Please focus on mukbang"), one viewer sends a message to other viewers because they are chatting about something that is not relevant to the current mukbang (those viewers' messages are not shown). By calling attention to mukbang, the viewer signals that it is a shared activity in mutual participation that is expected (i.e., viewers should watch mukbang, not do something unrelated to mukbang). In other words, these other messages are distracting from the main activity or frame at hand.

Lastly, in line 5 ("Why are you using chopsticks like that? It really bothers me"), a viewer criticizes how the BJ is holding the chopsticks. As chopsticks are one of the main utensils that Koreans use to eat, using chopsticks properly is considered important to table manners and this chat message shows that table manners are applicable to mukbang. This also enhances framing mukbang as a shared mealtime in the sense that an eater is expected to display table manners for the benefit of others. Possibly, the last two chat messages (lines 4 and 5) mirror cultural expectations that Koreans have during shared mealtimes. According to Kim (2006), Korean family mealtime conversations are usually devoted to the current mealtime and include evaluating prepared dishes, negotiating eating actions (i.e., what and how much to eat), and teaching table manners. Numerous discourse analytic studies also cite mealtime as an important site for socialization of politeness and social norms (e.g., Blum-Kulka 1997). Related to such studies, mukbang can be understood as a shared mealtime: Table manners are relevant and may be commented on.

In examples 1 and 2, I have demonstrated how mukbang participants use various linguistic, discursive, and multimodal resources and strategies to have eating (or drinking) companions and create virtual togetherness between online and online. Exchanging virtual toasts to drink together and viewers' integration of their own offline eating moments into the current online mukbang activity reproduce, in technology-mediated ways, aspects of physically eating together.

6.2 Virtually eating for another: Sharing food and the eating activity

As mentioned earlier, mukbang BJs can earn revenue: Viewers send star balloons (cryptocurrencies in AfreecaTV that can be converted into actual money) while watching. Although the two parties (eater and viewers) have different primary underlying motivations to eat food and watch mukbang – the eater seeks monetary benefits while the viewers meet vicarious satisfaction of food and eating (see Choe 2019 for details) – the basic mechanics of mukbang is that each party does something for the other: Viewers supply eating instructions for a BJ, and the BJ eats food for the viewers (in instructed ways). Previous examinations of how, in different contexts, one participant does something for someone else are relevant to explain what is going on in mukbang. Schiffrin (1993), in her analysis of sociolinguistic interviews, shows how "speaking for another" can be taken to be "chipping in" or interpreted as "butting in." Gordon and İkizoğlu (2017) examine an instance of "asking for another" that takes place in an online discussion thread started by a woman who asks for health advice regarding her boyfriend's picky eating. While some responses to her post view her asking-for-another act as caring, many interpret it as nagging. In other words, doing something for another person shifts alignments, or what Goffman (1981) calls footings, in interaction.

Extending such work, I demonstrate how participants align with each other to accomplish "eating for another" in mukbang, thus creating mutual participation. Example 3 illustrates ChangHyun doing virtual feeding, as he offers food to his viewer and then eats the food as if the viewer were eating. Example 4 shows ChangHyun following a viewer's typed instruction to eat food in a particular way. In both examples, ChangHyun and his viewers take up different footings simultaneously to jointly accomplish the eating-for-another action. Eating for another is mukbang's very own way to overcome the absence of physical co-presence and thus virtually achieves the practice of eating together. (The following examples are excerpted from Choe [2019], where I focus on how eating action is jointly and multimodally accomplished moment-by-moment, thus creating what I term "constructed action" originated from Tannen's 2007 notion of constructed dialogue.)

Example 3 Virtual feeding

ChangHyun is eating different kinds of boneless fried chicken, including creamy chicken, Korean BBQ-flavored chicken, and chicken with shrimp, along with pickled radishes. Preceding this excerpt, a viewer, called Bamboo, gave a number of star balloons to him. In this segment, the eater offers Bamboo the chicken as a gesture of gratitude. (Please see transcript.)

ChangHyun takes up two simultaneous footings through spoken and bodily actions as he creates pretend play: In one he is a food provider, and in the other he is a food receiver. First, as a food provider, he offers food in line 1 ("Okay, Bamboo, say ah") with his right hand bringing the chicken closer to the computer screen and camera and in line 3 ("Bamboo, try it"). ChangHyun even compliments the viewer – Bamboo, whom he is performing as, in line 12 ("our Bamboo is eating so well"), even though he is the one who eats the food. Second, embodying the food receiver (i.e., Bamboo-as-eater), ChangHyun performs bodily actions by chewing the chicken (line 12) and producing gustatory

IMAGE	BJ CHANGHYUN			VIEWERS		
	LINE	SPOKEN ACTION	BODILY ACTION	LINE	TYPED ACTION	ID
	1	자 우리 밤부먹자 "Okay, Bamboo, say ah"	Right hand brining boneless fried chicken closer to the computer screen			
	2		Waiting for 3 seconds	A	밤부님 냠 장전!!!! "Bamboo is ready to eat!!!!"	21bibi21
	3	밤부 냠 "Bamboo, try it"		B	순살인가? "Is it boneless chicken?"	krbfl433
				C	?	hwpgud1
				D	리얼사운드아니가? "Isn't it high quality sound?"	Djadmlwlo
	4	리얼사운드나고요? 네 리얼사운드죠 "Did you ask if it's high quality sound? Yes, it is"		E	BJ창현님의 방송 추천 1위 "BJ ChangHyun's broadcast is currently ranked as No.1 for the most recommended now"	website notification
	5	소리 왜요? "Is there any problem with the sound?"				

IMAGE	BJ CHANGHYUN			VIEWERS		
	LINE	SPOKEN ACTION	BODILY ACTION	LINE	TYPED ACTION	ID
	6		Right hand bringing back the chicken to him	F	썸네일이 다 브이젯어요 "Your video thumbnail would be all V gesture"	flyhigh277
	7	아유 추천 내가 1 등이구나 "Oh my god, my mukbang is being the most recommended now"		G	와우 "Wow"	Fniizndk
				H	어디치킨이에요 "Where did you order the chicken"	0622yung0622
	8		Mouth opening to eat the chicken	I	엥 "What"	solar3414
	9	음음 "Mmmm"	Eyes looking at the chat screen and ChangHyun chewing the chicken	J	앙! "Nom nom!"	Bamboo

IMAGE	BJ CHANGHYUN			VIEWERS		
	LINE	SPOKEN ACTION	BODILY ACTION	LINE	TYPED ACTION	ID
	10		Right hand passing over the chopsticks to the left hand	K	비트에 절여서 그래윰~ㄱ "It is because they are pickled with beets~ㄱ"	loveooojj
	11		Eyes looking at the right computer screen	L	우와 "Wow"	cjdnfwoo
				M	ㄱㄱㄱㄱㄱㄱ	ge2016zx051
				N	우와 "Wow"	tablove123
	12	음 잘 먹는다 우리 뱀부 아구아구 "Mmmm ah mmm our Bamboo eating so well nom nom"				

expressions in line 9 ("Mmmm") and 12 ("Mmmm ah mmm [...] nom nom"). In particular, in line 12 ("Mmmm ah mmm our Bamboo is eating so well"), ChangHyun rapidly changes his footing from the food receiver (the gustatory expressions part) to the food provider (the compliment part: "our Bamboo is eating so well"). Through this pretend play, ChangHyun achieves what can be described as "eating for another."

Also, in line J, Bamboo types the eating sound, "nom nom!" as if s/he were eating the offered chicken. The viewer's gustatory chat message not only enhances ChangHyun's footing as a food provider but also suggests Bamboo joins (and also reinforces) the frame of the shared mealtime. ChangHyun's spoken and bodily actions as well as Bamboo's typed actions virtually embody the act of feeding that happens in shared meals, such as when a parent feeds a child (e.g., Paugh & Izquierdo 2009; Bova & Arcidiacono 2014) or when an adult feeds a friend or partner (e.g., Chye & David 2006). Through the virtual sharing and feeding food, ChangHyun and his viewer co-create mukbang as a joint activity, evoking a sense of togetherness.

Example 4 Eat-as-I-type

Kendon (1990) describes a children's game called timmy wherein participants agree to imitate one another's action: One person, a challenger, initiates her or his instruction, touching each fingertip of their left hand with the index finger of their right hand, repeatedly saying "timmy" and asks the others, responders, to follow the challenger's performance, by saying "do as I do." The responders are expected to repeat the performance. Although the responders' imitation will never be exactly the same, the timmy activity suggests how children jointly and multimodally construct actions. Similarly, mukbang often shows such a joint moment which I term "eat-as-I-type," and this action, like virtual feeing, co-constructs "eating for another," a shared mealtime frame, and involvement.

In the following excerpt, ChangHyun is eating *tangsuyuk* (crispy sweet and sour pork), *possam* (steamed pork with vegetables) with *ssamjang* (Korean dipping sauce), and fried dumplings. Right before the following situation, a viewer (trtr5) has continuously asked him to eat *tangsuyuk* in a particular way. ChangHyun finally accepts the viewer's request and subsequently eats the food as the viewer types. To conserve space, I include only the messages of the viewer who makes this request and "controls" the BJ's eating (and I have not described all of the BJ's bodily actions because his spoken actions and images are enough to grasp his moment-by-moment actions that follow the viewer's chat messages). Other viewers' chat messages are included only if BJ mentions them while speaking.

IMAGE	BJ CHANGHYUN			VIEWERS		
	LINE	SPOKEN ACTION	BODILY ACTION	LINE	TYPED ACTION	ID
	1		Eyes reading the chat screen	A	상추탕수육 한번만 먹어주세요 "Could you please eat *tangsuyuk* wrapped with a lettuce leaf?"	trtr5
	2	음 "Umm"	Eyebrows frowning			
	3	이 조합 되게 안 어울릴 것 같은데 자꾸 부탁하시니깐 trtr5님께서 "I don't think this combination sounds good, but trtr5 keeps asking me to do so" [eating *tangsuyuk* wrapped with a lettuce leaf]				

IMAGE	BJ CHANGHYUN			VIEWERS		
	LINE	SPOKEN ACTION	BODILY ACTION	LINE	TYPED ACTION	ID
	4	상추에 탕수육이요? 요렇게? "Putting *tangsuyuk* on this leaf? like this?"				
	5	소스는 어떻게 해? 소스는 어떻게 해요? 쩍먹? "What about sauce? What about sauce? dipping?"				
	6	어떻게 해달라구요? "How do you want me to do?"				
	7	trtr5님 아니 trtr5님 "Hey trtr5 hello trtr5"				
	8	어떻게 해드려 쩍어줘? 쩍어서 올려 쩍먹 아니면 상추만 쩍먹 이렇게? 쿡? "Do you want me to dip? Dipping all or only the leaf? like this? Soaking in the sauce?"		B	쩍먹 "Dipping"	trtr5
	9	그다음에요? "What's next?"				

10	싸? "Should I wrap?"	
11	먹으면 돼요? "Can I eat now?"	
12	이거 맞아요? "Am I correct?"	
13	이거 맞아? "Am I doing it right?"	
14	맞아? "Right?"	C 쌈장 마늘요 trtr5 "Ssamjang and garlic"
15	쌈장 마늘이요? "Ssamjang and garlic?"	
16	쌈장하고 마늘? "Ssamjang and garlic?"	
17	때마침 우리 trtr5님을 위해 마늘이 하나만 남았네 딱 "You are lucky. There is one garlic left for you"	
18	쌈장? "Ssamjang?"	
19	올려 뒀어요? 맞아? "Here it is, right? am I right?"	

IMAGE	BJ CHANGHYUN			VIEWERS		
	LINE	SPOKEN ACTION	BODILY ACTION	LINE	TYPED ACTION	ID
	20	확실해? 됐어요? 이거 먹으면 돼요? 이제? "Are you sure? Am I done? Can I eat now?"		D	저 기억해주세요 창현님 내일 오면 반겨주세요~~~ "ChangHyun Please remember me and welcome me when I come tomorrow~~~"	phds8811
	21	끝이죠? 네! phds8811님 기억해드릴게요 고맙습니다. "Is it really done? Yes, I'll do, pdh8804, thank you"		E	아~~~ "Say ah~~~"	trtr5
	22	아 이제 먹으면 돼요? "Ahh can I eat now?"		F	네! "Yes!"	trtr5

This eating-for-another action, presumably for the viewer's vicarious pleasure, is carefully undertaken by ChangHyun. It is also a kind of joint participation between the BJ and his viewer, which not only accomplishes the eating performance but also virtually creates and enhances the shared mealtime frame.

ChangHyun and his viewer take up different footings simultaneously. The BJ assumes the footing of a puppet, as he does what he is instructed, and his viewer takes up a footing of a controller who mediates the BJ's eating action. The eat-as-I-type act starts with a request by the viewer, trtr5, in line A, "Could you please eat *tangsuyuk* wrapped with a lettuce leaf?" In accepting the viewer's request, ChangHyun continually and verbally seeks confirmation and visually demonstrates what he is doing. In other words, ChangHyun's spoken utterances and visual demonstrations serve as contextualization cues that indicate that he is accommodating the viewer, and that they are eating together. Specifically, he always seeks the viewer's confirmation with utterances such as "Do you want me to dip?" (line 8), "What's next?" (line 9), and "Should I wrap?" (line 10) regarding how to perform, or eat appropriately as instructed. ChangHyun also seeks confirmation that what he has just done is right like "Can I eat now?" (line 11), "Am I correct?" (line 12), and "Am I doing it right" (line 13) so he can correct his previous action, if he has made an error, before moving forward. Along with his spoken actions, ChangHyun also presents to the camera how he is following trtr5's instructions step-by-step: He 1) puts *tangsuyuk* on a lettuce leaf, 2) adds some sauce and garlic, 3) wraps it up, and finally 4) eats.

This type of eating for another is parallel to what happens in face-to-face interactions among family and friends during mealtimes. For example, numerous scholars (e.g., Ochs, Pontecorvo & Fasulo 1996; Paugh & Izquierdo 2009; Bova & Arcidiacono 2014) show that parents typically monitor their children during mealtime and instruct them on what and how to eat; Kim (2006) finds this pattern in Korean families specifically. The eat-as-I-type activity thus demonstrates how mukbang is a shared mealtime where participants influence and sometimes regulate what and how others eat, thus creating coordinated involvement.

In virtual feeding (Example 3) and the eat-as-I-type (Example 4), eating for another constructs, and is constructed by, joint participation between the mukbang BJ and his viewers that shifts footings, consequently realizing online commensality. Sharing and feeding food as well as instructing eating actions are part of the collaborative work between BJs and their viewers, constructing commensality as a central aspect of mukbang.

7 Conclusion

Orienting toward Korea's traditional culinary culture that values eating together and sharing dishes, I have demonstrated how mukbang accomplishes digital commensality, creating a sense of togetherness by connecting eating actions to communication about them online, and through mutual participation between mukbang BJs and their viewers. Extending prior research on eating as a collaborative activity, and bringing together Goffman's (1974, 1981) notions of frame and footing and Tannen's (2007) concept of involvement, this study contributes to our understanding of not only how eating is co-constructed online, but also how digital communication about and involving food serves as a means of realizing the cultural valuing of commensality.

The chapter has demonstrated that mukbang is more than voyeurism. Incorporating spoken, bodily, and typed actions, mukbang participants virtually share foods; drink and eat together; and request, direct, and perform eating actions. Mukbang interaction is thus an inherently collaborative activity where both BJs and viewers are mutually engaged. They virtually realize the practice and frame of eating together and co-construct their shared involvement in that frame. This demonstrates a new way of engaging in commensality that brings together food and digital discourse.

As a new way of being together, mukbang also simultaneously draws on and challenges traditional forms of eating practice. Involvement created through mukbang establishes a joint reclaiming of what it means to "eat alone" and "eat together." It turns what has been considered social stigma – not sharing a table or platter with another person – into a powerful interactional resource that binds physically separated people together through food and eating. My analysis of mukbang sheds light on how the ritual act of eating, which is generally conducted offline, can be jointly and multimodally performed on the internet and create a new context of, and for, sociability. Moreover, the chapter illuminates how Korean young adults make use of technological affordances and multimodalities to continue the cultural ideology embedded in eating in digital environments, without giving up the independence of living alone. Lastly, the current study not only bridges the gap between online and offline, and food and discourse, but also expands the scope of what constitutes eating together.

Notes

1. Although ChangHyun's mukbang clips are no longer publicly available, you can find Haetnim's mukbang on her YouTube page: https://www.youtube.com/channel/UC-Bsa2ivAGWq7bsSPrPGFVA
2. Please see abbreviations.

Abbreviations

ACC	Accusative particle	IMV	Imperative (clause type)
CIRCUM	Circumstantial	INT	Interrogative (clause type)
CUTE	Cute marker	NC	Numeral classifier
DEC	Declarative (clause type)	POL	Polite (speech level)
DEF	Deferential (speech level)	SH	Subjective honorific suffix
END	Sentence ender	TOP	Topical particle
EXH	Exhortative (clause type)		

Acknowledgments

I am very grateful to Dr. Cynthia Gordon and Dr. Alla Tovares for inviting me to be a part of this volume. Their perceptive insights and incisive editorial suggestions helped me to improve this chapter.

References

AFP/Relaxnews (2013), "Meok-Bang Trend in South Korea Turns Binge Eating into Spectator Sport." *Huffington Post*. Available online: http://www.huffingtonpost.ca/2013/12/18/meok-bang-trend_n_4467240.html.

Aronsson, Karin and Lucas Gottzén (2011), 'Generational Positions at a Family Dinner: Food Morality and Social Order', *Language in Society*, 40(4): 405–426.

Bateson, Gregory (1972), *Steps to an Ecology of Mind: Collected Essays in Anthropology*, Chicago: University of Chicago Press.

Beeman, William O. (2014), 'Negotiating a Passage to the Meal in Four Cultures', in Polly E. Szatrowski (ed.), *Language and Food: Verbal and Nonverbal Experiences*, 31–52, Amsterdam: John Benjamins Publishing Company.

Blum-Kulka, Shoshana (1993), '"You Gotta Know How to Tell a Story": Telling, Tales, and Tellers in American and Israeli Narrative Events at Dinner', *Language in Society*, 22(3): 361–402.

Blum-Kulka, Shoshana (1997), *Dinner Talk: Cultural Patterns of Sociability and Socialization in Family Discourse*, New York and London: Routledge.

Bova, Antonio and Francesco Arcidianocono (2013), Invoking the Authority of Feelings as a Strategic Maneuver in Family Mealtime Conversations', *Journal of Community and Applied Social Psychology,* 23(3): 206–244.

Bova, Antonio and Francesco Arcidiacono (2014), '"You Must Eat the Salad Because It Is Nutritious." Argumentative Strategies Adopted by Parents and Children in Food-Related Discussions at Mealtimes', *Appetite*, 73: 81–94.

Bruno, Antonetta L. (2016), 'Food as Object and Subject in Korean Media', *The Korean Cultural Studies,* 31: 131–165.

Cho, Wookyoun, Wakako Takeda, Yujin Oh, Naomi Aiba and Youngmee Lee (2015), 'Perceptions and Practices of Commensality and Solo-Eating among Korean and Japanese University Students: A Cross-Cultural Analysis', *Nutrition Research and Practice,* 9(5): 523–529.

Choe, Hanwool (2019), 'Eating Together Multimodally: Collaborative Eating in Mukbang, a Korean Livestream of Eating', *Language in Society,* 48(2): 171–208.

Choi, Jiwon (2015), 'South Korea's Passion for Watching Strangers Eat Goes Mainstream', *ABC news*. Available online: http://abcnews.go.com/International/south-koreas-passion-watching-strangers-eat-mainstream/story?id=30124160

Chye, David Yoong Soon and Maya Khemlani David (2006), 'Talking to Older Malaysians: A Case Study', *Multilingua*, 25(1-2): 165–182.

de Solier, Isabelle (2018), 'Tasting the Digital: New Food Media', in Kathleen LeBesco, and Peter Naccarato (eds), *The Bloomsbury Handbook of Food and Popular Culture*, 54–65, London and New York: Bloomsbury.

Erickson, Frederick (1981), 'Money Tree, Lasagna Bush, Salt and Pepper: Social Construction of Topical Cohesion in a Conversation among Italian-Americans', in Deborah Tannen (ed), *Analyzing Discourse: Text & Talk*, 43–70, Washington, DC: Georgetown University Press University Press.

Erickson, Frederick (2015), 'Oral Discourse as a Semiotic Ecology. The Co-construction and Mutual Influence of Speaking, Listening, and Looking', in Deborah Tannen, Heidi Hamilton and Deborah Schiffrin (eds.), *The Handbook of Discourse Analysis*, 422–446, Malden, MA: Wiley.

Galatolo, Renata and Letizia Caronia (2018), 'Morality at Dinnertime: The Sense of the Other as a Practical Accomplishment in Family Interaction', *Discourse & Society*, 29(1): 43–62.

Georgakopoulou, Alexandra (2011), '"On for Drinkies?" Email Cues of Participant Alignments', *Language@Internet* 8. Available online: https://www.languageatinternet.org/articles/2011/Georgakopoulou/georgakopoulou.pdf

Goffman, Erving (1974), *Frame Analysis: An Analysis on the Organization of Experience*, Cambridge, MA: Harvard University Press.

Goffman, Erving (1981), *Forms of Talk*, Philadelphia, PA: University of Pennsylvania Press.

Goodwin, Charles and Marjorie H. Goodwin (2004), 'Participation', in Alessandro Duranti (ed), *A companion to Linguistic Anthropology*, 222–244, Malden, MA: Blackwell Publishing.

Gordon, Cynthia (2009), *Making Meanings, Creating Family: Intertextuality and Framing in Family Interaction*, New York: Oxford University Press.

Gordon, Cynthia and Didem İkizoğlu (2017), 'Asking for Another Online: Membership Categorization and Identity Construction on a Food and Nutrition Discussion Board', *Discourse Studies*, 19(3): 253–271.

Graham, Sage L. and Scott Dutt (2019), '"Watch the Potty Mouth": Negotiating Impoliteness in Online Gaming', in Astrid Ensslin and Isabel Balteiro (eds), *Approaches to Videogame Discourse: Lexis, Interaction, Textuality*, 201–224, London: Bloomsbury.

Gumperz, John J. (1982), *Discourse Strategies: Studies in Interactional Sociolinguistics*, Cambridge: Cambridge University Press.

Hakimey, Husna and Rashad Yazdanifard (2015), 'The Review of Mokbang (Broadcast Eating) Phenomena and Its Relations with South Korean Culture and Society', *International Journal of Management, Accounting and Economics*, 2(5): 443–455.

Hu, Elise (2015), 'Koreans Have an Insatiable Appetite for Watching Strangers Binge Eat', *NPR*, March 24. Available online: http://www.npr.org/sections/thesalt/2015/03/24/392430233/koreans-have-an-insatiable-appetite-for-watching-strangers-binge-eat?utm_campaign=storyshare&utm_source=twitter.com&utm_medium=social.

Kendon, Adam (1990), *Conducting Interaction: Patterns of Behavior in Focused Encounters*, Cambridge: Cambridge University Press.

Kerner, Susanne, Cynthia Chou and Morten Warmind (2015), *Commensality from Everyday Food to Feast*, London, U.K.: Bloomsbury Academic.

Kim, Hyun-Jung (2006), 'Let's Have a Meal (and a Little Bit of Talk Too!): Conversations at Korean Family Mealtimes', PhD dissertation, Harvard University.

Kim, Sohee and Joyce Lee (2014), 'Korea Inc Targets "Golden Singles" amid Consumer slump', *Routers*. Available online: http://www.reuters.com/article/southkorea-economy-singles-idUSL3N0R20Z920141029#CjQcMyeFCPjQXImO.97

Kim, Yeran (2018), 'Sell Your Loneliness: Mukbang Culture and Multisensorial Capitalism in South Korea, in Lorraine Lim and Hye-Kyung Lee (eds), *Routledge Handbook of Cultural and Creative Industries in Asia*, 225–238, London: Routledge.

Kress, Gunther and Theo Van Leeuwen (2001), *Multimodal Discourse: The Modes and Media of Contemporary Communication*, London: Edward Arnold.

LeVine, Philip and Ron Scollon, eds. (2004), *Discourse and Technology: Multimodal Discourse Analysis*. Washington D.C.: Georgetown University Press.

Mandelbaum, Jenny (2014), 'How to Do Things with Requests: Request Sequences at the Family Dinner Table', in Paul Drew and Elizabeth Couper-Kuhlen (eds), *Requesting in Social Interaction*, 215–242, Amsterdam: John Benjamins.

Mondada, Lorenza (2009), 'The Methodical Organization of Talking and Eating: Assessments in Dinner Conversations,' *Food Quality and Preference*, 20(8): 558–571.

Ochs, Elinor and Carolyn Taylor (1995), 'The "Father Knows Best" Dynamic in Family Dinner Narratives' in Kira Hall and Mary Bucholtz (eds), *Gender Articulated*, 97–120, New York: Routledge.

Ochs, Elinor, Clotilde Pontecorvo and Alessandra Fasulo (1996), 'Socializing Taste', *Ethnos*, 61(1–2): 7–46.

Ochs, Elinor, Ruth Smith and Carolyn Taylor (1989), 'Detective Stories at Dinnertime: Problem-Solving through Co-narration', *Cultural Dynamics*, 2(2): 238–257.

Paugh, Amy and Carolina Izquierdo (2009), 'Why is This a Battle Every Night?: Negotiating Food and Eating in American Dinnertime Interaction', *Journal of Linguistic Anthropology*, 19(2): 185–204.

Pyun, Gwaynghyun (2017), 'Table for One?: How Dining Culture is Changing in South Korea', Korea Economic Institute of America. Available online: http://keia.org/table-one-how-dining-culture-changing-south-korea

Recktenwald, Daniel (2017), 'Toward a Transcription and Analysis of Live Streaming on Twitch', *Journal of Pragmatics*, 115: 68–81.

Schiffrin, Deborah (1993), 'Speaking for Another in Sociolinguistic Interviews', in Deborah Tannen (ed), *Framing in Discourse*, 231–263, Oxford: Oxford University Press,

Sicoli, Mark A. (in press), *Saying and Doing in Zapotec: Multimodality, Resonance, and the Language of Joint Actions*, London: Bloomsbury.

Steger, Isabella and Soo Kyung Jung (2017), 'Exhausted by the Herd: Single South Koreans are Gingerly Embracing the Yolo Lifestyle', *Quartz*, August 2. Available online: https://qz.com/1024923/exhausted-by-the-herd-single-south-koreans-are-gingerly-embracing-the-yolo-lifestyle/

Streeck, Jürgen, Charles Goodwin and Curtis LeBaron (2011), *Embodied Interaction: Language and Body in the Material World*, Cambridge: Cambridge University Press.

Tannen, Deborah (2005), *Conversational Style: Analyzing talk among friends*, 2nd edn, Oxford: Oxford University Press.

Tannen, Deborah (2007), *Talking Voices: Repetition, Dialogue, and Imagery in Conversational Discourse*, 2nd edn, Cambridge: Cambridge University Press.

Tannen, Deborah and Cynthia Wallat (1993), 'Interactive Frames and Knowledge Schemas in Interaction: Examples from a Medical Examination/Interview', in Deborah Tannen (ed), *Framing in Discourse*, 57–76, New York: Oxford University Press.

Tulviste, Tiia, Luule Mizera, Boel De Geer and Marja-Terttu Tryggvason (2002), 'Regulatory Comments as Tools of Family Socialization: A Comparison of Estonian, Swedish and Finnish Mealtime Interaction', *Language in Society*, 31(5): 655–678.

Vásquez, Camilla and Alice Chik (2015), '"I Am Not a Foodie...": Culinary Capital in Online Reviews of Michelin Restaurants', *Food and Foodways*, 23(4): 231–250.

Wiggins, Sally (2002), 'Talking with Your Mouth Full: Gustatory Mmms and the Embodiment of Pleasure', *Research on Language and Social Interaction*, 35(3): 311–336.

Wiggins, Sally (2013), 'The Social Life of "Eugh": Disgust as Assessment in Family Mealtimes, *British Journal of Social Psychology*, 52(3): 489–509.

Wiggins, Sally (2014), 'Family Mealtimes, Yuckiness and the Socialization of Disgust Responses by Preschool Children', in Polly E. Szatrowski (ed), *Language and Food: Verbal and Nonverbal Experiences*, 211–232, Amsterdam: John Benjamins Publishing Company.

Wiggins, Sally (2015), 'Producing Infant Food Preferences During Weaning: The Role of Language and Gesture in Parent-Child Interaction', Paper presented at *British Feeding and Drinking Group*, Netherlands.

Zappavigna, Michele (2014), 'Coffeetweets: Bonding around the Bean on Twitter', in Philip Seargeant and Caroline Tagg (eds), *The Language of Social Media: Identity and Community on the Internet*, 139–160, London: Palgrave Macmillan.

Part Three

Using Food as a Discursive and Material Resource for Online Activism and Political Engagement

7

Growing Online: Activist Identities in the "Grow Your Own" English Blogging Community

Nadine Pierce, Isidoropaolo Casteltrione, and Ana Tominc

1 Introduction

In recent years, there has been a rise in the number of people growing their own food both through community initiatives and individually (DEFRA 2010; Miller 2015; The National Allotment Society 2019). This trend could be an indication of significant and potentially influential practices and ideologies in Western societies that oppose the current globalized food system: Gardening can be seen as a grassroots space to express concerns related to finite and declining resources such as soil and water and a way of both reconnecting production and consumption and disengaging from the globalized neoliberal food system (Larder, Lyons & Woolcock 2014; McClintock 2014).

An increasing number of those who grow their own food – the activity known as "Grow Your Own" (hereafter GYO) – are sharing information about their growing and harvesting experiences through social media (Counihan & Siniscalchi 2013; Hearn et al. 2014), an umbrella term that refers to a variety of digital platforms such as social networking websites, photo and video sharing sites, virtual worlds, and blogs (Aichner & Jacob 2015). While technology writers have proclaimed the impending death of blogs, depicting them as outdated media, recent research has shown their vitality and long-lasting popularity, and attested to the uniqueness of these online social spaces where users learn from one another (Head, Van Hoeck & Hostetler 2017; Pettigrew, Archer & Harrigan 2016). Despite this, following a proliferation of academic studies focusing on blogs from 2004 to 2008 (Larsson & Hrastinski 2011), scholarly interest in this area seems to have somewhat decreased (Elega & Özad 2018), arguably due to the rise in popularity of competing, more recent online "self-publication" platforms such as microblogging and social networking websites that offer researchers new opportunities for exploration (Head, Van Hoeck & Hostetler 2017; Pinjamaa & Coye 2016). Although it is challenging to find accurate statistics about blogs due to their highly dynamic and decentralized nature (Schmidt 2007), recent figures provided by the blogging platform Tumblr show that, as of January 2019, the site had close to 456.1 million blog accounts, up from 392 million in the previous year (Statista 2019). Moreover, the blogosphere is not only well-populated but also active. For instance, a survey of British bloggers that aimed to measure activity on their blogs indicates that, of the 93 percent of respondents measuring activity on their blogs, 41 percent reported that they received between 1,000–10,000 unique visitors per month, with the most popular blog categories being lifestyle, parenting and family, fashion and beauty, travel, and food (Vuelio 2017). These figures demonstrate the enduring relevance of blogs in today's digital landscape and highlight the need for a revival of academic research in this area. Furthermore, while there have been studies that focus on food blogs, including those that approach them from a linguistic perspective (e.g., Diemer & Frobenius 2013), food blogs, especially their contributions to digital food activism, remain underexplored.

In this chapter, we focus on the GYO Blogging Community in England, and argue that GYO blogging represents a form of digital food activism, defined as "an internet-based, organized effort to change the food system or parts thereof in which civic initiators or supporters use digital media" (Schneider et al. 2018: 8). Through a detailed linguistic analysis using the tools of critical discourse analysis (CDA), we demonstrate how these bloggers construct themselves as "social actors" (Reisigl & Wodak 2001). We first identify sub-topics, grouped into three overall topics that provide an overview of discourse as evidenced in blogs on a macro level. As van Dijk (1977: 132) notes, "discourse topics seem to reduce, organize and categorize semantic information of sequences as whole" so that we cognitively perceive and memorize it in particular ways; these are linked to how on a micro level, discourse is constructed through specific linguistic strategies. Through the analytical lens of CDA, we then demonstrate how these bloggers construct their sense of self v. others through referential/predicational strategies (construction of social actors) (Reisigl & Wodak 2001) as they understand themselves as active, responsible and self-sufficient common-sense environmentalists, with the power to change current harmful practices in agriculture. They thus take on the "capitalist system of production, distribution, consumption and commercialization [in order] to change the food system by modifying the way that they produce, distribute and/or consume food" (Siniscalchi & Counihan 2013: 6).

One of the key ideas underpinning this study is that food is a critical resource through which activism is materialized and around which activist practices can be mobilized. There is a growing body of research on food activism, largely through the lens of community-based food production and ethical consumerism (e.g., Thompson 2012; Larder, Lyons & Woolcock 2014; McClintock 2014; Tornaghi & Van Dyck 2014; Adams, Hardman & Larkham 2015; Certoma & Tornaghi 2015; De Hoop & Jehlicka 2017), and a more recent strand of research looking specifically at digital food activism (e.g., Eli et al. 2016; Lewis 2018; Schneider et al. 2018). However, little attention, if any at all, has been given to the ways through which these activists emerge linguistically as drivers of social change and negotiate an identity that brings them close to other digital communities that strive to impact the way our capitalist world is run (see Svensson et al. 2015 for examples of other digital activist communities) and those who construct their lifestyle discursively through food-related texts (e.g., Johnston & Baumann 2015; Tominc 2017). Our paper is therefore a contribution at the intersection of food, discourse, and digital media studies in line with Androutsopoulos' (2011) call for a more ethnographically-grounded user-related approach to social media language (see also Thurlow & Mroczek 2011 and Bou-Franch & Garcés-Conejos Blitvich 2019).

This paper is composed of four parts. First, we review the literature related to blogging, digital activism, and digital food activism. The literature review is then followed by a description of our method and data. Next, we move on to provide an overview of the topics identified in the nine most influential food activists in England in 2016. This sets the stage for our critical discourse analysis of three selected blogs through which we study on a micro level (as opposed to a macro, topic level) how these writers linguistically construct themselves as part of an activist community. The final section briefly summarizes the key findings of the study and highlights its unique contribution to the field, as well as identifies avenues for further research.

2 Constructing identity through blogging: Grow Your Own as digital food activism

2.1 Building community identity through blogging

Over the last decade, social media platforms have become an integral part of many people's everyday lives (Fuchs 2017), supporting social interaction and community formation (Hunsinger & Senft 2013; van Dijck 2013). Blogs, the focus of the present study, are a particular type of social media; they are essentially personal and easy-to-manage websites presenting content in reverse chronological order (Schiano et al. 2004). Blogs have developed into a relevant component of modern-day popular culture (Baumer, Sueyoshi & Tomlinson 2008) and one of the most used and relied-on online information sources (Johnson & Kaye 2004, 2014).

Blogs also serve as tools for self-presentation. Goffman's (1959) dramaturgical approach is a fruitful framework through which to examine the dynamics of self-presentation on social media as performance (e.g., Azariah 2016; Dmitrow-Devold 2017). By understanding this in terms of a *front stage* and *back stage*, where the latter is the place where individuals retreat and step out of their roles and thus where a more *authentic self* resides, Goffman emphasizes the rather porous dichotomy between the *public* and the *private*. The private refers to the realm of personal intimacy, to something hidden or withdrawn, while the public (Goffman's *front stage*) constitutes what is open, revealed, or accessible (Weintraub 1997). On social media, however, a blurring of the public/private spheres is even more prominent (Boyd 2011), and the front stage is magnified, leading to *hyper-ritualization*, an editing of real life and an exaggeration of its rituals (Goffman 1979).

As social media becomes more and more embedded in people's daily routines, "material world" social practices are reformulated in texts and discussions online (Shaw 2012). Van Dijck (2013) discusses the implications of social media for self-presentation and highlights how these platforms can provide individuals with a stage for crafting a self-image and promoting such an image beyond their intimate circles. In particular, blogs, as Rose (1996) points out, are a form of social media often used by those pursuing personal fulfilment through expressing individual identities. Blogs, in fact, allow people to present highly selective versions of themselves to a variety of interconnected audiences (Mendelson & Papacharissi 2011), giving individuals greater freedom to express their hoped-for identities (Jung, Song & Vorderer 2012).

Guadagno, Okdie and Eno (2008) go a step further and, based on the theories of Foucault (1988), consider blogs a form of online self-presentation and self-expression. It has also been suggested that the essence of blogging is a form of vanity culture enacting social ranking, in a rat race for maximum attention and slick self-promotion (Lovink 2008). In a study looking at how Norwegian teenage female bloggers perform selves in their blogs over time, Dmitrow-Devold (2017) finds that the girls develop and perform a *blogging self*, an identity/

character that is not fixed but relational, situated in everyday interactions with the mainstream blogging community, and becoming, in certain cases, an integral part of the girls' offline experiences. Blogs also act as virtual megaphones for citizen journalists and institutional entrepreneurs (Kozinets, Patterson & Ashman 2016); they are the next step in a culture of burgeoning narcissism stemming from reality TV and other elements of the modern media environment (Lenhart & Fox 2006). Along the same lines, de Solier (2013) considers blogs a form of productive leisure – a way of expressing a sense of creativity and a feeling of "making something" in a post-industrial world.

However, while blogs operate as a medium for the expression of identity, they are also a means for community creation (Gurak & Antonijevic 2009). Considering blogs as genres that are characterized not by their content but by the "kinds of uses to which they are put, and the ways these uses define social identities and communities," Myers (2010: 15, 24) argues that successful bloggers write for people like themselves, creating a sense of community. In her study on feminist blogs, Keller (2012) argues that, through blogging, teenage girls are actively reframing participation in feminist politics, enacting political agency by sharing personal experiences, forming communities, and creating global networks through which feminist information can be disseminated. Keller's (2012) and Soon and Kluver's (2014) studies highlight the affordances of blogs for community creation, but also indicate how these platforms can aid digital activism, an issue discussed in the following section.

2.2 Blogs as platforms for digital activism

Digital activism encompasses different forms of activism that utilize digital technologies (Gerbaudo 2017) and can be defined as "social and political action exclusive to the Internet" (Vlavo 2017: 6). According to Gerbaudo (2017), since the late 2000s, digital activism has been shaped by a techno-political orientation, which he describes as *cyber-populism*, that considers the mass web of commercial services controlled by corporations such as Facebook and Google as spaces that, despite their inherent capitalist biases, activists need to harness so as to take advantage of their mass outreach capabilities. Hereof, Törnberg and Törnberg (2016) highlight the agenda-setting and framing affordances of social media that, like traditional mass media, can frame issues and events, shaping people's perceptions.

Activists increasingly wield the power of digital technologies to penetrate organizational boundaries and enable social and political change (Ghobadi

& Clegg 2015), and websites such as blogs can be important platforms for expressing dissent and expanding the realm of public free speech. Focusing on the informational affordances of blogs, Sánchez-Villar, Bigné and Aldás-Manzano (2017) establish that there is a clear connection between blog usage and political involvement and activism, and suggest that the more useful a blog is perceived the more influence it will have on individuals' political activism. Bloggers can stimulate online discourse around current critical issues and challenge traditional media and political authorities (Bar-Ilan 2005; Bosch 2010). In her study on the Australian feminist blogging community, Shaw (2012) discusses the notion of *discursive activism*, "speech or texts that seek to challenge opposing discourses by exposing power relations within these discourses, denaturalizing what appears natural" (Fine 1992: 221, cited in Shaw 2012: 42). Shaw (2012) finds that participation in this blog network is an expression of discursive activism in that it challenges and critiques the ideology of mainstream discourses aiming, at least in part, to change them. Collectively and independently of the country of origin, prior research on blogs and politics agrees that these platforms have effects that extend far beyond the personal sphere, with bloggers often cooperating, despite their individualized actions, to build collective identity and make a larger collective impact (Soon & Kluver 2014).

2.3 Grow Your Own as digital food activism

De Hoop and Jehlicka (2017) observe that there has been little academic connection to date between food self-provisioning, GYO, and food activism. This is surprising as foraging, GYO, the trading of food and treating food preparation as primary sources of pleasure and entertainment are practices congruent with local food movements and, in turn, food activism (Siniscalchi & Counihan 2013). Food activism is defined as "an action that takes aim at the capitalist system of production, distribution, consumption and commercialization" and considers people's discourses and actions to make the food system or parts of it more "democratic, healthy, ethical, culturally appropriate, and better in quality" (Siniscalchi & Counihan 2013: 6).

GYO blogs are essentially food blogs. In the last decade, food blogs have become one of the most popular and authoritative sources of food-related information, addressing the multiple meanings and motivations of food consumption, and informing and influencing consumers' opinions and purchases (Denveater 2009; Kilian, Hennigs & Langner 2012). As Schneider et al. (2018: 6) argue, by offering such information these sites often fill "an information gap" with facts that are otherwise "difficult to obtain," using "the digital realm to redefine and/or expand food transparency, and to disseminate otherwise "hidden" information to citizen-consumers who may share these concerns." In this sense, blogs emerge as online platforms "*fostering* and *mediating* activism" (Schneider et al. 2018: 8, italics original). GYO blogs, therefore, can be understood as venues that enable the emergence of digital food activism. As an internet-enhanced and/or internet-based activity (Vegh 2003), digital food activism encompasses forms of food activism that are both enabled and shaped by and through digital media and occur mainly on these platforms (Eli et al. 2018).

Although an increasing number of people are growing their own food (DEFRA 2010; Miller 2015; The National Allotment Society 2019), and sharing their GYO experiences and practices online through blogs and other social media (Counihan & Siniscalchi 2013; Hearn et al. 2014), there has been no published research connecting the online activity of people practicing GYO to digital food activism. As we note in the introduction, the intersection of the emerging body of research in the fields of GYO and digital food activism is an area of interest worthy of further study. There are significant numbers of individuals taking up domestic production and consumption of their own food and seeking to shorten supply chains. There are also significant numbers of people writing gardening and lifestyle blogs. This review of the literature has stressed the need for more empirical research into the blogging of GYO as an avenue of digital food activism, and it is hoped that this study may bring some new insights into this emerging field of study.

3 Method and data

This paper is based on critical discourse analysis (CDA), an umbrella term for a number of linguistic approaches to discourse analysis that pay critical attention to issues related to ideology and power in discourse. CDA aims to demonstrate how injustices or "social wrongs" are produced and reproduced through discourse, including the simplistic construction of identities (e.g., Fairclough 2001; Reisigl & Wodak 2001). Following Wodak and others' (e.g., Reisigl & Wodak 2001) discourse-historical approach to CDA, we first conduct topic analysis and report on the overall topics that appear in the corpus; these provide the "global meanings" of a specific discourse, define the overall coherence of a discourse and can thus affect the way it is memorized and reproduced (van Dijk 1987: 48; van Dijk 2009: 62). Further, a more detailed linguistic analysis of three selected texts is then performed, aiming to demonstrate qualitatively how GYO activist identities are constructed in digital discourse on a micro level.

The overall topic analysis is based on a corpus of blogs, written by GYO gardeners and found by searching "best GYO blogs" and "top UK garden blogs" in Google (June 2017). Purposive sampling was used to narrow down the material; all bloggers studied met a well-defined set of criteria to allow for reliable comparative analysis: All bloggers were British and primarily focused on the domestic growing of food within a private garden or allotment. These searches resulted in a number of curated lists from the mass media and businesses with a commercial interest in bloggers – such as those that sell blogger contacts to companies wishing to promote their products and PR agencies, e.g., Vuelio, Feedspot Blog, and more.

A number of blogs appeared on more than one of these lists, and therefore arguably can be perceived to be the most popular, and therefore influential, in the GYO blogosphere. A sample of nine blogs was then drawn, containing overall 218 blog posts collected over a six-month period from April 2016 until September 2016, coinciding with the main British food-growing season.[1] Of the selected blogs, two were written by men, five by women, one by a married couple, and one by two male friends. In this corpus of blogs, key sub-topics were distinguished and grouped within the three overarching topic categories of Environment, Economics, and Food & Health. Each sub-topic was identified as a key-word based on the available data by two authors of this paper; results were then compared and contrasted. The final categories were decided based on overlap of sub-topics in both analyses. As these categories are often interconnected and overlapping, environmental and economic concerns, for example, are often found in the same sentence. In many cases, all three categories can be found within a single blog post.

Three blog posts among those that demonstrated a form of activism were then randomly selected for further language analysis, although they were checked for representability of the overall corpus. These blog posts are "Why bread is so damn important" (from the blog "Life on a Pig Row," 1 April 2016), "Full of beans – a recipe for Broad Beans and Mint Hummus" (from the blog "Urban Veg Patch," 8 August 2016) and "Contaminated compost" (from the blog "Mark's Veg Plot," 22 September 2016).

4 Overview of blog topics: Environment, Economics, and Food & Health

While these topics – Environment, Economics, and Food & Health – may not mark the blogs as activist writing *per se*, sub-topics provide more evidence for anti-capitalist, change-advocating activism, as advocated by Counihan (2013). Within the environment category, recurring sub-topics across the nine representative blogs (identified by letters A-J) were wildlife, peat-free compost (peat is a substance primarily sourced from lowland raised bogs – an increasingly rare habitat in the UK and across Europe – and its extraction generates greenhouse gases), composting, organic methods, climate change, seed saving and heritage seeds, water saving, and food miles (i.e., the distance food travels from the place of production to the place of consumption, e.g., consumer's plate) (see Table 7.1).

Environmental issues and concerns were apparent throughout. Most of the bloggers explicitly state that they use organic methods and use products that are environmentally friendly. They also explain why they use them. In one of the blogs, Life on a Pig Row, the post "More Food Less Lawns: The Future of Micro-Farming is You" argues for the need to cut down on food miles, which harm the environment, and suggests that GYO is everyone's responsibility. Another blogger ("Mark's Veg Plot") is concerned with the environmental impact of importing bamboo, offering coppiced hazel (referred to as "they" in Example 1), as a local alternative:

> *Example 1*
> "they are made from renewable resources, grown locally, which is good because it removes all the negative aspects of importing bamboo [...] what about the environmental impact of shipping the goods? How much forest is felled to make way for plantations of bamboo?"

As seen in the example above, the blogger is concerned with the negative impact transportation and deforestation have on the environment.

Instances of food activism related to "economics" were produce-related costs and saving money, recycling and upcycling (i.e. reusing discarded objects or material to create a product of a higher quality or value than the original) of materials, large corporations (with a stance opposing them), shopping locally/alternative food networks (AFNs) and free products (that they may have received to review). This can be seen in Table 7.2.

Table 7.1 "Environment" category by blog identifier

Blog identifier	Attracting Wildlife	Peat-free Compost	Composting	Environment Organic Methods	Climate Change	Seed Saving/ Heritage Seeds	Water Saving	Food Miles
A	Y	Y	Y	Y		Y		
B	Y		Y	Y	Y		Y	Y
C	Y	Y	Y	Y	Y	Y	Y	Y
D	Y	Y	Y	Y		Y		
E		Y	Y	Y				
F			Y	Y		Y		
G	Y		Y	Y				
H	Y	Y	Y	Y	Y	Y	Y	
J	Y		Y	Y		Y	Y	Y

Table 7.2 "Economics" category by blog identifier

	Economics				
Blog identifier	Costs and Saving Money	Repurposing	Large Corporations	Shopping Locally/AFNs	Free Products
A	Y	Y			
B	Y	Y	Y	Y	Y
C	Y	Y	Y	Y	Y
D	Y	Y			
E	Y	Y		Y	
F	Y		Y	Y	
G		Y		Y	Y
H		Y	Y		
J	Y	Y	Y		Y

Many blogs, as the following extract from "Life on a Pig Row's" post demonstrates, encourage people to grow from seed rather than buying plants, stressing the economic side of the issue:

Example 2
"Is growing from seed worth it? Damn right it's worth it. This is hard economics, seed is cheaper and a way for us to learn the worth of plants."

Another blogger ("Mark's Veg Plot"), when comparing the price of willow poles (believed to be from Europe) and bamboo canes (from Asia) that retail at half the price, recognizes another economic problem and addresses the reader with a rhetorical question, "How much does a bamboo-grower or worker in the Far East earn for their efforts?" Through this, he points towards the exploitative nature of capitalism, where workers in certain non-European economies work at a fraction of the cost compared to those in Britain, often without environmental and other protection. As seen here, bloggers are generally very concerned about the capitalist system and its impact on the environment, making it difficult to separate the two discourses.

Within the Food & Health category, common sub-topics amongst the bloggers were the sharing of recipes, taste comparisons between home-grown produce and produce resulting from intensive farming methods, preserving food (e.g., jam making), and health concerns, such as the nutritional value or levels of chemicals in home-grown produce in comparison to shop-bought.

Table 7.3 "Food & Health" category by blog identifier

Blog identifier	Food & Health			
	Sharing Recipes	Taste Comparisons	Preserving Food	Health
A			Y	Y
B	Y	Y	Y	Y
C		Y	Y	Y
D		Y	Y	
E		Y	Y	Y
F	Y			Y
G	Y	Y	Y	
H		Y	Y	Y
J		Y		

Safety of food that is consumed, as well as dietary health, was a key consideration for the bloggers. There were many comparisons between the perceived taste and quality of home-grown produce and that purchased from supermarkets as well as the produce's nutritional value. In one post of "Dig my Veg" blog, the author states that she has decided to utilize her front garden for growing vegetables. This can be considered a form of direct activist stance and action in a society such as the UK, where traditionally one's front lawn is seen as a place for conforming with the neighborhood, e.g., front-staging, as opposed to back-stage activities of everyday lives (cf. Goffman 1959).

Concerns regarding food and health were also raised in the comments section of the blogs: In "Mark's Veg Plot," for example, the commenters discuss the safety of the chemical glyphosate found in genetically modified food and its potentially detrimental effect on the gut biome. Through the comments, these topics are further explored in detail and experiences are shared, as evident from blog post "Contaminated Compost" analyzed in the following section. Health was one of the main reasons given by one of the bloggers for becoming a vegan. She largely consumes her own home-grown fruits and vegetables and, as a result, believes her life to be less complicated, while also having health benefits. In Example 3 she links health (and body weight) to environment and ethics:

Example 3
"There has been no measuring, weighing or thinking about what I'm eating other than having fun creating things using as much produce from the garden.

I've loved the food knowing that it is totally cruelty-free and and I'm doing my bit for the environment."

It is perhaps not surprising that these topics – Environment, Economics, and Food & Health – were found to be discussed in GYO blogs; what is fascinating is the breadth and depth of knowledge about gardening and food preparation displayed in these blogs, and the tightly-knit sense of community and mutual support seen through posts and discussions. In the next section we turn our focus to community and support, as we unpack some of the posts in detail, demonstrating how these food activist bloggers discursively construct a positive sense of self as they contrast themselves with big corporations, supermarkets, and the capitalist food system in general.

5 Construction of activist identities in three GYO blogs

In this section we demonstrate how GYO bloggers discursively construct activist identities through three blog posts specified in the Method section. The blogs are written in a form of a diary with links to other websites; through them, their writers document their everyday lives focusing on gardening and other food-related activities as they reach out to the reader through an informal, often conversational style characteristic of the genre (Myers 2010). In so doing, they construct the reader as someone interested in GYO, although not yet necessarily part of the community: Some of their posts therefore function as tools through which to inform and convince. While the composition of the blog audience remains varied, the authors use linguistic devices, such as the inclusive pronoun "we," that reassure readers of inclusion (following Myers 2010). Most blogs also include comments from other bloggers, and there is clear evidence of a GYO community through these discussions, containing a sense of solidarity and support. It is also worth noting that as multimodal texts (Kress & van Leeuwen 2001; Thurlow & Mroczek 2011), all blogs also include images of gardening activity, often to demonstrate growth of plants, diseases or the final produce – the latter usually with some pride.

5.1 "You lunch out on lies": Construction of "us" and "them" in a food activist blog

"Why Bread is so Damn Important," asks the writer of the first blog post in the title of this highly persuasive text. Through it, he sets out to argue the case for home-baking bread. The blogger begins the post by metaphorically explaining that he will be dragging "a soapbox across the garden to the top of a hill" to set the stage for convincing the reader not to buy bread at the supermarket, but to make it at home. "Shouting from a soapbox" is metaphorically used in various forms throughout the blog: Speaking from an imagined podium, the author is aiming to persuade the readers to change their practices, but suspects that his persuasive power may not be strong enough (the soapbox "straining beneath our muddy feet," "creaking," we are "waggling in the wind"). Thus, other linguistic strategies are deployed through which the reader is gradually brought to the side of the writer.

Before bringing the reader to his side, the blogger constructs the reader as the other, as "you" who have been told about ingredients in supermarket bread, about the production of chicken and beef and how "fast food kills us" but have continued to perceive "food as fuel," that is, something that provides calories regardless of pleasure. "You" might even know the "lies," that is that supermarkets create farm names[2] and that Fairtrade certification is "shit" created for hipsters (possibly such as "you"):

> *Example 4*
> "It's another lie. You lunch out on lies. You eat lies. You shit lies. On a good day you'll tell people it's a lie as you dig into fairtrade chocolate that is about as fair about trade as you are about being asked to pay 5p for a plastic bag […] You know lies. […] You know best. You tell us everyday. It's your body. Your mind. Your planet. This is our bread."

As Example 4 demonstrates, the blogger creates a positive "we" group (those who bake "our bread") in contrast to a negative "you"– someone who is well aware of the ills of the contemporary food system but chooses to ignore them. The repetition of "you" to address and construct the audience is characteristic of blogs, making readers think they are being talked to directly, while projecting particular characteristics onto them. Myers (2010: 97) highlights how the use of pronouns in blogs engages readers and gives them a sense of participation in the group concerned. In example 4, the anaphora emphasizes the target subject ("you"), making audience members feel uncomfortable, with the aim of making them recognize the hypocritical ways they may act on a daily basis (e.g., buying Fairtrade products). The key word in this example, "lie," helps the author to construct "the other" as a superficial hipster who claims to be environmentally aware by purchasing – and even promoting – Fairtrade products, which is a marketing strategy that, according to the blogger, is not as fair as it claims to be.

The writer, however, cannot be fooled by the "feel good" environmentalists who claim "moral superiority," but are in fact driven not by necessity but by "hippy, dippy need to connect to the earth" and, as the author mockingly suggests, the fake need for a windmill in the garden to grind their home-grown barley.[3] As opposed to this, and stressing class differences, the author bakes bread at home not because this is a fashionable lifestyle choice, but because unlike today, when bread in supermarkets is "cheap, ridiculously cheap, [...] we came to making bread because we couldn't afford to go to the supermarket more than once a month."

Commodification of anti-capitalist sentiment and its often elitist lifestyle narrative, here represented through the image of the hipster, on the one hand, and the bloggers-activists analyzed in these blogs on the other, exposes friction around anti-capitalist activism online as discussed by Giraud (2018: 130). In this case, the bloggers disassociate themselves from the reader constructed online as "you." In turn, as the text turns towards "we," the tone of the narrative changes to highlight positive practices that contrast with the lies the constructed reader has been living by.[4] The activist lifestyle is presented as genuine and slow, and, as we will further show below, involving someone who does not enjoy supermarket food. Rather, real activists bake bread at home, and give it to their friends and family, and through this, "make them happy, make them smile." The reader, too, is now drawn into this idealized image of bread making by having qualities projected onto them that contrast to "lies": By receiving bread from the writer ("we give it to you with love, with care"), the hope is that "you will try" to do the same. Through baking their own bread, the readers will hopefully realize "that the time you put in was paid back to you a million fold." In other words, through bread-making the reader is transformed from the distant "you" to one of "us" in an effort to demonstrate that bread making transforms people, making them better and more informed citizens. Through baking bread, they become activists.

5.2 Supermarkets, food, and identity

One of the recurring concerns of bloggers throughout the corpus are supermarkets, presented mostly as the antithesis of the "natural" and healthy lifestyle that these bloggers seem to seek. Supermarkets are also a culprit when it comes to farming as their low pricing squeezes farmers and therefore reduces the quality of food. Thus, as the text from the "Urban Veg Patch" blog discusses a recipe for "Broad Bean and Mint Hummus," the ability to "easily make your own" hummus is opposed to the supermarket product that not only does not contain ingredients that "come from your own patch" but is, as one commenter of this text suggests, also too salty. This concern is further supported by the blog author herself, as she concludes that other supermarket food is also "overloaded with salt."

The blogger's solution is to "cook everything from scratch in my own kitchen with salt rarely added." This is part of her argument for home preparation of food, also put forth by other bloggers and commenters. Through contrast, the blogger shows that food grown/prepared at home is tastier: Broad bean hummus made of produce grown by oneself is always superior to the store-bought because it not only tastes better but also because growing and eating her own broad beans is a way of bypassing supermarkets' limited choice of produce. In discussion with other bloggers, the writer reveals in the comments section that she did not even like broad beans before she started growing her own because she hated "ordinary" broad beans for which she "developed a loathing [. . .] when dished up reheated in parsley sauce, with tough skin on, at school." Growing her own, however, she can choose to grow a variety she likes, as for example red broad beans, the growing of which she described in this post. Likewise, she can make hummus from a variety of vegetables and pulses (e.g., beetroot, which she mentions) that are not available in the supermarket.

The bloggers of "Life on a Pig Row" similarly shows disdain for supermarket food. They not only indicate that home-made bread is tastier than store-bought, but also claim that supermarket bread is "full of ingredients that could keep it white and fresh through a nuclear winter." To this image of everlasting white bread the authors juxtapose the bread prepared by themselves, which is not only "unique" (as opposed to mass-produced supermarket bread) but also therapeutic. Taking a philosophical stance, the authors notes that bread "saved us from a life of apathy, of never questioning, of accepting the status quo," especially in relationship to food and agriculture. Bread made at home can therefore "do" things for the bakers. It was the baking of bread that taught them how to slow down in life as they waited for it to rise and then bake. It was bread that "keeps you at home and stops you from window shopping or impulse buying in the supermarket." Here, the supermarket is negatively evaluated not only because it sells non-natural food, but also because it consumes time ("pointless wandering around supermarkets") and is disconnected from local communities (shopping centers are not comprised of "local identity"), while baking bread at home does the opposite.[5]

The contrast between "our" bread and that from the supermarket is further highlighted using the rhetorical device of repetition (epistrophe) where the idea of "our bread" is made increasingly important as the text progresses; at the end of every paragraph the author repeats "This is our bread" until it culminates with a direct address to the readers, directing them to action (bake bread themselves). Example 5 shows the final line in each paragraph of the blog post:

Example 5
This is our bread.
This is our bread.
This is our damn bread.
This is our bread, it saved us from a life of apathy . . .
Set yourself free, bake some bread.

Given the informal nature of blogs, Myers (2010) finds that questions and directives are used quite frequently. Similarly, in Example 5 the authors use the informal style to project their ideas onto readers by issuing unmitigated directives ("Set yourself free, bake some bread"). Such involvement of the reader into the discourse is commonly achieved through the rhetorical device of repetition, as Tannen (2007) finds for conversational and political discourse, a combination of which could be said to be the discourse in this blog.

5.3 "We must keep on trying": Growing food organically

The two analytic sections above are primarily concerned with the topics of health and economy, two of the corpus topics identified in the previous section. The text from the third blog, "Mark's Veg Plot," relates to the third, the environment. The blog is an example of a text written for a specific, very narrow audience in mind because the topic, herbicides in compost, is likely to attract a very limited group of readers (those interested in organic farming, hence familiar with technical vocabulary), another feature characteristic of successful blogs (Myers 2010: 91). Through discussion of compost contamination, the author and his blog readers create an online community of those concerned with such contamination as they discuss their own experiences as well as urge others to act. The blog post starts with a report on (and an embedded link to) a scientific article that highlights the finding that a "high proportion of commercial composts are contaminated with residues from weed-killers" which affect vegetables. The author urges "amateur gardeners" to read it, and everyone else to "raise the profile of this issue, and lobby" for this particular weed-killer to no longer be used.

Through the discussion, two groups – indexed by lexical choices – are created. An in-group consisting of "us" is constructed to represent the side of compost users ("we," "every amateur gardener," "everyday gardeners (millions of)," "growers"), while an out-group of "them" consists of compost producers ("producers," "compost manufacturers," "commercial brand," "companies," "Big Business"). "We" are represented as actively doing various things to tackle this problem: publicizing and lobbying about the problem, revealing the effects of contamination on plants, sharing the ways to test compost for contamination, encouraging a boycott of the product, involving a third party (e.g., a celebrity) to put on pressure through the media, posting on garden forums, contacting MPs and so forth, all telling examples of how online and offline lives and actions are intertwined. These efforts, however, are simultaneously portrayed as futile because "when big business is involved, the amateur gardener doesn't really have a strong enough voice" because the problem is denied and responsibility for contamination is hard to prove. It's a battle where one group, though numerous and engaged, is unable to take on the other, more powerful one.

Through their comments, other bloggers and commenters reconfirm their sense of shared identity as they commit to continuing their work, research and actively trying to change the system. By questioning even the most widespread labels that are seen to guarantee being friendly to the environment and health, they turn a critical lens on the label "organic," which they see as "another sales term with little other meaning."[6] The deconstruction of the term "organic," coupled with disappointment with contaminated compost, indexes a larger mistrust in labelling and British legislation, as the "gardening products do not fall under the EU" so there is no body or legislation to control composting of what is termed organic products (in Britain, however, the term organic is not certified). The discussion concludes with a reassurance that the group – the writer, "you" and "Sue" (another blogger commenting) – will continue fighting this problem through publicizing the issues. As Mark says at the end of the comments section, "[w]e must keep on trying" as he thanks others for doing "whatever [they] can" to spread information.

6 Conclusion

Our analysis demonstrates that bloggers in the present study are deeply passionate about producing their own food. Their use of language, especially positive self-representation strategies (as opposed to negative representation of others), constructs them as educated individuals who understand the wider neoliberal globalized food system. Through description of a range of activities, including establishing an informal group that allows for discussion of issues to do with gardening, they represent themselves as striving to learn new skills and techniques to improve their own production and consumption as well as production of food in post-industrial modernity. They also construct themselves as relative experts who provide guidance in these areas to others, inviting them into the fold of GYO. The acts of GYO and of blogging about it can be seen as creative production, or productive leisure (de Solier 2013), as both are important aspects of use of leisure time in a society which has been disconnected from the domestic growing of food (Tornaghi & Van Dyck 2014). Rewards appear to be reaped at the physical level and experienced through the senses, including pride in one's accomplishments and a connection to earth and the environment, as evidenced through the three main topics identified in the study: environment, economy, and food and health. The deep level at which they experience the activities of GYO (involving the senses and feelings of self-empowerment, such as, for example, through the evident camaraderie in the comments section of the blogs through which they support and encourage each other, e.g., "I agree with what you say," "long comments are a good sign," thanks for "thoughtful insight," etc.) suggest that GYO has the capability to move food activists beyond a consumer-oriented approach to politics and to develop a relationship to food more in line with the environmental beliefs of alternative food movements (Click & Ridberg 2010).

GYO blogs could be important platforms for expressing dissent and public free speech (Ghobadi & Clegg 2015) and have the potential to make audience members more attentive to social problems around them and more active in their own lives. The blogs can be seen as a critical vehicle in moving people from thoughts and ideas around food politics into action, as evidenced by the comments under analysis. In our qualitative analysis, we demonstrate how these writers – through various linguistic strategies such as referential and predication strategies – urge audiences to change their ways, shifting from their current harmful practices to more ethical and sustainable ones. As the analysis has shown, there are multiple layers of power within the discourse of these blogs – the authors exert influence over their readers by raising awareness of issues, educating them and influencing their actions and purchasing power. The authors also exert power over the businesses and organizations they are in apparent opposition to by challenging the labelling practices of big food industries, publicizing their own activities to shorten the food chain, saving money and encouraging others to do the same.

While this study offers some insight into an emergent online community, it is only a small contribution to what appears to be a growing area of interest in digital food discourse. The study would have benefited from the addition of in-depth interviews with GYO bloggers to ascertain more detailed information on their motivations and by investigating the practical and ideological outcomes of posting their narratives online. However, this study could be replicated on an ethnographic basis allowing researchers to compare discursive practices of similar communities across different countries and cultures and interrogate the impact of gender, race and class, which would make additional contributions to our understanding of GYO blogging and the construction of activist identities.

Notes

1. Ten blogs were initially selected, but as one was later removed from the internet, so the study was based on nine remaining blogs. The data was reduced from 218 (all blogs that demonstrated activism) to 18 (blogs selected for further topic analysis) by selecting two individual posts from each blogger (one representing implicit and one explicit activism, following Counihan's (2013) definition).
2. In 2016, some British supermarkets (Tesco), have branded products – especially imported ones – with invented farm names in order to make them sound more local (British).
3. "Hippy dippy" is defined by Oxford dictionary as an informal (and pejorative) expression for "[r]ejecting conventional practices or behavior in a way perceived to be vague and unconsidered or foolishly idealistic." The authors of this blog consider some people's rejection of conventional farming practices as shallow, although their categorization of such as "hipster" is generally rather stereotypical.
4. Although, for multiple possible meanings of collective deictics such as "we," see Reisigl & Wodak (2001).
5. This is an interesting argument, not least because it is generally thought that buying food in the supermarket actually saves time in making/preparing food.
6. Compare a similar critical observation related to the term "fair-trade" earlier on.

References

Adams, David, Michael Hardman and Peter Larkham (2015), 'Exploring Guerrilla Gardening: Gauging Public Views on the Grassroots Activity', *Local Environment*, 20(10): 1231–1246.

Aichner, Thomas and Frank Jacob (2015), 'Measuring the Degree of Corporate Social Media Use', *International Journal of Market Research*, 57(2): 257–275.

Androutsopoulos, Jannis (2011), 'From Variation to Heteroglossia in the Study of Computer-Mediated Discourse', in Crispin Thurlow and Kristine Mroczek (eds), *Digital Discourse: Language in the New Media*, 277–298, New York and London: Oxford University Press.

Azariah, Deepi Ruth (2016), 'The Traveller as Author: Examining Self-Presentation and Discourse' in the (Self) Published Travel Blog', *Media, Culture & Society*, 38(6): 934–945.

Bar-Ilan, Judit (2005), 'Information Hub Blogs', *Journal of Information Science*, 31(4): 297–307.

Baumer, Eric, Mark Sueyoshi and Bill Tomlinson (2008), 'Exploring the Role of the Reader in the Activity of Blogging', *Proceedings of ACM CHI 2008 Conference on Human Factors in Computing Systems*, 1111–1120. Available online: http://doi.acm.org/10.1145/1357054.1357229.

Bosch, Tanja (2010), 'Digital Journalism and Online Public Spheres in South Africa', *Communication*, 36(2): 265–275.

Bou-Franch, Patricia and Pilar Garcés-Conejos Blitvich, eds. (2019), *Analyzing Digital Discourse: New Insights and Future Directions*, Cham: Palgrave MacMillan.

Boyd, Danah (2011), 'Social Network Sites as Networked Publics Affordances, Dynamics, and Implications', in Zizi Papacharissi (ed), *A Networked Self: Identity, Community, and Culture on Social Network Sites*, 39–58, New York: Routledge.

Certoma, Chiara and Chiara Tornaghi (2015), 'Political Gardening. Transforming Cities and Political Agency', *Local Environment*, 20(10): 1123–1131.

Click, Melissa and Ronit Ridberg (2010), 'Saving Food: Food Preservation as Alternative Food Activism', *Environmental Communication*, 4(3): 301–317.

Counihan, Carole (2013), 'Women, Gender, and Agency in Italian Food Activism', in Carole Counihan and Valeria Siniscalchi (eds), *Food Activism: Agency, Democracy and Economy*, 61–76, New York: Bloomsbury Academic.

Counihan, Carole and Valeria Siniscalchi, eds. (2013), *Food Activism: Agency, Democracy and Economy*, New York: Bloomsbury Academic.

De Hoop, Evelien and Petr Jehlička (2017), 'Reluctant Pioneers in the European Periphery? Environmental Activism, Food Consumption and "Growing Your Own"', *Local Environment*, 22(7): 809–824.

de Solier, Isabelle (2013), *Food and the Self: Consumption, Production, and Material Culture*, London: Berg Publishers.

DEFRA (2010), *Food 2030*. Available online: http://appg-agscience.org.uk/linkedfiles/Defra%20food2030strategy.pdf

Denveater (2009), 'The Virtual Roundtable: Food Blogging as Citizen Journalism', *World Literature Today*, 83(1): 42–46.

Diemer, Stefan and Maximiliane Frobenius (2013), 'When Making Pie, All Ingredients Must Be Chilled. Including You: Lexical, Syntactic and Interactive Features in Online Discourse – A Synchronic Study of Food Blogs', in Cornelia Gerhardt, Maximiliane Frobenius and Susanne Ley (eds), *Culinary Linguistics: The Chef's Special*, 53–82, Amsterdam and Philadelphia: John Benjamins.

Dmitrow-Devold, Karolina (2017), 'Performing the Self in the Mainstream. Norwegian Girls in Blogging', *Nordicom Review*, 38(2): 1–14.

Elega, Adeola Abdulateef and Bahire Efe Özad (2018), 'New Media Scholarship in Africa: An Evaluation of Africa-Focused Blog Related Research from 2006 to 2016', *Quality & Quantity: International Journal of Methodology*, 52(5): 2239–2254.

Eli, Karin, Catherine Dolan, Tanja Schneider and Stanley Ulijaszek (2016), 'Mobile Activism, Material Imaginings, and the Ethics of the Edible: Framing Political Engagement through the Buycott App', *Geoforum*, 74: 63–73.

Eli, Karin, Tanja Schneider, Catherine Dolan and Stanley Ulijaszek (2018), 'Digital Food Activism: Values, Expertise and Modes of Action', in Tanja Schneider, Karin Eli, Catherine Dolan and Stanley Ulijaszek (eds), *Digital Food Activism*, 203–219, London: Routledge.

Fairclough, Norman (2001), *Language and Power*, 2nd edn, London: Pearson Education.

Fine, Michelle (1992), *Disruptive Voices: The Possibilities of Feminist Research*, Ann Arbor, MI: University of Michigan Press.

Foucault, Michel (1988), 'Technologies of the Self', in Luther H. Martin, Huck Gutman and Patrick Hutton (eds), *Technologies of the Self: A Seminar with Michel Foucault*, 16–49, New York: Vintage.

Fuchs, Christian (2017), *Social Media: A Critical Introduction*, 2nd edn, London: Sage Publications.

Gerbaudo, Paolo (2017), 'From Cyber-Autonomism to Cyber-Populism: An Ideological History of Digital Activism', *tripleC*, 15(2): 478–491.

Ghobadi, Shahla and Stewart Clegg (2015), '"These Days will Never Be Forgotten . . .": A Critical Mass Approach to Online Activism', *Information and Organization*, 25(1): 52–71.

Giraud, Eva (2018), 'Displacement, "Failure" and Friction: Tactical Interventions in the Communication Ecologies of Anti-Capitalist Food Activism,' in Tanja Schneider, Karin Eli, Catherine Dolan and Stanley Ulijaszek (eds), *Digital Food Activism*, 130–150, New York and London: Routledge.

Goffman, Erving (1959), *The Presentation of Self in Everyday Life*, New York: Anchor Books.

Goffman, Erving (1979), *Gender Advertisements*, Cambridge: Harvard University Press.

Guadagno, Rosanna E., Bradley Okdie and Cassie A. Eno (2008), 'Who Blogs? Personality Predictors of Blogging. Internet Empowerment', *Computers in Human Behavior*, 24(5): 1993–2004.

Gurak, Laura J. and Smiljana Antonijevic (2009), 'Digital Rhetoric and Public Discourse', in Andrea A. Lunsford, Kurt H. Wilson and Rosa A. Eberly (eds), *The SAGE Handbook of Rhetorical Studies*, 497–507, Thousand Oaks, CA: SAGE publications.

Head, Alison J., Michele Van Hoeck and Kirsten Hostetler (2017), 'Why Blogs Endure: A Study of Recent College Graduates and Motivations for Blog Readership', *First Monday*, 22(10). Available online: https://doi.org/10.5210/fm.v22i10.8065

Hearn, Greg, Natalie Collie, Peter Lyle, Jaz Hee-Jeong Choi and Marcus Foth (2014), 'Using Communicative Ecology Theory to Scope the Emerging Role of Social Media in the Evolution of Urban Food Systems', *Futures*, 62(Part B): 202–212.

Hunsinger, Jeremy and Theresa Senft, eds. (2013), *The Social Media Handbook*, New York: Routledge.

Johnson, Thomas J. and Barbara K. Kaye (2004), 'Wag the Blog: How Reliance on Traditional Media and the Internet Influence Credibility Perceptions of Weblogs among Blog Users', *Journalism & Mass Communication Quarterly*, 81(3): 622–642.

Johnson, Thomas J. and Barbara K. Kaye (2014), 'Credibility of Social Network Sites for Political Information among Politically Interested Internet Users', *Journal of Computer-Mediated Communication*, 19(4): 957–974.

Johnston, Josée and Shyon Baumann (2015), *Foodie. Democracy and Distinction in the Gourmet Foodscape*, 2nd edn, New York and London: Routledge.

Jung, Younbo, Hayeon Song and Peter Vorderer (2012), 'Why Do People Post and Read Personal Messages in Public? The Motivation of Using Personal Blogs and its Effects on Users' Loneliness, Belonging, and Well-Being' *Computers in Human Behaviour*, 28(5): 1626–1633.

Keller, Jessalynn Marie (2012), 'Virtual Feminisms: Girls' Blogging Communities, Feminist Activism, and Participatory Politics', *Information, Communication & Society*, 15(3): 429–447.

Kilian, Thomas, Nadine Hennigs and Sascha Langner (2012), 'Do Millennials Read Books or Blogs? Introducing a Media Usage Typology of the Internet Generation', *Journal of Consumer Marketing*, 29(2): 114–124.

Kozinets, Robert, Anthony Patterson and Rachel Ashman (2016), 'Networks of Desire: How Technology Increases our Passion to Consume', *Journal of Consumer Research*, 43(5): 659–682.

Kress, Gunther and Theo van Leeuwen (2001), *Multimodal Discourse: The Modes and Media of Contemporary Communication*, London: Arnold.

Larder, Nicolette, Kristen Lyons and Geoff Woolcock (2014), 'Enacting Food Sovereignty: Values and Meanings in the Act of Domestic Food Production in Urban Australia', *Local Environment*, 19(1): 56–76.

Larsson, Anders Olaf and Stefan Hrastinski (2011), 'Blogs and Blogging: Current Trends and Future Directions', *First Monday*, 16(3). Available online: https://doi.org/10.5210/fm.v16i3.3101.

Lenhart, Amanda and Susannah Fox (2006), *Bloggers: A Portrait of the Internet's New Storytellers*, Washington DC: Pew Internet & American Life Project. Available online: https://www.pewtrusts.org/en/research-and-analysis/reports/2006/07/19/bloggers-a-portrait-of-the-internets-new-storytellers

Lewis, Tania (2018), 'Digital Food: From Paddock to Platform', *Communication Research and Practice*, 4(3): 212–228.

Lovink, Geert (2008), *Zero Comments: Blogging and Critical Internet Culture*, New York: Routledge.

McClintock, Nathan (2014), 'Radical, Reformist, and Garden-Variety Neoliberal: Coming to Terms with Urban Agriculture's Contradictions', *Local Environment*, 19(2): 147–171.

Mendelson, Andrew L. and Zizi Papacharissi (2011), 'Collective Narcissism in College Student Facebook Photo Galleries', in Zizi Papacharissi (ed), *A Networked Self: Identity, Community, and Culture on Social Network Sites*, 251–273, New York: Routledge.

Miller, Wendy M. (2015), 'UK Allotments and Urban Food Initiatives: (Limited?) Potential for Reducing Inequalities', *Local Environment*, 20(10): 1194–1214.

Myers, Greg (2010), *The Discourse of Blogs and Wikis*, London: Continuum.

Pettigrew, Simone, Catherine Archer and Paul Harrigan (2016), 'A Thematic Analysis of Mothers' Motivations for Blogging', *Maternal and Child Health Journal*, 20(5): 1025–1031.

Pinjamaa, Noora and Coye Cheshire (2016), 'Blogs in a Changing Social Media Environment: Perspectives on the Future of Blogging in Scandinavia', *ECIS 2016 Proceedings*, Research Papers 17. Available online: http://aisel.aisnet.org/ecis2016_rp/17/

Reisigl, Martin and Ruth Wodak (2001), *Discourse and Discrimination: Rhetorics of Racism and Antisemitism*, London: Routledge.

Rose, Nikolas (1996), *Powers of Freedom: Reframing Political Thought*, Cambridge: Cambridge University Press.

Sánchez-Villar, Juan M., Enrique Bigné and Joaquín Aldás-Manzano (2017), 'Blog Influence and Political Activism: An Emerging and Integrative Model', *Spanish Journal of Marketing – ESIC*, 21(2): 102–116.

Schiano, Diane J., Bonnie A. Nardi, Michelle Gumbrecht and Luke Swartz (2004), 'Blogging by the Rest of Us', *Extended abstracts of the 2004 Conference on Human Factors and Computing Systems*, 1143–1146, CHI 2004, Vienna, Austria, April 24–29. Available online: https://dl.acm.org/citation.cfm?id=985921-

Schmidt, Jan (2007), 'Blogging Practices: An Analytical Framework', *Journal of Computer-Mediated Communication*, 12(4): 1409–1427.

Schneider, Tanja, Karin Eli, Catherine Dolan and Stanley Ulijaszek, eds. (2018), *Digital Food Activism*, London: Routledge.

Shaw, Frances (2012), 'The Politics of Blogs: Theories of Discursive Activism Online', *Media International Australia*, 142(1): 41–49.

Siniscalchi, Valeria and Carole Counihan (2013), 'Ethnography in Food Activism', in Carole Counihan and Valeria Siniscalchi (eds), *Food Activism: Agency, Democracy and Economy*, 3–12, New York: Bloomsbury Academic.

Soon, Carol and Randy Kluver (2014), 'Uniting Political Bloggers in Diversity: Collective Identity and Web Activism', *Journal of Computer-Mediated Communication*, 19(3): 500–515.

Statista (2019), *Cumulative Total of Tumblr Blogs from May 2011 to January 2019 (in millions)*. Available online: https://www.statista.com/statistics/256235/total-cumulative-number-of-tumblr-blogs/

Svensson, Jacob, Christina Neumayer, Alexander Banfield Mumb and Judith Schossböck (2015), 'Identity Negotiation in Activist Participation', *Communication, Culture & Critique*, 8(1): 144–162.
Tannen, Deborah (2007): *Talking Voices. Repetition, Dialogue, and Imagery in Conversational Discourse*. 2nd ed. Cambridge: Cambridge University Press.
The National Allotment Society (2019), *Brief History of Allotments*. Available online: https://www.nsalg.org.uk/allotment-info/brief-history-of-allotments/
Thompson, John (2012), 'Incredible Edible – Social and Environmental Entrepreneurship in the Era of "Big Society"', *Social Enterprise Journal*, 8(3): 237–250.
Thurlow, Crispin and Kristine Mroczek, eds. (2011), *Digital Discourse: Language in the New Media*, London: Oxford University Press.
Tominc, Ana (2017), *The Discursive Construction of Class and Lifestyle. Celebrity Chef Cookbooks in Post-Socialist Slovenia*, Amsterdam: John Benjamins.
Tornaghi, Chiara and Barbara Van Dyck (2014), 'Research-Informed Gardening Activism: Steering the Public Food and Land Agenda', *Local Environment*, 20(10): 1247–1264.
Törnberg, Anton and Petter Törnberg (2016), 'Muslims in Social Media Discourse: Combining Topic Modelling and Critical Discourse Analysis', *Discourse, Context and Media*, 13 (Part B): 132–142.
Van Dijck, José (2013), *The Culture of Connectivity: A Critical History of Social Media*, Oxford: Oxford University Press.
van Dijk, Teun A. (1977), *Text and Context: Explorations in the Semantics and Pragmatics of Discourse*. London: Longman.
van Dijk, Teun A. (1987), *Communicating Racism. Ethnic Prejudice in Thought and Talk*, Newbury Park, CA: Sage.
van Dijk, Teun A. (2009), 'Critical Discourse Studies: A Sociocognitive Approach', in Ruth Wodak and Michael Meyer (eds), *Methods of Critical Discourse Analysis*, 62–86, London: Sage.
Vegh, Sandor (2003), 'Classifying Forms of Activism', in Martha McCaughey and Michael D. Ayers (eds), *Cyberactivism. Online Activism in Theory and Practice*, 71–95, London: Routledge.
Vlavo, Fidele A. (2017), *Performing Digital Activism: New Aesthetics and Discourses of Resistance*, New York: Routledge.
Vuelio (2017), *UK Bloggers Survey 2017*. Available online: https://www.vuelio.com/uk/wp-content/uploads/2017/09/UK-Bloggers-Survey-2017.pdf
Weintraub, Jeff (1997), 'The Theory and Politics of the Public/Private Distinction', in Jeff Weintraub and Krishan Kumar (eds), *Public and Private in Thought and Practice: Perspectives on a Grand Dichotomy*, 1–42, Chicago: The University of Chicago Press.

8

Food, Activism, and Chips Oman on Twitter

Najma Al Zidjaly, Einas Al Moqbali, and Ahad Al Hinai

1 Introduction

Chips Oman is a savory national snack in Oman, an Arabian social monarchy located in the Arabian Gulf of the Middle East.[1] It is part of the Omani traditional breakfast and is commonly offered in Omani school cafeterias. Chips Oman is also popular in the neighboring countries, including the United Arab Emirates (UAE or the Emirates). Therefore, Omanis were stunned in the summer of 2019 when a trending video out of the Emirates featured a group of UAE children beating a bag of Chips Oman like a piñata. Omanis construed this as an indirect criticism of their traditionally peaceful nature. As (social) media posts and personal encounters indicate, Omanis' neutrality and preference for diplomatic solutions are often misconstrued by citizens of neighboring countries as apathy. Therefore, the Emiratis' action was taken to imply that, akin to a piñata that is hit with a stick to release its contents, Omanis too need to be "hit on the head" to be compelled to take sides, particularly in the context of divisive regional concerns (e.g., the 2015 war on Yemen and the 2017 economic boycott of Qatar, both led by the Kingdom of Saudi Arabia and the UAE). Oman's neutral diplomatic stance has caused much tension with the United Arab Emirates in particular, given the long history of conflicts between Oman and the UAE, especially regarding border disputes. As a result, Omani citizens responded by creating the Twitter hashtag #بطاطس_عمان (#Chips_Oman) to use food as a cover to engage indirectly in larger political discourses and concomitantly take a national stand against an offending party. However, what commenced as a reactionary act against the UAE (and a discussion of the moral contract between neighbors) ended up as a resource to negotiate internal conflicts and the Omani moral order among Omanis themselves.

In this chapter, we analyze eight representative tweets posted on #Chips_Oman to demonstrate how citizens in Oman in 2019 used this food-related hashtag to protest the use of a national Omani snack as a piñata by the children of the UAE and to engage in discussions of Omani national identity. To analyze the often insulting tweets, we draw upon moral approaches to impolite-oriented discourse (Kádár 2017a) and the Arabic cultural practice of "those who shall remain unnamed," or when the offense is so egregious that the offending party does not deserve to be referenced by name (even though they are known), to signal dismissal and emotional hurt. Specifically, we highlight the role that indirectness (linguistically realized through pronoun use and reference terms) and manipulation of the participation framework (Goffman 1981) can play in tandem with images and emojis to signal political dissent while saving Omani cultural face on Twitter. The findings cement food as a political and cultural resource in the Arabic context; show how political dissent is constructed indirectly on Twitter while managing cultural face; illuminate the role food can play in managing internal conflicts and national moral order; and show how indirectness and implicit references not only facilitate taking a stand against an offending party, but also act as calls for action.

The remainder of this chapter first provides, in two sections, background to contextualize the study: (a) a synopsis of political dissent in Oman and ongoing political tensions with neighboring countries and (b) the history of food (and social media) as an activism tool, especially in the Arabic context. Next, the data and analytical framework are introduced. This is followed by analysis and finally a discussion of the paper's contribution to scholarly understandings of digital (food) discourse, especially in the context of political activism.

2 Background to study

2.1 The Omani Arab Spring

Political dissent in Oman commenced in 2011 as part of the Arab Spring to demand improved living standards and an end to unemployment and government corruption (Al Zidjaly 2011; Katzman 2012).[2] While some measures were immediately implemented (e.g., deposing of government officials), disconnection between government and people remained. In a series of publications, Al Zidjaly documented how Omanis handled the dissent or the disconnection through tweets and memes posted on WhatsApp and Twitter from 2013 to 2019. For instance, Al Zidjaly (2014) demonstrated how Omani teachers used WhatsApp to demand the implementation of promises made in 2011 and observed that living standards of many Omani citizens subsequently rose. Nevertheless, unemployment and government officials' corruption persisted; the Sultan's health declined; and oil, Oman's economic mainstay, precipitously dropped in price. However, rather than protesting publicly, as Al Zidjaly (2017) showed, in 2015 Omanis took to WhatsApp again to request a new relationship between the government and citizens through a series of memes created and shared nationally. Their indirect reconciliation attempt fell on deaf ears (e.g., oil subsidiaries were lifted despite public condemnation, leading to deeper economic constraints). Al Zidjaly (forthcoming) illustrates how in 2016 a nationwide food scandal broke and a rift between the Omani public and government widened further when a major Indian/Omani company that wantonly sold expired food in the Omani market was pardoned by government officials despite Omani grassroots Twitter campaigns to boycott the company. Concurrently, news of financial government corruption continued to resurface. Omanis expressed their discontent by creating more hashtags to address government corruption and unemployment, but no resolution followed. By 2019, Omani citizens' sense of helplessness intensified.

2.2 Oman and the UAE

The major catalysts for existing tensions between Oman and UAE are border disputes and differing foreign policy (Saeed 2014; Kinninmont 2019). Oman shares borders with the UAE (northwest), Yemen (southwest), and Saudi Arabia (west). Valeri (2017) explains that although the nomadic nature of Arabian Gulf Bedouins meant that Oman and other Gulf states historically did not mark their borders, the discovery of oil reserves in the 1960s made the allocation of oil fills a matter of national economic importance. Thus, UAE-Oman tensions started with the decades-long Buraimi Crisis that involved the UAE's struggle to gain control of a strategic Omani border city (Al-Sayegh 2002). Concurrently, the UAE attempted to metaphorically annex the Omani provinces of Musandam and Al-Mahra through publishing maps on official websites that included parts of Omani land as part of UAE territory. Although the UAE expressly stated the mistake was unintentional, this event reignited Omanis' sharp discontent with the UAE. In addition to border disputes, the economic boycott of Qatar, because of contrasting foreign policies, and war on Yemen (both led by the Kingdom of Saudi Arabia and the UAE) escalated Oman's tension with its neighbors, as Oman condemned both acts while the Kingdom of Saudi Arabia and the UAE formed a coalition against Yemen and Qatar (Nagi 2019). Further adding to the tension, the UAE also was caught engaging in Oman-focused espionage (emiratesleaks.com). When caught, the UAE government retaliated by erecting a security fence spanning the entire border in order to allegedly stem the flow of illegal immigrants, drugs, and terrorism between the two countries (Al-Sayegh 2002). The wall's constraints on cross-border movement has also created negative social and economic repercussions (Al-Bolushi 2016). Omanis in return attempted to retaliate in 2018 by making requests to boycott Emirati food, but their efforts failed.

2.3 Food and identity politics

Bourdieu's (1984) seminal study on food in modern France has demonstrated how cuisines can be implemented as analytical lenses through which to view sociopolitical contentions. Although linguists have likewise drawn connections between food, language, and socio-politics (e.g., Ferguson 2006; Fellner 2013; Wright & Annes 2013; Tovares, this volume), the intricacies of these connections remain under-explored, observed as early as 2005 by Ron Scollon and as recently as 2017 by Rick Flowers and Elaine Swan, especially in the context of the Middle East (Avieli 2016) and as apropos to social media (Poulain 2017).

Gerhardt, Frobenius and Ley (2013) argue that the unprecedented global enchantment with food in the twentieth century led to novel meanings surrounding food culture, culminating in the birth of the food industry. Stajcic (2013: 13), moreover, explains that as food is "directly linked to both ritual and culture," the construction of food as a form of communication was inevitable, especially since food constitutes a nonverbal method of sharing meanings with others. This construction is supported by Fitrisia, Sibarani and Ritonga (2018: 24) who argued that cuisine, defined as an "exploration of culture through food," has verbal and nonverbal meanings expressible through symbols and other indications during cultural eating rituals. Anderson (2014: 26) further established that "food communicates class, ethnic group, lifestyles affiliation, and other social positions." Accordingly, food has been constructed as a key component of national identity, as it acts as both an analytical lens through which to examine political and cultural tendencies and a social variable (i.e., food serves as an identity marker). In particular, research has demonstrated that food can be both an affiliation tool (national emblem) (e.g., Duffy & Ashley 2012) and a boundary marking tool (a disaffiliation tool) or site of contestation (Hobbis 2017). Therefore, in addition to indexing national identity, representing culture, and creating relations and affiliation (Gerhardt 2013), food can mark boundaries and negotiate ethnicity, gender, and social roles (Avieli 2016).

Food-oriented discourse can additionally signal political dissent. Fellner (2013) presents a complex relationship between culinary narratives, politics, and identity. By examining three literary narratives of what he describes as culinary nostalgia by North American writers, the author argues that such narratives are not mere expressions of nostalgia; rather, they are political commentary, enabling narrators to reflect on the ambivalent relations they have with ethnicity. In other words, they are indirect expressions of political dissent. In a related vein, Wright and Annes (2013) argued for the need to examine food-oriented data through contextual frameworks that ground food discussions in larger political discourses. Specifically, the authors integrate multimodality with content analysis and ethnography to examine the political contentions that surrounded the introduction of Islamic halal or kosher menus to the French fast-food industry. The analysis of national newspapers revealed that resistance to "halalburgers" functioned as a form of defensive gastronationalism, or the idea that introducing Islamic meals would forever change French authentic identity at its core, as food is a symbol of national identity and a marker of (French) borders. The necessity to ground micro food-related discourses in macro political contentions has also been demonstrated by the incident of the "hummus wars" (i.e., laying claims on hummus as a national emblem) between Lebanese and Israelis, documented in Avieli (2016).

Research on the connection between food and politics in digital contexts remains scarce, with the majority of studies devoted to collecting a large corpus of tweets to predict latent population characteristics regarding health and consumption behavior (e.g., Fried et al. 2014; Blackburn, Yilmaz & Boyd 2018; Lupton 2018). Apps created by market research companies and designed to monitor food-related behavior subsequently proliferated (see İkizoğlu & Gordon's, this volume, analysis of threads from a discussion board affiliated with one such app). Linguistic research highlights the discourse of genetically modified food from a critical discourse analysis perspective (e.g., York & Brewster 2013) and identifies the linguistic strategies used in the construction of magazine discourse (e.g., Fuller, Briggs & Dillon-Sumner 2013) and food and health blogs (Gordon 2019). Food-related discourse as a digital tool of activism has received less attention, especially in Arabic contexts. A notable and especially relevant example is the previously mentioned study by Al Zidjaly (forthcoming) of a trending hashtag created by Omanis in 2016 to boycott an Omani/Indian company caught selling expired food in the Omani market. The study explores the part that food-related actions can play in signaling political dissent, highlighting the role of pronouns, as well as the interplay between text, image, and emoji, akin to the focus in this chapter. It also illustrates the shift in moral, political, and affective stances of the Omani public towards two "stance objects" (Du Bois 2007): the Omani/Indian company and the Omani officials who sided with the company against the public. Therefore, what started as a stance of "we the Omanis" against an offending "them" (the Omani/Indian company) ended with "we the Omani poor public" against "the rich Omani officials and their Indian business friends." Thus, the popular but short-lived hashtag ended with a complete shift in alignment, wherein the public aligned against the officials. The food boycott hashtag and action therefore became an implicit negotiation of Omani identity and the responsibilities thereafter. This negotiation of the national moral order or public responsibilities were picked up on #Chips_Oman, analyzed in this chapter.

3 Data and framework

The data set is extracted from a larger longitudinal and ethnographic project focused on Omani identity and social media, which the first author commenced in 2015 (with an emphasis on Omani political dissent).[3] In this chapter, we highlight a thread of 276 tweets on #Chips_Oman created by Omanis in the summer of 2019 after a video surfaced on Twitter of Emirati children playing the piñata game with a large package of Chips Oman. The discussions that unfolded on #Chips_Oman prompted numerous questions regarding the intent of the action by the Emiratis (i.e., was the video showing children hitting a Chips Oman box an innocuous faux pas, a childish game – as declared by the government of Oman – or an indirect act of insult to a main food emblem of the Omani national identity?). The thread additionally prompted questions about the reactions of Omanis (i.e., was the expressed moral outrage justified or misdirected?). These questions impelled the researchers to examine in detail the tweets on #Chips_Oman to understand the construction of ongoing political digital activism in Oman and the role that food can play in national identity debates, especially since this was the second time that Omanis resorted to Twitter to express political anguish through a food hashtag (the first was in response to the 2016 food scandal).

Analytically, we draw upon moral approaches to impoliteness, as theorized by Kádár (2017a), because morality features heavily in the discussions on #Chips_Oman. Kádár (2017a: xii) defines moral order as a "cluster of social and personal values that underlie people's production and interpretation of (im)polite action." In other words, moral order can be defined as ritualistic practices or ideologies engrained in the historical body of people (Nishida 1958; see Al Zidjaly 2019 for a discussion of the moral order in Arabic contexts). Therefore, investigating impolite-oriented discourse, including the tweets analyzed here, requires considering the perception of morality and interpersonal relationships within the broader context and rituals in which they are based, especially since, as postulated by Kádár (2017a), a ritual, in particular, can trigger polite or impolite evaluations, as rituals maintain the order of things and tend to imply a moral stance. The process of negotiation, response, or evaluation of perceived attacks is referred to by Kádár (2017a) as "the rites of moral aggression," or the ritualized ways of responding to a perceived public attack. We thus situate the analysis in this chapter both socially and culturally in observing that the tweets draw upon a to-date undocumented Arabic cultural practice named by the Arabian Gulf people, "those who shall remain nameless." Akin to all linguistic strategies, following Tannen (1994), this ritualistic discursive practice is concurrently ambiguous (has unclear meaning) and polysemous (has more than one meaning at once); uttered in interaction it can signal hurt, dismissal, and moral indignity. In this way, "those who shall remain nameless" functions as a type of what Kádár (2017b) calls "implicit ritualistic insult." Implicitness in this Arabic case is not a means of mitigating face threat; rather, given the value of naming in Arabic culture, it is an offense.

In the historically tribal Arabic societies (Hofstede, Hofstede & Minkov 1990), naming is a sign of respect, as one's surname or title is a key component of one's identity. That is so because a name signals one's tribe and, in turn, one's standing in society. Therefore, the worst thing that could happen to one in Arabia is to not be given a name, as it connotes nonexistence, insignificance, or shame. Consequently, the strategy of "those who shall remain nameless" (i.e., intentionally not naming a person whose name is known) in Arabic discourse is an act of disrespect, linguistically realized through generic or indirect reference (e.g., "their direction" instead of "Emiratis' direction" in Example 3), the use of third person pronouns (i.e., "they" or "them"), or the use of general descriptive categories (e.g., "the neighboring country"). It can also function through the manipulation of Goffman's (1981) participation framework (i.e., including both addressed and unaddressed ratified participants). Indirectness or implicitness is often related to politeness (Lakoff 1973; Khaffaf, Safwat & Al-Jawadi 2016); however, given the nonexistence of a direct relationship between linguistic strategies and politeness (Upadhyay 2010), in Arabic countries (and in Israel too, see Sertbulut 2012), indirectness is associated with impoliteness, signaling both emotional hurt and dismissal. Therefore, using ambiguous and/or general reference terms and indirectly addressing ratified participants in the context of the strategy of "those who shall remain nameless" interactionally (and collectively) accomplish much more just than indexing a particular group (note that Schegloff 2007 argues that this is often the case with reference terms, that they signal stance and/or alliances in addition to group reference).

Van Dijk (1997), in his discussion of political manipulation through language, further illustrates the use of implicit or indirect referencing to enact the interactional goal of insulting an attacker while managing face. For instance, linguistic strategies such as pronouns, active and passive constructions, general categories, variations of word order, uses of specific syntactic categories, nominalizations, clause embedding, and sentence complexity can convey implicit meanings, including creating an "us" versus "them" stance. They can further signal alliances or misalliances (Fowler et al. 1979). Such linguistic indirectness, coupled with the manipulation of the participation framework, works best in conflict situations as it helps manage or mitigate the conflict without the speaker being held accountable and/or it helps to save face (Khaffaf, Safwat & Al-Jawadi 2012). In this chapter, we show how tweeters draw upon personal pronouns; evoke the strategy of "not naming the offending party directly," though the instigator (the UAE) is known; or opt for general descriptive terms or euphemisms (e.g., the nation), which construct a sense of distance (Tannen 2005) or create a separate stance (Du Bois 2007). We illustrate how this distancing or separation, which evokes the unaddressed ratified participant role, is used to manage conflicts and release emotion but also to act as a call for public protest against the government, as Omanis did in 2011. In other words, we show how the polysemous and ambiguous linguistic and multimodal strategies Omanis drew upon in #Chips_Oman helped them construct a collective stance against an intruder party and against each other while maintaining face and evading responsibility. Put another way, tweeters worked to signal political dissent on a digital platform through how they constructed their food-related communication.

4 Analysis of tweets

In this section, we analyze eight tweets that represent the feelings of Omanis towards the Emiratis, each other, and the Omani government as expressed on a food-related hashtag during the summer of 2019 (#Chips_Oman). We specifically highlight the role that implicit referencing and personal pronouns (in conjunction with visual modes) play in enabling Omanis to manage political concerns while saving face.

The first tweet (Example 1) was selected for analysis because it turned a national hashtag used by Omanis into a trending hashtag in the Gulf region, as the person tweeting is an influencer from Saudi Arabia sharing with his 16,000-plus followers (while tagging #بطاطس_عمان [#Chips_Oman]). The tone of the tweet is sarcastic: After reporting the incident where several Emirati children are being encouraged by family members to hit a Chips Oman package like a piñata, the author of the tweet informs his followers that Omanis requested Emiratis to issue an apology because of the "abuse" directed at "their potatoes." The tweet includes a short version of the original video of the incident. The author of the tweet includes a caption on the video that reads "The toys of the neighboring country," which is the title of a poem an Omani poet created in response to the Chips Oman incident in which he laments Omanis. In the screenshot of Example 1, the tagged comment/the title of the poem that the author pasted appears top left. The square brackets in this and the following translations enclose comments added to clarify the text.

Example 1

Translation

#Chips_Oman

The tweet: Trending in the Sultanate of Oman: A clip of Emirati children playing a game called "piñata," the idea of which is to fill a carton [in the clip, a shipping carton from the company Chips Oman] with sweets, which the children beat, and whoever manages to break it open wins what is inside. The Omanis are asking the Emiratis for an apology for abusing their potatoes.

The tag on the video (appears top left): "The toys of the neighbouring country" by the poet, Said Al-Mishiqri.

Implicit references are embedded in Example 1 to indirectly, and sarcastically, call out the Emiratis' action and the Omanis' response. On the surface, the tweet's text is a factual description of the situation and a joke that Omanis' requested apology from the Emiratis was for "abusing their potatoes." In reality, Omanis were the target of the (indirect) abuse. The author's metacomment (i.e., stating that Omanis were upset because their potatoes were abused) seems to downplay the incident (only potatoes were hurt) and/or indirectly criticize Omanis (for their sensitivity). As strategies can be potentially both ambiguous and polysemous, the metacomment can also be more jocular in tone, signaling the triviality of the incident.

In formal Arabic (posted by the author of the tweet on the top left corner of the video image) is the title of a poem written by Omani poet Saeed Al-Mishiqri, "The toys of the neighboring country." The formal register and lack of emojis index formality. The poem's title appears to lament the Emiratis' action but also indirectly criticizes Omanis for becoming "a toy" at the hands of the neighboring country. Al-Mishiqri's (and, consequently, the Saudi tweeter's) choice to refer to the UAE as "the neighboring country" rather than to directly name it accomplishes two aims: First, both the Saudi author of the tweet and the quoted Omani poet absolve themselves from any responsibility in the conflict, especially since the government of Oman has warned Omani citizens from clashing with UAE citizens (and the Saudi government was and remains in coalition with the Emirati government). Second, the term invokes the Arabic cultural practice of insult of "those who shall remain nameless." (Although the lack of directness may also be intended to mirror the Omani government, which avoids publicly acknowledging the UAE government's intrusive acts). The poet's (and, subsequently, the Saudi tweeter's) use of the term "toys" additionally implies that Omanis themselves have become toys in the hands of UAE citizens, in the sense that Omanis remained publicly unresponsive to previous aggressive acts of the UAE, including their appropriation of Omani heritage symbols such as the dagger.

The Omani government's official response came in the form of a clarifying tweet by @Oman_event explaining that the incident was a harmless game that should not be taken as creating regional tensions and that Omanis are not to engage in divisive discourse with the Emiratis. Others' responses to the triggering Saudi tweet were divided. In what follows, we examine what Kádár (2017a) calls "the rites of moral aggression" or the ritualized responses to the presumed attack which we divide into three types: tweets of people who took a stand against the Emiratis, the offending third party, or the unaddressed but ratified participant (Examples 2 and 3); tweets of those who took a stand against Omanis – either for caring about a trivial snack-related incident or for failing to stand up to their own government (Examples 4-6); and tweets of those who took a stand against the Omani government (Examples 7 and 8). All negotiations took place through indirect references and generic pronouns, even when Omanis attacked each other.

4.1 Omanis versus Emiratis

Example 2 is representative of the tweets by Omanis who, in opposition to the official position of the government of Oman on @Oman_event, contended that the piñata incident was neither harmless nor unintentional. As demonstrated, these tweets rely on implied references that highlight indirect offense toward a long-time aggressor; they also indirectly evoke the moral code of neighbors.

Example 2

Translation

Taking into consideration the history of the neighboring country's interference in the Sultanate, in obstructing its projects, abusing its citizens at the borders, and planting espionage cells, and other things, the matter doesn't seem accidental, even if I might hope it were.

#Chips_Oman

This tweet summarizes the feeling of many Omani citizens regarding the supposedly harmless food game: That it was an intentional, aggressive act, not an innocuous food game as suggested by the government of Oman on @Oman_event. According to the tweeter, this position is justified by the UAE's past actions (e.g., espionage of internal Omani affairs, disruption of Omani economic projects, redrawing official maps to include some Omani lands in the UAE, abuse of Omani citizens on the border). Meanwhile, the author's use of "even if I might hope it were [innocuous]" is a mitigative or softening strategy that could signal, albeit indirectly, his or Omanis' preference for peace, giving the Emiratis the benefit of the doubt, and honoring the Omani government's request to refrain from judgement by hoping the act was not intentionally aggressive.

Identifying the UAE as "the neighboring country" is a polysemous and ambiguous linguistic strategy that accomplishes several interactional goals: The implicit reference dismisses Emiratis as unworthy of mention because the unspecified descriptive category evokes the Arabic insulting ritual of "those who shall remain nameless." The term in addition signals Emiratis' breach of the moral code between neighbors (i.e., bordering countries are expected to refrain from aggressive acts against each other). The tweet thus serves as a lament consisting of an indirect reproach and an indirect request for "the neighboring country" to abide by neighboring laws, as the term "neighboring" indexes closeness. Because the Arabic practice of "those who shall remain nameless" is used by those who feel hurt, the metacomment "the neighboring country" could further work as Omanis putting themselves at the mercy of a higher agent (the UAE), thereby invoking a second Islamic/Arabic ritual known as "getting the lower hand" (Beeman 1986; Al Zidjaly 2006). In so doing, Omanis call upon the UAE government and the country's people to stop all aggressive acts and mend the broken relationship in addition to lamenting the bad relationship and criticizing the Chips Oman incident. Implicit referencing moreover relieves Omanis of responsibility and saves their face (and that of the Emiratis' too). In this sense, indirectness by Omanis in this context could be an example of what Tannen (1994), based on Lakoff (1973), terms a "defensiveness" strategy. It is defensive because, as Tannen explains, indirectness provides a way out through allowing speakers to rescind (or not admit to) what was said indirectly if it is not met positively. Indirectness can also be a bonding strategy, as argued by Tannen (1994), enabling Omanis to experience rapport because they all know who is being talked about without "the neighboring country" being named directly (i.e., akin to sharing an insider joke).

The sentiment expressed in Example 2 is echoed in Example 3, wherein a second Omani tweeter concurs with the government that the act should not be commented on (indicating a preference to take the high ground). However, doubts about the intention of the Emiratis linger, and implicit or indirect referencing again creates an us-versus-them stance.

Example 3

مريم ||
@maryamli03

صح إنه الموضوع م يستحق التعليق بس
بعد نيتي م عادت صافية إتجاه أي شيء
يطلع من صوبهم هذا مستواهم ولا تنحدروا
لمستواهم

#بطاطس_عمان

Translation

True, the matter doesn't deserve comment, but I am still disquieted by anything that comes from their direction [or side]. This is their level [of discourse]; don't descend [or stoop] to their level.

#Chips_Oman

Example 3 is written in Omani Arabic dialect to construct closeness (i.e., it is an in-group strategy); in the case of Arabic, as well as other diglossic languages, the formal variety indexes distance and the colloquial variety indexes familiarity and connection (Bassiouney 2009). The tweet begins by agreeing with the official Omani government's stand that the Chips Oman incident is unworthy of commentary. The tweet author proceeds to deliver insults in several ways. First, Emiratis are referenced obliquely through "their direction" and "their level." Refusal to directly name and acknowledge the culprit country is a linguistic retaliation that reduces that country's identity and can be read as disrespectful. Second, expressing distrust can be interpreted as an indirect accusation toward the UAE regarding their many actions against Omanis. Third, the tweet constructs Omanis as metaphorically above the aggressors by asking Omanis not to "descend [or stoop] to their (i.e., the UAE's) level." The tweet's collective impact is constructing Emiratis as immoral. As a result, the author's opening statement (indicating that the topic is not worth commenting on) has various implicit meanings: (a) the subject deals with Emiratis, who are not worth Omanis' time; (b) the Chips Oman game is of no consequence and the spread of the hashtag that engages with it is ridiculous; and/or (c) Emirati actions do no not warrant attention. The part about not trusting anything from their (Emiratis') direction demonstrates a tense relationship between the citizens of the two countries.

4.2 Omanis versus Omanis

As Omanis continued constructing the Chips Oman "game" as a moral insult and moral indignity, they also began to retaliate against each other. Example 4, written by an Omani tweeter whose username is "Sultan Al Abri," in standard modern Arabic and without emojis, signals the graveness of the matter. His tweet refers to serious Omani concerns (e.g., corruption, unemployment), which had not received the same attention as #Chips_Oman had; in so doing, he attacks Omanis for misguided activism and calls for a refocus of energy.

Example 4

Translation

#Chips_Oman
#Chips_Oman

We've left aside the announcement of Sultan [bin Majid] Al-Ibri
We've left aside the issue of unemployment
We've left aside the issue of corruption
To concentrate on a trivial issue like
Playing with Chips Oman becoming a hashtag
Upgrade your thinking and your issues so that the country [homeland] can be upgraded with you and by you

In Example 4, reminiscent of the style of memes Omanis created in 2015 to signal dissent through repetition that created rhythm and emphasis (see Al Zidjaly 2017), insults toward Omanis are used to construct the piñata event as not being worthy of attention. First, the #Chips_Oman hashtag is posted twice to perhaps indicate the unwarranted attention the hashtag has received or the momentum the hashtag has generated. Second, serious Omani concerns (e.g., corruption and unemployment), which had not received the same attention as #Chips_Oman had, are listed along with reference to a revelation of corruption by an Emirati company in charge of developing Mutrah waterfront in Oman's capital city. The revelation was announced by an Omani parliament member during the trending period of the hashtag. The reference acts as a reminder that Omanis have more important issues to address, evoking the collective moral responsibility to address corruption. The switch between "we" to "upgrade or rise" (which implicitly reads as "you upgrade or rise") accomplishes more than reference to a group of people: *We* indexes the responsibility of all, including the author of the tweet, towards the ailments of the country; "upgrade [rise]" or "you upgrade [you rise]" constructs Omanis as a separate group from the author of the tweet; the latter has claimed the higher moral ground instructing the rest of Omanis to focus on the consequences of discovering corruption and the legal measures that need to be taken in response. Third, the UAE is not mentioned – this time, to indirectly signal the insignificance of the act of children hitting the Chips Oman package. Accordingly, the tweet demonstrates the tweeter's frustration with the absurdity of the attention given to the insignificant potato chips incident. The call to morally rise in thought and action (in conjunction with the call not to "descend or stoop" in Example 3) makes use of the metaphor that *good is up* and *bad is down* akin to *virtue is up* and *depravity is down* (Lakoff & Johnson 1980). The tweet and reference choices are therefore an attack on Omanis and a call for action against internal corruption, as well as an assertion of morality.

Example 5 makes use of the address term "you" to expresses moral indignation through questioning Omanis' loyalty by listing a number of immoral features of Omani citizens themselves; consequently, it also identifies the moral code of a proper Omani citizen.

Example 5

Translation

You are defensive of your country; you saw a video of children beating a box emblazoned with a local brand name, so you rose in defense of it with the hashtag #Chips_Oman. But you go to work late, and you pilfer supplies from your work for your own personal use, and you throw garbage everywhere, and you mistreat foreign workers for the sake of financial gain.

Put simply, you are choosing the type of patriotism that suits you 😅

This Omani tweeter delivers attacks on Omani character in Standard Arabic, mitigated with an emoji that is often employed to express embarrassment or awkwardness to soften the blow. According to Bassiouney (2009), using standard Arabic indexes seriousness and objectivity (in contrast to Omani colloquial dialect which indexes closeness and lightheartedness – see Example 6). The choice of formal code also references preaching discourse used on Omani official media outlets (for more on this discourse, see Al Zidjaly 2017). An image of Chips Oman is attached to make the tweet eye-catching, which helps get viewers and likes. Like the tweeter of Example 4, this tweeter constructs himself (the accuser) as separate from others (the accused Omanis). Yet, neither Emiratis nor Omanis are directly named. The first sentence constructs an insulting position by questioning other Omanis' ("your") patriotism towards the country ("your country"); the tweeter is excluded from this group (by "our" not being used instead). The indirect message is that Omanis (but not the author of the tweet who claims the moral high ground) are hypocrites: While outraged about an innocuous food-related incident, they commit a host of immoral behaviors, including not taking work seriously, disrespecting public space, and committing financial fraud. The tweet attempts to raise Omanis' consciousness that patriotism begins with caring for national interests and becoming better citizens who exhibit moral behavior in everyday actions.

Example 6 continues this type of call to action; it involves Omanis taking stances of opposition vis-à-vis other Omanis and also provides an expanded list of immoral behaviors committed by officials from the Omani government. This tweet constructs Omanis as a separate distant identity by constructing them as "the nation." In other words, here the contrast is between "them-the unmentioned (Omani) government or government officials" against "you-the nation." Keywords for analysis are underlined in the translation.

Example 6

Translation

#Chips_Oman

—Money is looted and treasures are <u>stolen</u> (as our Kuwait brethren say)
—Imaginary schools, that we have neither seen nor known
—[The price of] Petrol goes up and down
—They've even <u>raised</u> the price of the Pepsi that one drinks to cool one's troubled heart

And the nation makes a trending hashtag about a [mere] <u>carton of chips</u>!!

Several linguistic strategies are noticeable in this tweet to argue (albeit playfully) for the need to refocus dissent energy on what actually matters. First, the tweeter mixes standard Arabic with Omani colloquial dialect and one term from the Kuwaiti dialect (e.g., stolen); the intentional code-switch, or *heteroglossia with awareness* (Bakhtin 1981; Tovares 2019), acknowledges the hashtag's regional reach and indirect referencing of Arabian Gulf identity. The switch also creates humor; the humor in turn is intensified by the use of other amusing colloquial terms that are underlined in the translation (e.g., "carton of chips" and the Omani colloquial term for *raised* in "raised the price"). Juxtaposing various dialects and formal sentence construction with colloquial terms creates playfulness but also an indirect signaling of disapproval, as the linguistic style of this tweet is reminiscent of the style of the memes Omanis created in 2015 during the height of Omani dissent wherein humor was mixed with formal sentence construction and topics to signal disconnection with the Omani government (see Al Zidjaly 2017). In the same manner, the tweet's humor in this example is juxtaposed with references to government corruption (e.g., embezzlement by the Omani Ministry of Education, fluctuating gas prices); the author's use of the concessive conjunct "even" both indicates the addition but also the surprising nature of the next thing (i.e., "even the Pepsi one drinks" has become more expensive). This signals sarcasm toward the aggressiveness of the Omani tax system that prevents Omanis from enjoying the only drink they consume to forget troubles (to "cool" their "troubled heart[s]").

In his last sentence, the tweeter signals the triviality of Omanis' reactions by contrasting the harsh Omani government actions towards its citizens (which received little disapproval) with Omanis' reaction to the Chips Oman piñata incident. The disconnection between the two is highlighted by the use of an extra line space between the two parts, which visually separates the first part of a list of serious aggressions by the Omani government towards its people, from the "nation's" response to an insignificant incident. The disconnection is further realized through a second juxtaposition between the use of a passive sentence construction in the first part of the tweet (e.g., "money is looted") and active sentence construction at the end (e.g., "the nation makes"). By using a passive construction, the government is not directly accused of theft, which absolves the author from responsibility for any perceived aggression. It also saves face and mitigates the attack. The people in contrast are directly accused of the crime of turning a blind eye to government aggression. They are therefore constructed as active but misguided because they are "the nation." The term "the nation" references "the Arabic nation," a political imagined and abstract construction that refers to twenty-three divergent countries connected by religion and different varieties of Arabic (Nydell 2005). When insulting each other, Omanis humorously use "the nation" to refer to themselves to signal they are not actual citizens with rights and moral responsibilities but rather an abstract, imagined construct. Also, stating "the nation" instead of "you" or "we the nation" indexes the tweeter's stance as an objective analyst of the situation. Therefore, in the first part of the tweet, the patient is highlighted (and the agent is left unnamed – no direct government criticism). In the second part, "the nation" becomes the agent and the action is criticized. The exclamation marks signal absurdity and the tweeter's disapproval of Omanis (i.e., how is this even possible?). In this tweet therefore even though corrupt actions by the government in Oman are listed, it is the Omani people who are blamed (and attacked) because of misguided activism.

4.3 Omanis versus the Omani government

Omanis' call to refocus the discussion to create real change is taken up by other tweeters, including Omani intellectuals. In Example 7, an Omani citizen and influencer redirects the conversation to focus on Omani governmental actions by presenting a novel idea. His argument goes as follows: The reported actions by the UAE are made-up actions by the Omani government to distract Omanis from news of Omani government corruption. In other words, there is no Emirati conspiracy against the Omanis. It is simply a plot that unfolds as follows: The Omani media reports (fake) acts of aggression; the Omanis get worked up; meanwhile, and covertly, the Omani government continues its attacks on the Omani public while, overtly, attempting to calm them down. By the time they quiet down, news of another conspiracy breaks. And the cycle continues. In this tweet therefore "the conspiracy" refers to the Omani government's construction of UAE people's actions as a conspiracy against Omanis. Put differently, the author argues that it is not the UAE government and people who are conspiring to fool Omanis but rather it is the Omani government itself conspiring against its citizens by continually distracting them through news of external insignificant aggression while national riches are looted.

Example 7

Translation

The conspiracy is not the insult of #Chips_Oman

The conspiracy is how you made [or how you transformed] a simple game into an issue of public opinion.

And how the interest in Chips Oman
has become more important than interest in **#Sultan_Qaboos_port**
in Mutrah

And **#Duqm_port**

#Conscience_relieved

This Omani tweeter redirects the conversation by accusing the Omani government of using the Chips Oman incident to conceal their own corruption and crimes against the citizens of Oman (i.e., "how you made" or "transformed"). He specifically references two Omani port development projects (Duqm, the largest Omani project for 2019, and Sultan Qaboos Port at Mutrah), which have been marred with reports of financial corruption and embezzlement. Indirectly, he asks Omanis to address this corruption, especially since news about it failed to earn as much attention as did the Chips Oman incident. He, therefore, urges Omanis indirectly to address and report government corruption, evidenced by his inclusion of #Conscience_relieved, a hashtag created by Omanis in 2019 for this purpose. The use of *you* in this context is direct address and also direct blame because Omanis afforded a snack incident unwarranted attention. The hashtag and the tweet signal awareness and national self-reflexivity. Others supported this tweeter's argument, as shown in Example 8, which retweets (and comments on) a tweet by an Omani academic and social influencer (Dr. Haider

Al-Lawati), who originally tweeted Edward Herman and Noam Chomsky's (1988) political analysis of how governments distract nations, thereby accusing the Omani government of doing the same ("through diverting public attention from real fateful concerns to insignificant ones").

Example 8

Translation

    Comment on retweeted tweet: @drazmi6: Exactly. A tiny country suffers from the highest rates of unemployment and poverty in the Arabian Gulf, and poor services, and corruption, and the control of the country's wealth by a small group ... and it daily distracts its people with issues [like] #Chips_Oman, alleged spy cells and [other] external matters, to keep the ground-down [crushed. Beaten] nation from coming out [to the streets] or [to revolt] again, as they did in 2011.

    Original tweet: @DrAl_Lawati: Among the strategies of media manipulation according to Chomsky [sic – actually Herman and Chomsky]:
    The strategy of distraction and entertainment by way of directing the general public's attention away from truly crucial matters.

The tweeter @drazmi6's retweet serves as a reminder to Omanis of the distraction strategy that governments use to manipulate their citizens, as per the teachings of the linguist and political activist Noam Chomsky and economist Herman. In his comment, the tweeter uses the descriptor "tiny country" to refer to Oman – more specifically, to the Omani government that misappropriated the nation's riches. He compares Oman to all other Arabian Gulf countries and concludes Oman has the highest unemployment and poverty rates. He only indirectly references the Omani government by saying a small group controls the country's wealth and then inserting three dots either because it requires no explanation, or to avoid the government's wrath, or to signal disrespect through not directly naming them. He does not accuse the UAE government and people; instead he shifts the blame to Omani government officials for using the incident to divert public attention away from their own misdeeds and to avoid revolts like that of 2011. Note that the UAE spies that were asserted to exist in the tweet shown in Example 2 are here suggested to be a created rumor or a distraction strategy of the Omani government. Using passive syntactic constructions (e.g., the agent of the fabrication is not named) enables Omanis like this tweeter to concomitantly insult and evade responsibility. This tweet further acts as an indirect request for Omanis to protest publicly because it references the protests of 2011 and the government's expressed fear of their return. Specifically, the adjective "ground-down, crushed, or beaten" references the mental state of Omanis as beaten down by continuous abuses by their own government, and acts, albeit indirectly, as a reminder to the officials, and the Omanis themselves, that Omanis have reached their limit; therefore, officials are forewarned to beware. These kinds of tweets made many Omanis realize they were overreacting to the Chips Oman incident and that their anger and frustration were misdirected.

5 Discussion and conclusion

In this chapter we examined eight representative tweets left on #بطاطس_عمان (#Chips_Oman) to explore how a food-related hashtag was appropriated by Omanis in 2019 to address national and regional conflicts, following a potentially harmless (but unclear) incident involving "the abuse" of Omani food packaging (Example 1). We identified indirectness as the main linguistic strategy used in the tweets on the hashtag and illustrated how it was realized through the use of 1) general, impersonal, descriptive categories (e.g., "the neighboring country," "the nation," "a tiny country"); 2) collective (generic) pronouns (e.g., "they," "you," "their"); 3) agentless or passive sentence constructions (e.g., "money [is] looted," "riches [are] stolen"); and 4) the manipulation of the Goffmanian (1981) participation framework (e.g., constructing the UAE and the Omani government as unaddressed but ratified participants). The analysis was motivated by research that demonstrates the interconnectedness of food and identity politics (Fellner 2013; Avieli 2016; Hobbis 2017), which highlights that conversations about food are often about so much more (as pointed out in this volume's introduction). Accordingly, we examined the identified strategies through the lens of Arabic cultural practices; adopted a moral approach to impolite-oriented discourse, as defined by Kádár (2017a, 2017b); and highlighted the complexity of linguistic strategies, building on prior studies (e.g., Tannen 1994; van Dijk 1997; Schegloff 2007). Specifically, we illustrated how Omanis evoked the to-date undocumented Arabic cultural practice of "those who shall remain nameless," which, in Arabic interaction, signals hurt, dismisses the offending party, and evokes moral indignation. We also argued that the strategy helps evoke a second documented Arabic Islamic practice of putting oneself at the hands of a more powerful agent to correct the offense or reverse it, in addition to signaling the moral obligation of all parties involved, (see Beeman 1986; Wilce 2005; Al Zidjaly 2006 for more on Islamic and Arabic cultural practices). Collectively, the identified strategies signaled political dissent and presented the Omanis the opportunity to mobilize their outrage and engage in more fruitful discussions on digital platforms. This in turn created a call for a more morally inclined, responsible citizen who can and does defend Oman by standing up to corruption.

Perceived insults or face-attacks are often followed with the rites of moral aggression, defined by Kádár (2017a) as ritualistic means of engaging in conflict and managing face-loss. In this chapter, we identified three types of responses by Omanis to face-attacks by the neighboring country (the UAE), and their request for an apology for the abuse "their potatoes" received (Example 1) (Omanis rites of moral aggression): attacking back the UAE (Omanis versus Emiratis), self-attacks (Omanis versus Omanis), and government attacks (Omani public versus Omani government officials). It is worth noting that Al Zidjaly (2012), in a study on how Arabs responded to face-attacks to their identity, identified self-attacks as the prominent strategy by which Arab cultural face was managed in digital discourse. Al Zidjaly explained the findings through the lens of the Islamic cultural practice of lamenting, highlighting the necessity to take an expansive view of impolite-oriented discourse and explicating the displayed self-hatred leading up to the 2011 Arab Spring.

Those who believed that the piñata incident was an intentional offending act (Examples 2 and 3) resorted to implied references (e.g., "the neighboring country" and "they") to respond to the known aggressor (the UAE). Omani tweeters, in addition, referenced past aggressive actions by the offending party to justify their moral stance. In so doing, they further, but indirectly, evoked the moral code of neighbors through constructing the unnamed UAE as "the neighboring country" (i.e., they are still neighbors to Omanis though they might not act neighborly). Indirectness in these examples also served to save face and evade responsibility in addition to using the insulting "those who shall remain nameless" strategy. These first two examples demonstrate lingering doubts about the intention of the Emiratis, signaling moral indignation; indirectness further cemented an us-versus-them stance. They also used different language varieties to address different audiences – formal Arabic in Example 2 (to address all Omanis, government officials included) and Omani Arabic dialect in Example 3 (to address everyday Omani citizens in a way that creates alignment and closeness in the face of an "other" [the UAE]).

All examples evoked the strategy of "those who shall remain nameless," including Example 1 which was analyzed to signal the wide reach of the hashtag of a food snack scandal involving neighboring countries. In the second category (Examples 4, 5 and 6), Omanis hurled insults at their fellow Omanis who constructed the Chips Oman piñata event as worthy of attention, underscoring the unwarranted momentum the hashtag had generated. To refocus the activism energy, those tweets included reference to serious Omani concerns (e.g., corruption, unemployment), which had not received the same attention that #Chips_Oman had. The tweets also included calls to act by reminding Omanis of their moral and political responsibility to stand up to internal corruption. Omanis were referenced as "you," "the nation," "a tiny country" and as a "crushed [beaten] nation,"[4] separating the tweeters from the rest of the nation. In these tweets, passive syntactic constructions were used to evade direct accusation (and direct responsibility) when referencing government crimes. They were also used to signal the passivity of Omanis towards internal problems. The tweets in this section thus constructed division among Omanis. Example 5 in particular, in its use of the address term "you" and listing a number of bad acts of Omani citizens, both separated some Omanis from others and identified the moral code of a proper Omani citizen.

The redirection of misguided activism was further taken up in section 3, the final category in the rites of moral aggression (Examples 6–8), by tweeters who created disalignment with Omani officials, accusing the Omani government of using the Chips Oman incident to conceal their own crimes against Oman and its citizens. The "you" in examples such as "how you transformed" could reference either the Omani public or the government officials, again drawing upon vague or generic pronouns to evade responsibility but call out immoral actions at the same time. Altogether, all offending parties, including Omanis with misguided actions, are constructed as immoral and unworthy of mention. The examples signal political dissent and pose calls for action, requesting Omanis to go back to the streets as they did in 2011 during the first wave of the Arab Spring (the second wave started in 2019 and ended in January 2020).

Overall, the snack food incident served as a catalyst, spurring tweeters to collectively construct political dissent, engage in democratic discourse to build

Oman, and negotiate the moral ethics of citizenship which include morally rising above it all and ending corruption. It hinged on some tweeters identifying the attack on an Omani food item as an attack on Oman itself, which underlines the strong link between food and cultural identity (though others saw the incident as innocuous). It also set the stage for the food-related communication on Twitter on #Chips_Oman to become moral and political: #Chips_Oman was mobilized by Omanis to exercise agency, affording them a license to indirectly take issue with a continually aggressive neighboring country and, in doing so, take a stand against their own government and reprehensible actions of their fellow citizens. In this chapter, we thus highlighted the role that the linguistic strategies of indirectness and personal pronouns played in enabling Omanis to manage political concerns while saving face, demonstrating how food, and communication about it, can serve not just as a political and cultural lens but also as a moral lens that facilitates discussion of national concerns and underscores neighborly responsibilities and good citizenship.

Notes

1. "The Middle East" refers to the 23 and counting countries that speak the Arabic language whose territories extend from the Arabian Gulf to North and West Africa. The Arabian Gulf comprises six countries: the Kingdom of Saudi Arabia, Bahrain, Kuwait, Qatar, the United Arab Emirates, and Oman.
2. "The government" refers to the officials in charge of government institutions, not the publicly adored and revered past and current supreme leaders of Oman.
3. The strategic project, funded by Sultan Qaboos University in Oman, is named "The impact of social media on Omani youth: A multimodal project" (SR/ART/ENGL/15/01) –2015–2020.
4. It was pointed out to us by Cynthia Gordon that instead of the common cliché "you are what you eat" (as discussed e.g. by Lakoff 2006), in the #Chips_Oman piñata example, there is no "eat," only "beat." In other words, there are identity implications for Emiratis if, rather than eating Omani food, they beat it.

Acknowledgments

We are forever indebted to David Wilmsen for his translations of the data in this chapter and in other publications by the first author. We are additionally thankful to the valuable comments received from Cynthia Gordon and Alla Tovares on various drafts of this chapter.

References

Al Zidjaly, Najma (2006), 'Disability and Anticipatory Discourse: The Interconnectedness of Local and Global Aspects of Talk', *Communication & Medicine*, 3(2): 101–112.

Al Zidjaly, Najma (2011), 'From Oman with Love', *The New York Times*, March 8. Available online: https://www.nytimes.com/2011/03/08/opinion/08al-zidjaly.html?mtrref=www.google.com&gwh=BC5009075A9D1C27B64CA17ABF7644C0&gwt=pay&assetType=REGIWALL

Al Zidjaly, Najma (2012), 'What Has Happened to Arabs? Identity and Face Management Online', *Multilingua*, 31(4): 413–439.

Al Zidjaly, Najma (2014), 'WhatsApp Omani Teachers? Social Media and the Question of Social Change', *Multimodal Communication*, 3(1): 107–130.

Al Zidjaly, Najma (2017), 'Memes as Reasonably Hostile Laments: A Discourse Analysis of Political Dissent in Oman', *Discourse & Society*, 28(6): 573–594.

Al Zidjaly, Najma (2019), 'Divine Impoliteness. How Arabs Negotiate Islamic Moral Order on Twitter', *Russian Journal of Linguistics*, 23(4): 1039–1064.

Al Zidjaly, Najma (forthcoming), 'Multimodal Stance and Food Boycott on Twitter in Oman', *Discourse Studies*.

Al-Bolushi, Maryam (2016), 'The Effect of Omani-Iranian Relations on the Security of the Gulf Cooperation Council Countries after the Arab Spring', *Contemporary Arab Affairs*, 9(3): 383–399.

Al-Sayegh, Fatma (2002), 'The UAE and Oman: Opportunities and Challenges in the Twenty-First Century', *Middle East Policy*, 9(3): 124–137.

Anderson, Eugene N. (2014), *Everyone Eats: Understanding Food and Culture*, 2nd edn, New York: New York University Press.

Avieli, Nir (2016), 'The Hummus Wars Revisited: Israeli-Arab Food Politics and Gastromediation', *Gastronomica: The Journal of Critical Food Studies*, 16(3): 19–30.

Bassiouney, Reem (2009), *Arabic Sociolinguistics*, Edinburgh: Edinburgh University Press.

Bakhtin, Mikhail (1981), *The Dialogic Imagination*, Austin: University of Texas Press.

Beeman, William (1986), *Language, Status, and Power in Iran*, Bloomington, IN: Indiana University Press.

Blackburn, Kate G., Gamze Yilmaz and Ryan L. Boyd (2018), 'Food for Thought: Exploring How People Think and Talk about Food Online', *Appetite*, 123: 390–401.

Bourdieu, Pierre (1984), *Distinction. A Social Critique of the Judgment and Taste*, trans. Richard Nice, Cambridge: Harvard University Press.

Du Bois, John (2007), 'The Stance Triangle', in Robert Englebretson (ed), *Stancetaking in Discourse: Subjectivity, Evaluation, Interaction*, 139–182, Amsterdam: John Benjamins.

Duffy, Andrew and Yang Yuhong Ashley (2012), 'Bread and Circuses: Food Meets Politics in the Singapore Media', *Journalism Practice*, 6(1): 59–74.

Fellner, Astrid M. (2013), 'The Flavors of Multi-Ethnic North American Literatures: Language, Ethnicity and Culinary Nostalgia', in Cornelia Gerhardt, Maximiliane Frobenius and Susanne Ley (eds), *Culinary Linguistics: The Chef's Special*, 241–260, Amsterdam and Philadelphia: John Benjamins Publishing Company.

Ferguson, Priscilla Parkhurst (2006), *Accounting for Taste: The Triumph of French Cuisine*, Chicago and London: The University of Chicago Press.

Fitrisia, Dohra, Robert Sibarani and Mara Untung Ritonga (2018), 'Traditional Food in the Perspective of Culinary Linguistics', *International Journal of Multidisciplinary Research and Development*, 5(2): 24–27.

Flowers, Rick and Elaine Swan (2017), 'Seeing Benevolently: Representational Politics and Digital Race Formation on Ethnic Food Tour Webpages', *Geoforum*, 8(4): 206–217.

Fowler, Roger, Bob Hodge, Gunther Kress and Tont Trew (1979), *Language and Control*, London: Routledge & Kegan Paul.

Fried, Daniel, Mihai Surdeanu, Stephen Kobourov, Melanie Hingle and Dane Bell (2014), 'Analyzing the Language of Food on Social Media', *2014 IEEE International Conference on Big Data (Big Data)*. Available online: https://arxiv.org/pdf/1409.2195.pdf

Fuller, Janet M., Janelle Briggs and Laurel Dillon-Sumner (2013), 'Men Eat for Muscle, Women Eat for Weight Loss: Discourses about Food and Gender in Men's Health and Women's Health magazines', in Cornelia Gerhardt, Maximiliane Frobenius and Susanne Ley (eds), *Culinary Linguistics: The Chef's Special*, 261=N280, Amsterdam and Philadelphia: John Benjamins Publishing Company.

Gerhardt, Cornelia (2013), 'Food and Language–Language and Food', in Cornelia Gerhardt, Maximiliane Frobenius and Susanne Ley (eds), *Culinary Linguistics: The Chef's Special*, 3–49, Amsterdam and Philadelphia: John Benjamins Publishing Company.

Gerhardt, Cornelia, Maximiliane Frobenius and Susanne Ley, eds. (2013), *Culinary Linguistics: The Chef's Special*, Amsterdam and Philadelphia: John Benjamins Publishing Company.

Goffman, Erving (1981), *Forms of Talk*, Philadelphia: University of Pennsylvania Press.

Gordon, Cynthia (2019), '"You Might Want to Look up the Definition of 'Continental Breakfast'": Other-Initiated Repair and Community-Building in Health and Weight Loss Blogs', Special Issue, Najma Al Zidjaly (ed), *Multilingua*, 38(4): 401–426.

Herman, Edward S. and Noam Chomsky (1988), *Manufacturing Consent: The Political Economy of the Mass Media*, New York: Pantheon Books.

Hobbis, Ketterer (2017), '"The Comic and the Rule" in Pastagate: Food, Humor and the Politics of Language in Quebec', *Food, Culture & Society*, 20(4): 709–727.

Hofstede, Geert, Gert Jan Hofstede and Michael Minkov (1990), *Cultures and Organizations: Software of the Mind,* New York: McGraw-Hill.

Kádár, Dániel (2017a), *Politeness, Impoliteness and Ritual: Maintaining the Moral Order in Interpersonal Interaction,* Cambridge: Cambridge University Press.

Kádár, Dániel (2017b), 'Indirect Ritual Offence: A Study on Elusive Impoliteness', in Piotr Cap and Marta Dynel (eds), *Impoliteness: From Lexis to Discourse,* 177–199, Amsterdam: John Benjamins.

Katzman, Kenneth (2012), *Oman: Reform, Security, and U.S. Policy.* New York: Congressional Research Service, August 30. Available online: https://www.everycrsreport.com/files/20120830_RS21534_83256c59254d7e90d71d42623079327cc80a504a.pdf

Khaffaf, Suha, Suhair Safwat and Areej Al-Jawadi (2016), 'The Translation of The Implicit Organizational Meaning from English into Arabic in "Obama's 2015 State of the Union Address"', *International Journal of Humanities and Cultural Studies,* 3(2): 1919–1934.

Kinninmont, Jane (2019), 'The Gulf Divided: The Impact of the Qatar Crisis', *Middle East and North Africa Programme, Future Dynamics in the Gulf.* Available online: https://www.chathamhouse.org/publication/gulf-divided-impact-qatar-crisis

Lakoff, George and Mark Johnson (1980), 'The Metaphorical Structure of the Human Conceptual System', *Cognitive Science,* 4: 195–208.

Lakoff, Robin (1973), 'Language and Women's Place', *Language and Society,* 2: 45–79.

Lakoff, Robin (2006), 'Identity à la Carte: You Are What You Eat', in Anna De Fina, Deborah Schiffrin and Michael Bamberg (eds), *Discourse and Identity,* 142–165, New York: Cambridge University Press.

Lupton, Deborah (2018), 'Cooking, Eating, Uploading: Digital Food Cultures', in Kathleen LeBesco, and Peter Naccarato (eds), *The Bloomsbury Handbook of Food and Popular Culture,* 66–79, London and New York: Bloomsbury.

Nagi, Ahmed (2019), 'Oman's Boiling Yemeni Border', March 22. Available online: https://www.ispionline.it/it/pubblicazione/omans-boiling-yemeni-border-22588

Nydell, Margaret (2005), *Understanding Arabs: A Guide for Modern Times,* 4th edn, Boston: Intercultural Press.

Nishida, Kitarō (1958), *Intelligibility and the Philosophy of Nothingness,* Tokyo: Maruzen.

Poulain, Jean-Pierre (2017), *The Sociology of Food: Eating and the Place of Food in Society,* trans. Augusta Dörr, New York: Bloomsbury.

Saeed, Basma Mubarak (2014), 'Oman, Iranian Rapprochement and a GCC Union', Al Jazeera Center for Studies. Available online: http://studies.aljazeera.net/en/reports/2014/01/20141218365065800.html

Schegloff, Emanuel A. (2007), 'Categories in Action: Person Reference and Membership Categorization', *Discourse Studies,* 9: 433–461.

Scollon, Ron (2005), 'The Discourse of Food in the World System: Toward a Nexus Analysis of a World Problem', *Journal of Language and Politics,* 4(3): 465–488.

Sertbulut, Zeynep (2012), 'The Culinary State: On Politics of Representation and Identity in Israel', *Hagar: Studies in Culture, Polity & Identity*, 10(2): 49–76.

Stajcic, Nevana (2013), 'Understanding Culture: Food as a Means of Communication', *HEMISPHERES*, 28: 5–14.

Tannen, Deborah (1994), *Gender and Discourse,* New York: Oxford University Press.

Tannen, Deborah (2005), *Conversational Style: Analyzing talk among friends*, 2nd edn, Oxford: Oxford University Press.

Tovares, Alla (2019), 'Negotiating "Thick" Identities through "Light" Practices: YouTube Metalinguistic Comments about Language in Ukraine', *Multilingua*, 38(4): 459–484.

Upadhyay, Shiv R. (2010), 'Identity and Impoliteness in Computer-Mediated Reader Responses', *Journal of Politeness Research*, 6: 105–127.

Valeri, Marc (2017), 'So Close, So Far. National Identity and Political Legitimacy in UAE-Oman Border Cities', *Geopolitics,* 23(3): 587–607.

van Dijk, Teun A. (1997), *Discourse as Structure and Process*, London: Sage Publications.

Wilce, James M. (2005), 'Traditional Laments and Postmodern Regrets: The Circulation of Discourse in Metacultural Context', *Journal of Linguistic Anthropology,* 15(1): 60–71.

Wright, Wynne and Alexis Annes (2013), 'Halal on the Menu?: Contested Food Politics and French Identity in Fast-Food', *Journal of Rural Studies*, 32: 388–399.

York, Elizabeth and Christopher Brewster (2013), 'The Representation of Food in the Social Media Forum Twitter', Paper presented at the Efita-WCCA-CIGR Conference "Sustainable Agriculture through ICT Innovation", Turin, Italy. Available online: https://www.academia.edu/6351005/The_representation_of_Food_in_Social_Media_Forum_Twitter

Parmesan and Patriotism on YouTube: Food as Ideology in Today's Russia

Alla Tovares

1 Introduction

Food and communication about food are linked to global and local politics and often serve as a reflection of the relationships between people and countries. Depending on the circumstances, the same foods can be up or down on the sociopolitical scale, creating the sentiments of commonality or difference (Ferguson 2006). For instance, French cuisine was perceived and valued as "an exemplar for revolutionary action" in the nineteenth century but became a symbol of non-action and a target of anti-French sentiments at the onset of the U.S. war in Iraq (2003), hence the political euphemism "Freedom fries" instead of the familiar "French fries" (Ferguson 2006: 81–82). Perianova (2018: 12) describes a more recent example, and one that is even more closely related to the context of this study: There was a time (2014) when eating an apple in Poland was "perceived as a sign of protest against Russian sanctions proscribing the imports of EU [European Union] products, including Polish apples, to Russia." Therefore, as a material object and discursive resource, food can be used to index both local identities and beliefs and larger – global – sociopolitical issues. The interconnected nature of the local and global has been heightened and accelerated by the processes of globalization and development of new digital media. Social media in particular have created spaces where global issues play out in local contexts and local topics are discussed in global forums. In this regard, communication about food on social media platforms offers a window into how participants use linguistic strategies to index identities and ideologies that highlight food but also transcend it.

In this chapter, I explore the intersection of digital discourse, food, politics and ideology by focusing on how Russia's ban on imported Western foods is discussed on social media. Specifically, I analyze written comments posted in reaction to two YouTube videos to demonstrate how through lexical choices and the construction of evaluative stances, gastronomy, or the practice and knowledge of eating (good) food, is constructed as an ideology against the backdrop of the Russian/Ukrainian geopolitical conflict and the ensuing food sanctions. Both videos and their comments focus on Parmesan, an ideologically loaded food item with a long history in Russia; one video is satirical and the other belongs to the documentary genre. As an interactive platform that allows its users to create, post, and comment on videos, YouTube is a relatively new context and a productive site for investigating the ideological construction and contestation of food and taste, and, by extension, of sociopolitical conflicts.

In my analysis of written YouTube comments, I mobilize the notion of stance (Ochs 1996; Du Bois 2007) and I draw on Bourdieu's (1984) conceptualization of taste, more specifically his distinction between the *taste of necessity* and the *taste of luxury/liberty*; his notion of capital is also considered (Bourdieu 1986). I additionally rely on Bakhtin's (1975, 1981, 1986) theorizing on dialogicality, especially his notions of polyvocality, heteroglossia, and addressivity, to explore the role of previous discourse in shaping online contributions, in particular how discussion of the current food situation in Russia invokes voices of the past. Finally, I also build on insights from prior studies that explore food, politics, and ideology in the Russian context (Glants & Toomre 1997; von Bremzen 2013; Wengle 2016) to demonstrate how by using food as a discursive resource, YouTube commenters engage in promoting and challenging existing policies and ideologies in and about Russia that go beyond taste and gastronomy.

I begin by discussing prior studies that address food, politics, and society. Then, to situate this study and make some analytically important intertextual references and linkages salient, I offer a brief survey of food in Russia. Next, I connect Bakhtin's work with research on stance. After introducing the data and methodology, I analyze representative examples of YouTube comments to demonstrate how communication about food, Parmesan in particular, constructs different ideological alignments to Russia and different identities for Russians. My analysis also points to a complex heteroglossic sociopolitical situation in Russia in which its citizens are torn between the state-sanctioned and widely promoted patriotism, nationalism, and traditionalism on the one hand and their diminishing livelihoods and shrinking freedoms, including their freedom as consumers, on the other. This chapter also demonstrates that YouTube, as a type of interactive digital media, serves as productive site for investigating the (re)construction of identities and ideologies in food-related communication.

2 Background

2.1 Food, politics, and society

Chef and writer Anthony Bourdain (2017) poignantly observed that nothing is "more political than food" and added that when asked about what they like to eat, people "will tell you extraordinary things, many of which have nothing to do with food." In other words, talking about food is talking about politics. Similarly, DeSoucey (2016: xiii), building on Appadurai (1981), observes that gastropolitics not only pervades social trends, discourses, and institutions, but it is also a part of everyday life where food consumption, and I would add food-related communication, "can quite literally create bonds or erect barriers between people."

Food, as a lens for investigating sociopolitical issues, has attracted a number of researchers, most prominently Pierre Bourdieu (1984) who studied taste and class in modern France. Bourdieu (1984: 6) suggests that taste serves as a marker of class and that judgments of taste are acts of social positioning through which social subjects "distinguish themselves by the distinctions they make." Such distinctions are located along the dichotomy of the *taste of necessity* and the *taste of luxury/liberty*. While the *taste of necessity* stems from adjusting to deprivation and thus values the "most 'filling' and most economical foods" (Bourdieu 1984: 6, 177), the *taste of luxury/liberty* presupposes freedom of choice and places emphasis on the quality of food and the aesthetics of its presentation and consumption. Related, in a study situated in the U.S., Lakoff (2006: 165) observes that daily activities make and change people's identities, including what she terms "minor identities" such as "culinary preferences and sophistication," and suggests that how people construct their discourse about and around food creates distinctions between sophisticated "foodies" on the one end of the continuum and someone who might be labeled as "a bit of an oaf," or unsophisticated, on the other.

Because food is filled with both material and symbolic value, it can be also viewed through Bourdieu's (1986) notion of capital. Capital, Bourdieu theorizes, operates within social contexts, or fields, in which every human action is a part of a struggle for resources, power, and privilege. Two forms of capital, economic and cultural, are especially relevant to the discussion of food and taste. While not mutually exclusive and typically indicating privileged positions in society, economic capital is linked to purchasing power, and cultural capital indexes one's command of cultural knowledge, including of food. Thus, everyday actions of buying, preparing, consuming, and communicating about food (the focus of this study) construct and contest identities and ideologies as well as index one's economic and/or cultural capital. The next section traces the trajectory of food in Russia and its socio-political underpinnings.

2.2 Food is Russia: From necessity to luxury and back

Some early accounts (e.g., Fletcher [1591] 1966) describe the Russian diet as abundant but plain, consisting of meat, roots, onions, garlic, and cabbage. However, like many countries in Europe, in the nineteenth and early twentieth century Russia experienced a rapid development of gastronomy, which was described, and romanticized, in several memoirs, most notably by Gilyarovsky (1926). Gilyarovsky vividly depicts the 1901 opening of Moscow's famous *Yeliseyevsky* gourmet grocery store, which was reportedly dubbed by Muscovites as the "Temple of Gluttony." In his description, the author includes a then popular anonymous poem that lists various mouth-watering items found in the store:

> Countless people are attracted by a dazzling
> Display of sausages, pastries, and delicacies,
> Rows of ham, smoked and boiled,
> Turkey, stuffed geese,
> Sausages with garlic, pistachios and pepper,
> Cheeses of all ages – and Chester, and Swiss
> And gooey Brie, and granite-like Parmesan.
>
> Gilyarovsky 1926: 346, my translation

The poem's mentioning of "granite-like Parmesan" (in the last line) indicates that this Italian cheese, *Parmigiano Reggiano®* (protected designation of origin), along with other Western cheeses (Cheddar, Swiss, Brie), was viewed as a refined food. Noteworthy, during the deprived Soviet times, Gilyarovsky's sumptuous accounts became "food porn" devoured by readers, their stomachs growling (von Bremzen 2013: 19), their minds imagining the never-before-seen luxury foods. The opening of the *Yeliseyevsky* store was an important step in popularization and, to a degree, democratization of gourmet food and taste in Russia. In contrast to the hidden gastronomic indulgences of the Russian nobility who enjoyed fanciful feasts in the privacy of their residences (Selivanova 1933), the store offered access, albeit only voyeuristic to most, to an array of exotic and exquisite (often imported) foods, or what Bourdieu (1984) identifies as the *taste of luxury*.

While many citizens of pre-revolutionary Russia could not afford gourmet foods, the revolution of 1917 and the ensuing Soviet regime did not improve their access to quality foodstuffs. Instead, the centralized economy (with its uneven, politically laden distribution of goods), inept agricultural policies, bad crops, civil war and the Second World War brought famine and food rations (Medvedev 1988; Lih 1990; Osokina 2015). For most Russians, Soviet times were the years of food shortages, empty store shelves, and long lines (Glants & Toomre 1997; Borrero 2003). In the 1990s, during Russia's transition from a centralized to a market economy, the lack of food supplies even led to the reinstatement of food rations (officially abolished in 1947) that included such staples as butter, meat, sausage, and grains. In sum, most people in Soviet Russia (1917–1991) and in the early post-Soviet period (1991–1999) had (often limited) access only to basic foods, the *taste of necessity*.

The start of the twenty-first century brought a drastic change to food in Russia – its quality, availability, and consumption (Bruschi et al. 2015). A market economy, high oil prices, and strong currency resulted in fully stocked stores, an abundance of imported foodstuffs, and a proliferation of Western and local restaurants. Seemingly overnight many Russians gained access to the *taste of luxury*: "yesterday we were [...] thinking Levis and powdered milk were the height of luxury, and now we're surrounded by luxury cars and jets and sticky Prosecco" (Pomerantsev 2014: 19). While not everyone in Russia became rich, quality foods, including imported items such as Italian Parmesan, Spanish *jamon*, and Norwegian salmon, became an affordable luxury for many.

Russia's food situation was altered again in 2014 when the West introduced sanctions against Russia for its annexation of Crimea, a Ukrainian territory. In a retaliatory move, Russia banned the import of Western goods, including foodstuffs. Sanctioned foods became "contraband" and were publicly destroyed: Tons of imported products, including cheeses, were either incinerated or bulldozed into the ground (Kramer 2015). As part of its larger security initiatives,[1] Russia introduced "*importozameshchenie*" (import substitution), a program aimed at the replacement of Western imports, including foods, with Russian products (Zinchuk et al. 2017). After being reelected to a third term (in 2012), Russian President Putin "brought a renewed emphasis on Russian nationalism" and made food security (privileging production and consumption of domestic food) and nationalism (infusing food with moral qualities) mutually reinforcing (Wegren, Nikulin & Trotsuk 2018: vii).

While Soviet citizens lusted after inaccessible luxury foods, such as Parmesan, at the turn of the twenty-first century, Russians became accustomed to seeing imported foods in their local supermarkets. The embargo made Russians aware that their food preferences included imported goods. The post-embargo posts on popular social media platforms (*Instagram, Facebook,* and *YouTube*), mostly as satirical and humorous memes, have indicated that Russians simultaneously miss and mock Western delicacies. For instance, a widely circulated meme of a mock food ration card includes *jamon, foie gras*, smoked salmon, Parmesan and other Western delicacies (see Appendix 1). Through interdiscursive and intertextual linkages to actual food ration cards of the past, this meme – in a joking key or tone – indirectly points to, and criticizes, the fact that Western foods have become the "taste of necessity" to some, if not many, Russians.

Not only is the taste of imported food being missed, but also its quality.[2] Some studies (e.g., Wegren, Nikulin & Trotsuk 2018: 33) report "a significant problem with 'counterfeit' food in Russia, which refers to food products that have additives that should not be there." In fact, it was revealed that because dairy, an imported commodity from the West, has become prohibitive, cheap East Asian palm oil has turned into an easy substitute, and, as a result, "over two thirds of Russian cheese contains palm oil" (Wengle 2016: 285). In contrast to treating domestic food with suspicion, Russians tend to trust the quality of foreign, especially Western, food imports (Bruschi et al. 2015). All this underscores that food in Russia – its availability, consumption, and perception – has always been intertwined with politics, and communication about food is bound to have political and ideological overtones.

2.3 Dialogicality and taking up stances

Bakhtin (1975, 1981, 1986) understands human interaction as fundamentally dialogic: People react to and anticipate the words of others, and all words carry echoes from prior usages. Moreover, dialogic engagements bring together different voices and diverse points of view, the phenomena he describes as polyphony and heteroglossia. Bakhtin (1986: 95) also puts forth the notion of addressivity to indicate that every utterance is "directed to someone" and points out that an addressee could be any entity, from "an immediate participant-interlocutor" to "unconcretized other" and may include like-minded people and opponents, subordinates and superiors and so on. He goes on to suggest that each speech genre "has its own typical conception of the addressee, and that defines it as a genre" (Bakhtin 1986: 95). This (inter)relationship between the addressee and the (speech) genre is particularly relevant for this study as the two YouTube videos selected for analysis are of different genres (a satirical performance and a documentary) and produce different reactions by their respective addressees, the commenters.

Bakhtin understands language not as an abstract system of rules but rather as a heteroglossic view of the world, and indicates that "[a]ll words give off the scent of a profession, a genre, a direction, a party, a particular work, a particular person, a generation, age, a day and an hour" (1975: 106, my translation; see also Todorov 1988: 56).[3] Thus, words are not neutral but are socially saturated and reveal – intentionally or not – the ideological views of the speakers (or writers) and contribute to constructing and displaying their self-images and those of others. This is also true of food-related communication. Certain foods, and mentions of them, become associated with certain voices and certain categories of people. For instance, eating "beige," bland foods indexes child and child-like identities (Gordon & İkizoğlu 2017) and is also often linked to "picky eaters" (see İkizoğlu & Gordon this volume).

The question of how identities are indexed through the use of language lies at the heart of prior studies of stance (especially Ochs 1990, 1996; Du Bois 2007). In their theorizing of stance, both researchers foreground its socio-cultural dimensions, and in this way their work is linked to that of Bakhtin. Ochs (1990: 2) defines stance as "a socially recognizable disposition" and differentiates between epistemic stance ("socially recognized way of knowing") and affective stance ("socially recognized feeling, attitude, mood, or degree of emotional intensity"). Du Bois (2007: 163), in his three-part model (the stance triangle), defines stance as "a public act by a social actor, achieved dialogically through overt communicative means, of simultaneously evaluating objects, positioning subjects (self and others), and aligning with other subjects, with respect to any salient dimension of the sociocultural field." In this chapter, stance is deployed as both a theoretical concept and an analytical tool to investigate how, in communication about YouTube videos that center on food, commenters index their sociopolitical ideologies and identities.

2.4 YouTube as a public forum for negotiating identities and ideologies

As other chapters in this volume demonstrate, communication about food often occurs online. Rousseau (2012: 36) observes that we live in an information-saturated "post-idea world" and tend to "prefer knowing to thinking because knowing has more immediate value." While it might be the case that we are information-driven – and often don't digest the information properly – the comment function of new media, its interactive capability (Herring 2013), offers a space for the exchange of ideas, or thinking, and YouTube is one platform that facilitates these kinds of exchanges. Because its users create, share, and engage with both video content and one another via comments, YouTube has been dubbed as *a site of participatory culture* (Burgess & Green 2009) and a *participatory spectacle* (Androutsopoulos 2013). Herring (2013: 13) points out that YouTube comments tend to be "prompt focused"; that is, they are posted in reaction to an initial video prompt and (less frequently) to the comments in the same thread. Jones and Schieffelin (2009: 1062) observe that while YouTube comments may not be as influential as mass media, they are fairly democratic spaces where users engage with the topic of the video and other users. These and other scholars (e.g., Chun & Walters 2011; Hachimi 2013; Tovares 2019a) suggest that YouTube comments offer researchers a window into how users tackle larger sociopolitical issues online. Building on, and advancing, prior work on YouTube as a type of interactive media, my analysis demonstrates that YouTube comments offer a productive site to investigate how ideologies of food and taste are dialogically constructed and contested online.

3 Data and methods

As noted above, this study centers on written comments that follow YouTube videos about food in post-sanctions Russia. Before selecting the data samples for analysis, I conducted a three-month (August-October 2016) netnography (Nissenbaum & Shifman 2015) of YouTube and other popular social media platforms – primarily *Instagram, Facebook,* and *Odnoklassniki* (*Classmates*) – to gain a better understanding of the circulating discourses about food in Russia. My observations point to the heteroglossic nature of such discourses: from patriotic stances offering support for Russia's food independence and promoting "*importozameshchenie*" (import substitution) to missing Western imports and treating the quality of all domestic products with suspicion. In the context of Russia's embargo and import substitution, Western foods – cheeses especially – gained symbolic value. One cheese that has become a collective symbol of the *taste of luxury* and is inevitably mentioned in connection with sanctions in various media is Parmesan.

For this work, I selected two YouTube videos about Parmesan that are of two different genres and represent contrasting views on the post-sanctions food situation in Russia. One, titled "Belarusian Parmesan" (*uploaded on March 27,*

2016; https://www.youtube.com/watch?v=3qHeRkgJkCw), is a video-recording of a live performance of well-known Russian actor Mikhail Yefremov in which he recites a satirically reworded popular Soviet song. The song's title ("Belarusian Parmesan") references the open secret that Belarus, an ally of Russia that shares borders with Russia and the West, has become a space for "re-exporting," or smuggling, banned Western food to Russia.[4] The original song, titled "There, far away, across the river," is set during the post-revolutionary civil war (1918–1922) and depicts the death of a young Red (Soviet) Army soldier whose squad was ambushed by counter-revolution forces. The contemporary satirical version, written by Russian poet Andrei "Orlusha" Orlov, known for his critical stance toward Putin's regime, portrays Parmesan, *jamon*, mozzarella and other Western foods as a squad of "partisans" (resistance fighters) trying to reach Russia via Belarus only to be captured and burned (or secretly eaten) by a Russian "food patrol." In the song, before his "death," Parmesan wished that it were given to, and eaten by, old Russian people (pensioners) or homeless people; instead, Parmesan was first partially eaten by the food patrol and then incinerated following the orders of those in power. It is worth noting that like "Orlusha," Mikhail Yefremov – whose father (Oleg Yefremov) was also a famous Russian (Soviet) actor – is a vocal critic of Putin and his politics. The genre of the video can be classified as a satirical political commentary.

In the other video (*uploaded on October 22, 2015; https://www.youtube.com/watch?v=2Iwk7wQ3kQk)*,[5] an actual Russian cheesemaker, Oleg Sirota, welcomes sanctions as an incentive to develop the Russian food industry and promotes various cheeses, including "Russian Parmesan," that he makes in his creamery also named "Russian Parmesan." The genre is different, as it is a more documentary-style presentation of a person's work. In contrast to the actor, the cheesemaker is an enthusiastic supporter of Putin's political agenda:[6] In several media appearances and interviews, Sirota has indicated that he became a firm supporter of Putin after Russia's 2014 annexation of Crimea (a Ukrainian territory) when the Russian government started helping Russian farmers to (re) build the national food industry in order to counter the effects of the embargo on Western foods. The cheesemaker even invited Putin to the grand opening of his creamery (the President did not attend). Furthermore, Sirota's creamery – in full support of Russia's aggressive policies toward Ukraine – displayed the flag of Novorossiya (New Russia), an unrecognized self-proclaimed pro-Russian confederation of several regions in Eastern Ukraine, the territory of an active geopolitical conflict where the separatist movement is allegedly supported by Russia's armed forces (https://www.youtube.com/watch?v=xnU3Uc2yg3s).

Thus, the actor and the cheesemaker are known for and associated with divergent stances toward Putin and his politics and policies.

As of July 2017, when the data were collected, "Belarusian Parmesan" had over 330,670 views, 642 comments; "Russian Parmesan" amassed 43,650 views, 133 comments. For this analysis, having uploaded all user comments (newest first), I first identified recurrent themes and grouped these in several larger categories. Both sets of comments cluster around two topics: 1) the identities of the key figures (the actor and the cheesemaker) signaled through the choice of referring terms and 2) food. For the qualitative analysis of the comments about food, I have selected nine representative excerpts in which the commenters disagree with the main themes of the videos. In this way, I was able to capture a range of stances that the commenters take up toward the ban of Western food (the *taste of luxury*) and the return to the *taste of necessity* in Russia.

4 Analysis

In this section, I first analyze the written comments that appear below the "Belarusian Parmesan" video and then turn my attention to the posts in reaction to "Belarusian Parmesan." I begin by showing how, through lexical choices in reference to the actor, the commenters index the heteroglossic views of what it means to be a "true" citizen in Putin's Russia. I then consider several examples in which the commenters, in reaction to the actor's satire, downplay the food situation in Russia and equate patriotism with the *taste of necessity*. The second analytical subsection centers on how the cheesemaker's identity is indexed in the comments, which simultaneously praise his patriotism and question his motives and skills. This is followed by an analysis of the excerpts that shows how, by taking evaluative stances toward Russian and Western cheeses, Parmesan in particular, the commenters – indirectly and perhaps inadvertently – criticize Putin's politics that deprive them of the *taste of luxury/freedom* for the sake of nationalism and patriotism. The analysis shows that in reaction to both videos the commenters dialogically engage with prior discourses regarding the *taste of luxury* and the *taste of necessity* and how they are interconnected with Russian identities over time.

4.1 "Belarusian Parmesan": Patriotism and the taste of necessity

The analysis shows that the comments on the "Belarusian Parmesan" video are polarizing, of a discourse-counterdiscourse nature, in which pro- and anti-Putin views clash, both referencing Russian-Ukrainian geopolitical conflict and concomitant Western sanctions, but to different ends. Many comments focus on the personality of the actor featured in the video (who is known for his anti-Putin sentiments): He is alternatively portrayed as either a traitor or a true citizen of Russia who goes against Putin's authoritarian rule. Table 9.1 demonstrates the conflicting evaluative stances taken by the commenters toward the actor (here and throughout the paper, all translations of the data are mine).

While Table 9.1 shows both discourse and counterdiscourse, it is worth noting that overall there are more negative than positive comments about the actor whom the commenters try to discredit by attacking his personality. In their negative stances, made prominent by triple exclamation points, the commenters position the actor as a "sell out" to the West because of his satirizing of Russia's ban on Western food. Such stances also echo prior discourse in Russia, specifically its Soviet period when Western values – even food and clothes – were viewed as divergent from and incompatible with communist ideals.

Table 9.1 YouTube comments about the actor that construct polarization

Comments displaying negative stances	Comments displaying positive stances
• Предатель *a traitor*	• настоящий гражданин России *a true citizen of Russia*
• Деградант *a degraded person*	•Бесподобно … умница …)))[7] *Wonderful … a smart person …)))*
• бездарность и обыкновенная пьянь *mediocrity and an ordinary drunkard*	• респектуха тебе мужик! *respect to you, man!*
• убог и жалок *wretched and miserable*	• Молодец Михаил *Attaboy Mikhail*
• теперь он чмошный клоун *he is now a freakish clown*	• талантище *huge talent*
• продался как последняя БЛЯДЬ!!! *sold out like a cheap WHORE!!!*	• Браво Михаилу! Не посрамил память своего гениального отца, в наше время соединить в одном лице блистательного актера, гражданина и человека с большой буквы, ой как непросто! *Bravo to Mikhail! He is worthy of the memory of his brilliant father, in these times to combine in one person a brilliant actor, a citizen and a man with a capital letter is oh so difficult!*
• таких уродов гнать надо. Алкоголь засушил ему мозг!!! *such freaks must be driven away. Alcohol has drained his brain!!!*	
• американский холуй и пропагандист, … купленная шкура … *An American buffoon and propagandist, … a sell-out …*	

In the comments, the food situation in Russia is also discussed, with a focus on the ban on Western imports. Similar to the comments about the actor, those about food are polarizing: Some criticize Putin for depriving Russians of the *taste of luxury* and destroying "banned" Western foods while others (and such are the majority) align in their support of the Russian President's "standing up to the West" even if this means going back to the *taste of necessity*. As the following excerpts show, to deflate the actor's satire, the commenters tend to "deproblematize" (Kazun 2016) the Russian food situation by downplaying its seriousness. To do so, some draw attention to the problems in other countries, Ukraine especially, as Excerpt 1 demonstrates.

Excerpt 1
Если производство украины добито евросоюзом и сельское хозяйство пришло в упадок ... то в рф подьем сельского х. 70% + и в 2015 с первого места по экспорту зерна отодвинули сша.

While Ukrainian production was killed by the European Union and its agriculture fell into disrepair ... in the RF [Russian Federation] the increase in agricultural production went up by 70% + and in 2015 it outperformed the USA and took first place in grain production.

To deproblematize the food situation in post-sanctioned Russia, the commenter whose discourse is shown in Excerpt 1 creates a contrast by drawing attention to the downfall of Ukrainian agriculture while highlighting the success of Russia's agribusiness. At the same time, as Labov (2001) suggests in the context of narrative analysis, it is important to pay attention not only to what is mentioned but also, and even more so, to what is omitted. In this regard, the commenter selectively omits the fact that while the production of some foodstuffs (e.g., grain) in Russia has increased, the production of others, such as milk and dairy products, has fallen behind (as documented by Wengle 2016; Zinchuk et al. 2017). Moreover, it is worth pointing out that it was cheese (as well as other Western delicacies such as *jamon*) and not grain that was the key topic of the satirical portrayal. Thus, by shifting the topic of the discussion to focus on Russia's success and omitting its shortcomings in food production and portraying the European Union with its food imports as "a killer" of Ukrainian agriculture, the commenter constructs the Russian embargo on Western food as a positive step in developing Russian food production.

Another commenter dismisses the embargo problem altogether by arguing that because Italians started producing their (Italian) cheeses in Russia, their products are considered local and thus are not sanctioned, as shown in Excerpt 2.

In this way, the commenter – by taking up an affective stance to express his/her happiness that the ban on Western cheese has been resolved so easily – also displays an anti-elitist stance (for a discussion of elite discourse, see Mapes this volume) by challenging the view that Italian cheese, the *taste of luxury*, can be made only in a few specific areas in Italy.

Excerpt 2
Теперь данные сыры делают в России итальянцами, кои сообразили как выйти из положения. А это радует. А вы сами то хамон кушаете каждый день? Мне лично не нравится эта ветчина совсем.

Now these cheeses are made in Russia by Italians who have figured out how to resolve the situation. And this makes me happy. And you, do you yourself eat jamon every day? I personally do not like this ham at all.

By posing a rhetorical question (*And you, do you yourself eat jamon every day?*) and pointing out a personal dislike of *jamon* and calling it "ham" (using a common, not gourmet, word) the commenter in Excerpt 2 indirectly states that not all of the sanctioned food is missed, and it is not missed by all. In so doing, the commenter, through anti-elitist stances, deproblematizes the food embargo situation even further and creates alignments with others who do not miss, or even like, Western foods.

While commenters in Excerpts 1 and 2 – by highlighting Russia's agricultural success and minimizing or ignoring the negative effect of the embargo on the food choices of Russians – show their alignments with Putin's policies indirectly, a number of commenters displayed overt pro-Putin stances. In such comments, the ideology of national pride is placed above one's taste or even one's need of food as shown in Excerpt 3.

Excerpt 3
сам пенсионер, но эту парашу жрать не буду … лучше с голоду с дохнуть чем унижаться […] я за Путина, правильно делает!!!

I am a pensioner myself, but I will not eat this shit … it is better to starve to death than to degrade oneself […] I am for Putin, he is doing it right!!!

By stating that even though he is a pensioner himself he would not eat Western food, the commenter dialogically engages with the text of "Belarusian Parmesan" that criticizes destroying banned foods instead of distributing them to the needy, such as elderly people who have notoriously meager pensions. By proclaiming that he'd rather "starve to death" than "degrade" himself, the commenter takes up a defiant stance and in so doing aligns with the discourses circulating in Russia of patriotism, national pride, and the importance of Russia to stand up to the West (discourses also dialogically linked to the Soviet period). All of these are inextricably connected to Putin and his leadership (White 2017; Wegren, Nikulin & Trotsuk 2018).

In a number of comments, Putin – presented as independent and strong – is contrasted with the Ukrainian president (then Petro Poroshenko) who is portrayed as a Western puppet. In her study of Russian politics and ideology, Chebankova (2017: 81) observes that the "concept of state sovereignty [...], or political development free from external influence, has become the principle unifying factor in Russia," and many Russians subscribe to this patriotic trajectory, even if it requires tightening their belts. Therefore, it is not surprising that some commenters equate the abundance of (Western) foodstuffs with selling out and being unpatriotic, as Excerpt 4 demonstrates.

Excerpt 4
Просто для либерастов и хохлов колбаса в изобилии дороже родины.

Simply put, for liberasts [a derogatory term, a blend of "liberals" and "child molesters"] and khokhols [a derogatory term for Ukrainians] the abundance of sausage is valued more than the motherland.

Here, the derogatory terms for liberals and Ukrainians "give off the scent" (Bakhtin 1975) of the rapidly growing state-promoted ideology of conservatism and nationalism in Russia. Specifically, by taking a critical stance, the commenter indexes the higher moral standing of Russians as compared to the "sell-out" Ukrainians and brings into sharp relief the contrast between patriotic and traditional Russians (who reject the *taste of luxury* for the sake of the nation) and the liberals, who in Russia are often linked to the "immoral" Western lifestyle.

Many comments, similar to Excerpts 3 and 4, are vitriolic and deploy offensive language. This phenomenon can be explained through the lens of Bakhtin's (1986) addressivity: The satirical genre of video was perceived as criticism directed at pro-Putin Russians and an external attack on Russia's public image (the performance was in Ukraine by a political outsider known for his anti-Putin rhetoric). This also supports and builds on Herring's (2013) finding that as video-prompted discursive phenomena, YouTube comments are influenced – in their content and key – by the "prompt." In response to the biting satire of "Belarusian Parmesan," many commenters "closed ranks" and engaged in saving a collective face (Ting-Toomey 2004; Al Zidjaly 2012) by constructing stances in favor of Russia and Putin, even if this meant a return to the *taste of necessity*. In so doing, they aligned with the official discourse of the Kremlin and took a symbolic "if you are not with us, you are against us" stance in which Russian independence, nationalism, and traditionalism need to be defended against the West and pro-Western liberals. In this context, Western food – as a material and symbolic representation of Western lifestyle and values – is not only banned by the government but also voluntarily rejected by Putin's supporters.

4.2 "Russian Parmesan": A poor substitute for the taste of luxury

In contrast to the adversarial posts below the "Belarusian Parmesan" video, the comments about "Russian Parmesan" are offered in a friendly key. The Russian cheesemaker featured in the video is, for the most part, portrayed positively, and the relatively small number of negative comments are not as damning as those directed at the Russian actor (see Table 9.2).

Table 9.2 YouTube comments about the cheesemaker that construct non-confrontation

Comments displaying positive stances	Comments displaying negative stances
• образец настоящего русского мужика. *an example of a real Russian guy*	• клоун *clown*
• мужественный молодой человек *a high-spirited young man*	• пропагандист *propagandist*
• Молодец. Успехов тебе! *Attaboy. Good luck to you!*	• балабол *Bullshitter*
• горжусь такими гражданами России *I am proud of such citizens of Russia*	• Бородатый идиот! *Bearded idiot*
• Человек дела! Побольше бы таких в России! *Man of business! Russia needs more people like this!*	• дебил *moron*
• подерживаю этого парня! ... побольше таких добряков *I support this guy! ... we need more good-natured people like this*	• трепло *blabber*
• такими гордиться надо, таких мало в нашей стране и слава Богу они есть. *we should be proud of such people, there are few of them in our country and thank God we have them.*	

In contrast to the depiction of the actor as either a patriot or traitor, the cheesemaker is overwhelmingly portrayed as a patriotic person who has answered the call of his country and stepped up to solve the problems with food in Russia, both immediate (the lack of Parmesan) and long-term (Russia's dependence on food imports). At the same time, some of the commenters are also skeptical about the cheesemaker's ability to produce quality cheese and/or portray him as an opportunist who is using the sanctions for personal gain.

While in reaction to "Belarusian Parmesan" the commenters' political stances were clearly marked (either pro- or anti-Putin), the comments about "Russian Parmesan" are not confrontational or polarizing. Namely, most commenters praise the cheesemaker's efforts (as we can see in Table 9.2, left column); many also criticize high prices and the poor quality of Russian cheeses. Many of the comments follow a "yes but" format; namely, they first compliment the cheesemaker and his efforts to make high-quality cheeses in Russia, but then counter with a problem as shown in Excerpt 5.

Excerpt 5
Молодец! Только бабушке с пенсией в 6 тыс не купить его сыр. Простым мужикам с ЗП в 20 тыс – тоже не купить. А таких в России большинство.

Attaboy! But a grandma with a 6 thousand [rubles] pension cannot buy his cheese. Ordinary guys with a 20 thousand [rubles] salary cannot either. And such are the majority in Russia.

This commenter, after taking up a positive affective stance toward the cheesemaker, expresses frustration with his cheese being out of reach for many fixed- or low-income Russians. Several studies have found that after sanctions, Russian "consumers have purchased less meat and dairy in terms of weight, but they have paid more in ruble terms" (Wengle 2016: 285) because the embargo on Western food was compounded by inflation and reduction of discretionary income, and, as a result, "economic access to food worsened for the majority of the public" (Shagaida & Uzun 2017: 212). In sum, Russian people were (and are) buying less but paying more for their food. Thus, the commenter, while appreciating the efforts and enthusiasm of the cheesemaker, does not view "Russian Parmesan" as a solution to a larger problem: High food (dairy particularly) prices in Russia, and a "yes but" construction captures this ambivalence. Another commenter (Excerpt 6 below) uses markers of temporality (see Vásquez 2015 for a discussion of temporality online) to create a contrast between *before* (before sanctions) and *now* (after sanctions) and in so doing highlights the difference not only in price but also in cheese quality.

Excerpt 6
"импортозамещение" говорите? Скажем так, раньше европейский пармезан продавался по 600, а сейчас [...] вонючий российский по 1200-1500!!!

you say "import substitution"? Let's say before European parmesan used to be sold for 600, and now [...] foul Russian cheese costs 1200–1500!!!

Here, the commenter also questions the "substitution" part of the import substitution program by comparing banned European (of proven high quality, see Bruschi et al. 2015) Parmesan with "foul" (not a reference to the famous "stinky" cheeses, but to poor quality) Russian cheese. The three exclamation points at the end – which we have seen in a number of posts, especially those creating negative stances – further emphasize the commenter's negative stance. As it can be gleaned from this post, if "substitution" presupposes offering a replacement of equal quality and price, the more expensive and of poorer quality Russian cheese is anything but.

As noted earlier, many in Russia are concerned with food safety; therefore, it is not surprising that several commenters pointed out that they noticed a fly in the video of the cheese being made. Others were unhappy that in the video neither the cheesemaker nor his workers were wearing gloves. In making such observations, the commenters align in their negative stances by intertextually referring to and dialogically engaging with the discourses of suspicion of the quality of Russian food "substitutes." Yet, even more commenters zeroed in on the taste and aligned together in their shared mourning of the loss of high-quality scrumptious *real* Parmesan as the following excerpts, Excerpts 7 and 8, demonstrate.

Excerpt 7
вот сколько я не покупала "пармезан" и уругвайский, и эстонский, и русский ну нифига не то))итальяшки какой то секретный ингредиент добавляют ,поэтому настоящий пармезано реджано или грани подано такой вкусный,что не передать словами,и ни с чем его не сравнить!!!!

no matter how many times I bought Uruguayan, Estonian, and Russian "parmesan", no way, not the same)) Italians add some secret ingredient that's why real Parmigiano-Reggiano or Grana Padano is so indescribably tasty, it cannot be compared it with anything!!!!

While complaining about other cheeses not measuring up to the real Parmesan, the commenter not only indexes her economic capital (she is able to buy various types of cheese), but also her cultural capital (her familiarity with the *taste of luxury*) by using Italian "technical terms" for Parmesan (Parmigiano-Reggiano®) and comparable Italian cheese (Grana Padano). In referring to the Italian cheese as *real*, the commenter displays the negative stance toward "parmesan" (used in air quotes to index its inauthenticity) made elsewhere. Another poster, in Excerpt 8, also expresses skepticism about making *real* Parmesan in Russia and in so doing dialogically engages with the cheesemaker who in the video describes sanctions as a fortuitous opportunity to start making "Russian Parmesan" at his creamery.

Excerpt 8
Повеселило: если б не санкции ... ну тут скорее правда, – конкуренцию настоящих сыроваров он хрен выдежит ну и главное – не возможно в рф изготовить настоящий пармезан. это будет не пармезан, а простой почти твердый сыр.

I was amused: thanks to the sanctions ... well this is probably true, – no shit he'll withstand the competition and what is more important – it is impossible to make in RF [Russian Federation] real parmesan. It won't be parmesan, but some ordinary almost-hard cheese.

The focus on *real* Parmesan in Examples 7 and 8, the *taste of luxury*, allows the commenters to simultaneously index their identities as sophisticated people with refined tastes, or their cultural capital (Bourdieu 1986; see also Lakoff 2006), and indirectly criticize the situation in Russia where they have to be satisfied with the meager – of poor quality but more expensive – substitutions for the sake of national pride and sovereignty. The use of the words "ordinary" and "almost-hard cheese" to describe "Russian Parmesan" (Excerpt 8), in contrast to "real parmesan," underscores this involuntary switch from the *taste of luxury* to the *taste of necessity*, from higher class, modernity, and sophistication to lowliness that is reminiscent of the Soviet era.

While for some, such as the cheesemaker in the video, the ban on Western foods is a business opportunity, for others, it is not only a personal but also professional loss. Excerpt 9 provides one such example.

Excerpt 9
Будучи ещё профессиональным поваром, я очень скучаю по некоторым санкционным продуктам

Being also a professional chef, I really miss some of the sanctioned foodstuffs

An overt identity claim of being a professional chef both adds an expert evaluation of the high quality of Western foods and, albeit indirectly, criticizes the sanctions as disruptive in his line of work. The use of the intensifier *really* constructs for the chef a critical stance toward a new reality in Russia; he misses the *taste of luxury* for personal and professional reasons.

Despite the often-critical stances of the commenters, posts about "Belarusian Parmesan" are more civil than those about "Russian Parmesan," which often led to mutual insults between pro-Putin and anti-Putin commenters. This can be explained by the fact that the "Russian Parmesan" video was perceived by the commenters as a non-critical portrayal of Russia's import substitution in action; therefore, the commenters did not feel the need to "rally around the flag" and instead were free to not only voice their support for the cheesemaker, but also – without being afraid to be labeled as unpatriotic – air their complaints about the high prices and poor quality of available cheeses. While many commenters to the first video overtly defended Putin's actions, the everyday complaints about cheese in the second video offer an indirect criticism of the Russian president who is making Russians pay (metaphorically and literally) for his geopolitical ambitions by having them to return to the *taste of necessity*.

5 Conclusion

In this chapter, I have explored the intersection of discourse, politics, and ideology by focusing on how Russia's ban on imported Western foods is discussed online. My analysis demonstrates how YouTube can be used as a productive site for investigating gastronomy, or the knowledge and practice of eating (good) food, as ideology in online communication about food and taste. Specifically, I show how sociopolitical ideologies and identities are constructed, and contested, in written comments that appear below two different YouTube videos about Parmesan, a food item with a very long and complex history in Russia. Similar to when in the early 2000s in the U.S. French fries were renamed Freedom fries (by some) to symbolize political discord between France and the U.S., the trajectory of Parmesan in Russia – from a gastronomic delight immortalized in Gilyarovsky's memories, to an affordable and available luxury of Russian foodies, to a banned item in post-sanctions Russia – is inextricably linked to Russian sociopolitical history, especially its relationship with and orientation to the West. Put differently, the YouTube comments animate the ongoing heteroglossic dialogue about food and Russia. Through lexical choices made in referring to and describing foods, as well as other linguistic strategies that create evaluative stances, commenters invoke and evaluate Russia's history and current relationships with Parmesan, other foods, and the West.

I have also shown that a YouTube video as a prompt, especially its genre, can help shape the subsequent discussion, both in terms of its content and key (the tone and tenor). Namely, perceived as an external attack on Russia's public image, the satirical video "Belarusian Parmesan" prompted the commenters to take up confrontational stances and engage in collective face-saving by 1) portraying the actor as a traitor and attacking him personally, 2) downplaying the Russian food situation, and 3) rejecting Western food to promote Russian sovereignty, nationalism, and traditional values against pro-Western liberals and the West in general. In contrast, the "Russian Parmesan" video was a non-critical portrayal of one man's effort to make Parmesan in Russia. The written comments posted in reaction to this video are more measured in tone and varied in content: While some praise the cheesemaker's efforts, others 1) criticize the poor quality and high prices of Russian cheeses, 2) mourn the loss of Western foods, and 3) indirectly criticize Putin for making Russians pay for his policies toward Ukraine and the West. For both of these videos, the interactive capabilities of YouTube facilitate its users' engagement in polyphonic and heteroglossic discussions that offer researchers an opportunity to observe and analyze how food is constructed as ideology in online environments.

In light of Bakhtin's (1986) work on addressivity, it can be suggested that the comments after the first video were addressed to political adversaries; thus posters and their intended audience were typically located on opposite sides of the political spectrum (e.g., pro-Putin v. anti-Putin, patriots v. traitors, pro-Western v. anti-Western, etc.). The comments after the second video were intended for those interested in food, cheese in particular, and appear to be more nuanced, often containing both praise and criticism in one message. Taken together and viewed though the material and symbolic lenses of Parmesan, the comments point to a complex heteroglossic sociopolitical situation in Russia in which its citizens are torn between the state-sanctioned and widely promoted patriotism, nationalism, and traditionalism on the one hand and their diminishing livelihoods and shrinking freedoms, including their freedom as consumers, on the other.

My analysis of online comments reveals a peculiar situation regarding the *taste of necessity* and the *taste of luxury/ liberty* (Bourdieu 1984) in Russia. While during Soviet times the majority of people had access only to basic local foods (necessity), in post-Soviet Russia many were able to enjoy high-quality Western foods (luxury/liberty). Such foods, and Parmesan as its collective representation, have come to symbolize class, prestige, and (consumer) freedom. Russia's food embargo has literally and figuratively confiscated the *taste of luxury/liberty*, and it is unclear how long Russians will be satisfied with patriotism as a condiment to the – ironically expensive – *taste of necessity*.

Notes

1. Presidential Decree "On the Application of Special Economic Measures in Order to Ensure the Security of the Russian Federation," no. 560 of August 6, 2014.
2. A number of Russian newspapers, TV programs, and YouTube videos address the poor quality of the cheeses that have appeared on Russian supermarket shelves after the introduction of the "import substitution" program:

    a) Roscontrol (a magazine dedicated to quality control) https://roscontrol.com/journal/tests/30-iz-46-torgovih-marok-sira-i-masla-falsifikati-itogi-ekspertizi/
    b) YouTube videos: https://www.youtube.com/watch?v=KPcQsxmDyE8;
    c) Russian TV program, Russia, (available on YouTube): https://www.youtube.com/watch?v=DCtqHw8-GtE

3. My translation is closer to that of Todorov's (1988), who renders Bakhtin's (1975: 106) "пахнут/пахнет" as "give(s) off the scent," in contrast to Emerson and Holquist's "taste" in "Discourse in the Novel" (1981: 293), which is an apt sensory metaphor but an imprecise translation.
4. https://belarusdigest.com/story/belarus-smuggles-eu-food-to-russia-despite-sanctions/
https://www.globsec.org/wp-content/uploads/2017/11/Think-Visegrad-Analysis-by-Andrei-Yeliseyeu_Belarusian-shrimps-anyone-GLOBSEC-2017.pdf
https://themoscowtimes.com/news/russia-cracks-down-on-belarusian-food-imports-57324
5. Since then, the video has been taken offline.
6. https://meduza.io/feature/2015/08/28/parmezan-novorossii; https://www.ntv.ru/video/1673602/?from=newspage; https://www.youtube.com/watch?v=sVEnN6SaugI
7. Here and elsewhere in this chapter, (multiple) parentheses refer to smiling/laughter. Because of the keyboard layout of the Cyrillic alphabet, the "smiley/laughing" emoticon has lost its "eyes" in Russian/Ukrainian digital discourse (see Tovares 2019b for more information).

Acknowledgments

I am thankful to Cynthia Gordon for her insightful comments and suggestions. I also thank Najma Al Zidjaly for her comments on an earlier draft of this paper. I am forever grateful to Raul Tovares for his love and support.

References

Androutsopoulos, Jannis (2013), 'Participatory Culture and Metalinguistic Discourse: Performing and Negotiating German Dialects on YouTube', in Deborah Tannen and Anna Marie Trester (eds), *Discourse 2.0. Language and New Media*, 47–71, Washington, DC: Georgetown University Press.

Al Zidjaly, Najma (2012), 'What Has Happened to Arabs? Identity and Face Management Online', *Multilingua*, 31(4): 413–439.

Appadurai, Arjun (1981), 'Gastro-Politics in Hindu South Asia', *American Ethnologist*, 8(3): 494–511.

Bakhtin, Mikhail (1975), Slovo v romane (Discourse in the novel). In *Voprosy literatury i estetiki (Questions of Literature and Aesthetics)*, 72–232, Moskva: Khudozestvennaya Literatura.

Bakhtin, Mikhail (1981), *The Dialogic Imagination*, Austin: University of Texas Press.

Bakhtin, Mikhail (1986), *Speech Genres and Other Late Essays*, Austin: University of Texas Press.

Borrero, Mauricio (2003), *Hungry Moscow: Scarcity and Urban Society in the Russian Civil War, 1917–1921*, New York: Peter Lang.

Bourdain, Anthony (2017), 'On "Appetites," Washing Dishes and the Food He Still Won't Eat', *NPR, Fresh Air*, October 20. Available online: https://www.npr.org/2017/10/20/558792269/anthony-bourdain-on-appetites-washing-dishes-and-the-food-he-still-wont-eat

Bourdieu, Pierre (1984), *Distinction. A Social Critique of the Judgment and Taste*, trans. Richard Nice, Cambridge: Harvard University Press.

Bourdieu, Pierre (1986), 'The Forms of Capital', in John G. Richardson (ed), *Handbook of Theory and Research for the Sociology of Education*, 241–258, New York: Greenwood.

Bruschi, Viola, Ksenia Shershneva, Irina Dolgopolova, Maurizio Canavari and Ramona Teuber (2015), 'Consumer Perception of Organic Food in Emerging Markets: Evidence from Saint Petersburg, Russia', *Agribusiness*, 31(3): 414–432.

Burgess, Jean and Joshua Green (2009), *YouTube: Online Video and Participatory Culture*, Malden, MA: Polity Press.

Chebankova, Elena (2017), 'Ideas, Ideology & Intellectuals in Search of Russia's Political Future', *Daedalus*, 146: 76–88.

Chun, Elaine and Keith Walters (2011), 'Orienting to Arab Orientalisms: Language, Race, and Humor in a *YouTube* Video', in Crispin Thurlow and Kristine Mroczek (eds), *Digital Discourse: Language in the New Media*, 251–273, Oxford: Oxford University Press.
DeSoucey, Michaela (2016), *Contested Tastes: Foie Gras and the Politics of Food*, Princeton, NJ: Princeton University Press.
Du Bois, John (2007), 'The Stance Triangle', in Robert Englebretson (ed), *Stancetaking in Discourse: Subjectivity, Evaluation, Interaction*, 139–182, Amsterdam: John Benjamins.
Ferguson, Priscilla Parkhurst (2006), *Accounting for Taste: The Triumph of French Cuisine*, Chicago and London: The University of Chicago Press.
Fletcher, Giles ([1591] 1966), *Of the Russe Commonwealth*, Cambridge, MA: Harvard University Press.
Gilyarovsky, Vladimir (1926), *Moskva i Moskvichi (Moscow and Muscovites)*, Moskva: Vserossijskij Soyuz Poetov.
Glants, Musya and Joyce Toomre (1997), 'Introduction', in Musya Glants and Joyce Toomre (eds), *Food in Russian History and Culture*, xii–xxvii, Bloomington: Indiana University Press.
Gordon, Cynthia and Didem İkizoğlu (2017), '"Asking for Another" Online: Membership Categorization and Identity Construction on a Food and Nutrition Discussion Board', *Discourse Studies*, 19(3): 253–271.
Hachimi, Atiqa (2013), 'The Maghreb-Mashreq Language Ideology and the Politics of Identity in a Globalized Arab World', *Journal of Sociolinguistics*, 17(3): 269–296.
Herring, Susan (2013), 'Discourse in Web 2.0: Familiar, Reconfigured, and Emergent', in Deborah Tannen and Anna Marie Trester (eds), *Discourse 2.0: Language and New Media*, 1–25, Washington, DC: Georgetown University Press.
Jones, Graham and Bambi Schieffelin (2009), 'Talking Text and Talking Back: "My BFF Jill" from Boob Tube to *YouTube*', *Journal of Computer-Mediated Communication*, 14: 1050–1079.
Kazun, Anastasia (2016), 'Framing Sanctions in the Russian Media: The Rally Effect and Putin's Enduring Popularity' *Demokratizatsiya*, 24(3): 327–350.
Kramer, Andrew E. (2015), 'Russia Destroys Piles of Banned Western Food', *The New York Times*, August 5. Available online: https://www.nytimes.com/2015/08/07/world/europe/russia-destroys-piles-of-banned-western-food.html
Labov, William (2001), 'Uncovering the Event Structure of Narrative', in Deborah Tannen and James E. Alatis (eds), *Linguistics, Language, and the Real World: Discourse and Beyond*, 63–83, Washington, DC: Georgetown University Press.
Lakoff, Robin (2006), 'Identity à la Carte: You Are What You Eat', in Anna De Fina, Deborah Schiffrin and Michael Bamberg (eds), *Discourse and Identity*, 142–165, New York: Cambridge University Press.
Lih, Lars T. (1990), *Bread and Authority in Russia, 1914–1921*, Berkeley: University of California Press.
Medvedev, Zhores A. (1988), *Soviet Agriculture*, New York: W. W. Norton & Co.

Nissenbaum, Asaf and Limor Shifman (2015), 'Internet Memes as Contested Cultural Capital: The Case of 4chan's/b/board', *New Media & Society*, 19(4): 483–501.

Ochs, Elinor (1990), 'Cultural Universals in the Acquisition of Language', *Papers and Reports on Child Language Development*, 29: 1–19.

Ochs, Elinor (1996), 'Linguistic Resources for Socializing Humanity', in John Gumperz and Stephen Levinson (eds), *Rethinking Linguistic Relativity*, 407–437, Cambridge: Cambridge University Press.

Osokina, Elena (2015), *Our Daily Bread: Socialist Distribution and the Art of Survival in Stalin's Russia*, trans. Kate Transchel and Greta Bucher, New York: Routledge.

Perianova, Irina (2018), '"Something Borrowed, Something New": Memory and Oblivion in Food Discourse in Post-Soviet Eastern Europe', *International Journal for History, Culture and Modernity*, 6(1): 1–20.

Pomerantsev, Peter (2014), *Nothing is True and Everything is Possible: The Surreal Heart of the New Russia*, New York: Public Affairs.

Rousseau, Signe (2012), *Food and Social Media: You Are What You Tweet*, Lanham, MD: AltaMira Press.

Selivanova, Nina Nikolaevna (1933), *Dining and Wining in Old Russia*, New York: E. P Dutton and CO, INC.

Shagaida, Natalya and Vasiliy Uzun (2017), 'The Food Embargo and Choice of Priorities', *Problems of Economic Transition*, 59(1–3): 202–217.

Ting-Toomey, Stella (2004), 'The Matrix of Face: An Updated Face-Negotiation Theory', in William B. Gudykunst (ed), *Theorizing about Intercultural Communication*, 71–92, Thousand Oaks, CA: Sage.

Todorov, Tzvetan (1988), *Mikhail Bakhtin: The Dialogical Principle*, trans. Wlad Godzich, Minneapolis: University of Minnesota Press.

Tovares, Alla (2019a), 'Negotiating "Thick" Identities through "Light" Practices: YouTube Metalinguistic Comments about Language in Ukraine', *Multilingua*, 38(4): 459–484.

Tovares, Alla (2019b), 'Trolling as Creative Insurgency: The Carnivalesque Delegitimization of Putin and his Supporters in Online Newspaper commentary', in Andrew Ross and Damian Rivers (eds), *Discourses of (De)legitimization: Participatory Culture in Digital Contexts*, 228–247, New York: Routledge.

Vásquez, Camilla (2015), '*Right Now* Versus *Back Then*: Recency and Remoteness as Discursive Resources in Online Reviews', *Discourse, Context & Media*, 9: 5–13.

von Bremzen, Anya (2013), *Mastering the Art of Soviet cooking: A Memoir of Food and Longing*, New York: Crown Publishers.

Wegren, Stephen K., Alexander Nikulin and Irina Trotsuk (2018), *Food Policy and Food Security: Putting Food on the Russian Table*, Manham, MD: Lexington Books.

Wengle, Susanne (2016), 'The Domestic Effects of the Russian Food Embargo', *Demokratizatsiya*, 24(3): 281–289.

White, David (2017), 'State Capacity and Regime Resilience in Putin's Russia', *International Political Science Review*, 39(1): 130–143.

Zinchuk, Galina Mikhailovna, Marina Yegorovna Anokhina, Alexey Vladimirovich Yashkin and Svetlana Arkadievna Petrovskaya (2017), Food Security in the Context of Import Substitution', *European Research Studies Journal*, 10(3A): 371–382.

Appendix 1 A mock food ration card

Jamon	Olives	Parmesan	Foie gras	Smoked salmon
Smoothie	Food rations, Moscow, Fall 2014			Prosciutto
Coca-Cola	Type II, Hipsters and Office workers			Oysters
	1. Valid only when an iPhone is presented 2. If lost, "like", "share" and maximally repost			Mozzarella
Big Mac	Avocado	Sprats	Camembert	Broccoli

Afterword
Food, Language, and Social Media: Past, Present, and Future

Alla Tovares and Cynthia Gordon

This volume was initially inspired by "Food for thought and social action: Constructing ideologies in food-related communication across digital and cultural contexts," a panel organized by Cynthia Gordon for the 15th International Pragmatics Association (IPrA) Conference in Belfast, Ireland. The panel's papers – most of which appear in this volume, along with several additional invited papers – identified online food-related communication, or digital food discourse, as an area that is ripe for academic exploration. Language and food have dynamic intersections online and on social media, and food-related actions and communication have gone digital. Lewis (2018: 213) observes that except for several pioneering studies (e.g., Rousseau 2012; Choi, Foth & Hearn 2014; de Solier 2013, 2018; Lupton 2018), "the growing entanglements between the digital and the world of food" remain largely understudied.

Furthermore – and as we suggested in our introduction – digital food discourse, despite its proliferation, has only relatively recently begun to attract scholarly attention from linguists and scholars in closely allied fields (e.g., Sneijder & te Molder 2005; Brandt & Jenks 2011; Diemer, Brunner & Schmidt 2014; Jurafsky et al. 2014; Zappavigna 2014; Vásquez & Chik 2015; Chik & Vásquez 2017). The chapters in this book contribute to the growing body of work on digital food discourse by lending insight into how identities and ideologies are constructed, and contested, on a number of different popular social media platforms. Specifically, the chapters have examined food-related communication on blogs, discussion boards, Facebook, Instagram, Twitter, and YouTube, while also considering diverse cultural contexts and language varieties, including Arabic, Dutch, French, German, Korean, Russian, and English (American, British, and Canadian). Thus, by investigating digital food discourse in a number of sociocultural and sociolinguistic contexts, the studies in this book contribute not only to our understanding of digital communication about food, but also to research on "the multilingual Internet" (Danet & Herring 2007; see also Locher, Bolander & Höhn 2015), which hosts a wealth of food-related discourse.

Locher, Bolander and Höhn (2015) suggest that the division between online and offline actions, communities, and identities masks their intertwining nature, and the chapters in this volume collectively demonstrate that digital food discourse moves between and links online and offline life, from considering and implementing the individual action of altering one's food preferences (İkizoğlu & Gordon, Chapter 1) to using food as a resource in negotiating collective sociopolitical stances (Tovares, Chapter 9). Thus, with the development of digital and mobile technologies and their interactive features, the growing integration of the digital world into everyday food-related actions and communication merits continued scholarly attention. One such area of attention is the increasing monetizing of (food) social media. As extant research (e.g., Couldry 2015; Lewis 2018) suggests, it is important to understand the digital realm not only as a space for sharing daily food experiences and "ordinary expertise," but also as a place where people's "everyday digital food engagements can unwittingly become forms of free labour for corporations and marketers" (Lewis 2018: 216). The digitization of food-related communication also influences businesses, including how they interact with their customers, as made apparent by Vásquez (Chapter 5) who showed how restaurants use various linguistic strategies to engage in public online reputation management in response to customers' food complaints and negative reviews on *Yelp* and *TripAdvisor*. In other words, while customers' free labor of posting online reviews can help promote restaurants, their negative reviews "may represent an uninvited additional encroachment of technology" into restaurants' professional activities (Vásquez this volume). Choe (Chapter 6) focuses her analysis on online commensality, a primarily social endeavor, but also notes that mukbang exists for financial reasons: Viewers send money to the eaters. Continued exploration of food-related digital discourse would lend further insight into how online user content is exploited by corporations and marketers as well as into the impact of everyday digital food (inter)actions on the food industry and individual food entrepreneurs.

In a related vein, Thurlow (2013: 228–244) contends that the collapsed boundaries between public and private, social and corporate, and personal and institutional on social media sites represent further commodification of communication, where, through pseudo-sociality – or stylizing themselves as interactive and participatory – corporations and institutions exude influence over individuals, including their tastes. It is through such pseudo-social engagements and using interactive capabilities of new social media platforms that old media, such as newspapers, maintain their influence over consumers' taste preferences. For instance, Mapes (Chapter 3) showed how the food section of the *New York Times*, an influential "elite" newspaper, uses Instagram #tbt (throwback Thursday) posts to "school" their readers in the dominant values of food and consumption and in so doing (re)inscribes class distinctions presented as "good taste." That seemingly egalitarian social media platforms are also spaces for the (re)construction of social hierarchies highlights the need for future inquiries into how class distinctions are created, and normalized, in online communication about food. Put differently, examinations of digital food discourse can reveal how ambient, pseudo-social online interactions are also spaces for monetization and class (re)inscription. Moreover, such investigations uncover the increasing fluidity between "old" and "new" media, precipitated by media convergence, or the merger of "old" mass media outlets through digital media platforms. According to Jenkins (2004: 34), because of "the portability of new computing and telecommunications technologies, we are entering an era where media will be everywhere and we will use all kinds of media in relation to each other." Similarly, Rousseau (2012: xiii) observes that "contrary to the idea of new media replacing or usurping traditional platforms, we are in the midst of a constantly evolving – and constantly challenging, and always fascinating – dialogue of accommodation and adaptation." In this volume, Declercq, Tulkens, and Jacobs (Chapter 2) investigate the dialogic relationship between traditional and social media by exploring how social media (Facebook and Twitter) users interact about an infotainment TV show about food that aired in Belgium. Their chapter highlighted the many roles and aspects of food of importance to viewers (its taste, health, ethical, and environmental dimensions) and how this multidimensionality is negotiated on social media by the TV audience, revealing changing patterns of food-related tastes and beliefs.

Taste is always evolving and "never neutral: It reflects a vision of the world that defines what is and is not desirable" (Vercelloni 2016: 150). Indeed, various researchers (e.g., Lang & Heasman 2004; Norberg-Hodge 2016; Vercelloni 2016) suggest that in modern societies old tastes and ways of eating are vulnerable and suseptable to change. Digital environments contribute to new food-related engagements, including those based on traditional cultural contexts and values such as eating together, as Choe's (Chapter 6) analysis of Korean mukbang livestreaming showed. Herring (2013: 21) suggests that digital discourse "offers a rich field of investigation for discourse analysts" and underscores the urgency of "integrated multimodal analysis." In this regard, both Choe's and Mapes's (Chapter 3) integrations of visual and textual analyses heed the call and contribute to the growing area of multimodal discourse analysis. Al Zidjaly, Al Moqbali, and Al Hinai (Chapter 8), who also acknowledge the multimodal nature of digital food discourse in their analysis of #Chips_Oman tweets, contribute to research on digital activism by exploring the role food can play in an Arabic cultural context. Specifically, their study demonstrated how Omani citizens, in responding to a perceived attack perpetrated by another country on their national snack food, also indirectly engaged in larger political discourses and addressed not only international but also national conflicts and concerns.

The intersection of food and digital activism also takes center stage in the chapter by Pierce, Casteltrione, and Tominc (Chapter 7) who use Critical Discourse Analysis (CDA) to demonstrate how members of a Grow Your Own (GYO) blogging community construct activist identities and ideologies that are in opposition to centralized, dehumanized, expensive, and unsustainable capitalist food practices. Specifically, their chapter highlighted how GYO activists mobilize language to drive social change through online promotion of alternative practices of growing and consuming food. Attention to the linguistic construction of opposition, or discourse-counterdiscourse, is also central to Tovares's (Chapter 9) investigation of communication about food, Parmesan in particular, in the context of Russian politics. By zeroing in on how Russia's ban on imported Western foods is discussed in YouTube comments, Tovares demonstrates how through lexical choices and evaluative stances, food and taste are constructed as ideology. Indeed, the theme of discourse-counterdiscourse, or like-dislike, or us-them emerges throughout the volume; in the realm of food, this general theme can be traced back to Bourdieu's (1984) discussion of taste and "distinction," a notion which has gained prominence in contemporary linguistic understandings of identity construction (e.g., Bucholtz and Hall 2005).

The widespread notion that "you are what you eat" – or, in the context of linguistic studies, "you are what you say you eat, and how you communicate about food" – and the ideological underpinnings of this, is another theme of the volume. Gerhardt's (Chapter 4) analysis of adjectives and modifiers in vegan blogs shows how through lexical borrowings, such as "vegan," lifestyle ideas are spread online and offline. While language reflects and contributes to changing global food (and eating) trends, such as veganism, Gerhardt contends that language is also indicative of traditional omnivore cuisines and eating ideologies, thus making the use of animal-based concepts unavoidable as evidenced from her analysis of three blogs from different cultures and different languages

(English, French, and German). İkizoğlu and Gordon's (Chapter 1) analysis of communication about "picky eating" in an English-language online discussion board similarly reveals a tension between change and reification: In constructing and problematizing their identities as picky eaters, and aiming to transform their eating practices, posters draw on and reinforce ideologies that picky eating is inappropriate for adults; that food consumption is an individual choice; and that the healthy, socially responsible, and moral thing to do is refrain from picky eating.

Read à la carte, each of the volume's chapters mobilizes detailed linguistic analysis to approach online food-related communication. Collectively, the chapters contribute to our understanding of not only language and food but also of digital discourse. They reinforce Riley and Paugh's (2018: 65) identification of social media as rich sources of mediated food-related texts that offer researchers opportunities "for examining ideas about food" as well as "the linguistic forms they take." Additionally, this volume lends insight into contemporary, ever-changing social practices across various platforms, cultural groups, and languages, and thus answers Androutsopoulos' (2017: 241) call "to develop new perspectives on how language in the media [. . .] changes in the context of swiftly changing mediascapes." The chapters also contribute to our increasingly nuanced understanding of how "online" and "offline" blend together, especially (but not only) in the realm of food. Future studies should continue to investigate how online actions influence those offline, especially in contexts where – for political, religious, or cultural reasons – some action, such as dissent, is initially possible only online. In addition, online-offline influence should be explored in contexts where individual people attempt to communicate online about food consumption decisions that they make offline, a theme that is touched upon in some way in multiple chapters. In their analysis of food blogs, Diemer, Brunner, and Schmidt (2014) point out the links between "old" and "new" media, such as blogs and printed recipes, and suggest that references to personal, regional, and temporal contexts unite the two. While all chapters in this volume have addressed the interconnected nature of the contemporary multimodal digital food discourse and its various antecedents – and in a variety of cultural and linguistic contexts – the evolving nature of digital (food) discourse offers an exciting opportunity for a continued exploration of how time, place, authenticity, ideologies, and personal and collective identities are negotiated in an increasingly globalized world.

Rousseau (2012: 97) observes that while it is important to consider "how or whether the Internet is affecting how we think about food," it is also essential to acknowledge "how social media provide us with many more virtual locations for thinking about food, and for expressing our thoughts." In this volume, we have offered a buffet of analyses that use various approaches to the study of discourse to address food-related communication occurring across diverse social media platforms, involving multiple modalities, embedded in diverse cultural contexts, and occurring in multiple languages. With food being "an increasingly prominent subject of engagement online, from the aesthetics of cooking to the ethics of shopping" (Schneider et al. 2018: 1), we believe that this volume is a timely addition to the growing body of work that explores digital food discourse.

References

Androutsopoulos, Jannis (2017), 'Style, Change, and Media: A Postscript', in Janus Mortensen, Nikolas Coupland, and Jacob Thøgersen (eds), *Style, Mediation, and Change: Sociolinguistic Perspectives on Talking Media*, 239–250, Oxford: Oxford University Press.

Bourdieu, Pierre (1984), *Distinction: A Social Critique of the Judgement of Taste*, Cambridge: Harvard University Press.

Brandt, Adam and Christopher Jenks (2011), '"Is it Okay to Eat a Dog in Korea . . . Like China?" Assumptions of National Food-Eating Practices in Intercultural Interaction, *Language and Intercultural Communication*, 11(1): 41–58.

Bucholtz, Mary and Kira Hall (2005), 'Identity and Interaction: A Sociocultural Linguistic Approach', *Discourse Studies*, 7(4–5): 585–614.

Chik, Alice and Camilla Vásquez (2017), 'A Comparative Multimodal Analysis of Restaurant Reviews from Two Geographical Contexts', *Visual Communication*, 16(1): 3–26.

Choi, Jaz Hee-jeong, Marcus Foth and Greg Hearn, eds. (2014), *Eat, Cook, Grow: Mixing Human-Computer Interactions with Human-Food Interactions*. Cambridge, MA: MIT Press.

Couldry, Nick (2015), 'The Myth of "Us": Digital Networks, Political Change and the Production of Collectivity', *Information, Communication & Society*, 18(6): 608–626.

Danet, Brenda and Susan C. Herring, eds. (2007), *The Multilingual Internet: Language, Culture, and Communication Online*, New York: Oxford University Press.

de Solier, Isabelle (2013), *Food and the Self: Consumption, Production and Material Culture*, London: Bloomsbury.

de Solier, Isabelle (2018), 'Tasking the Digital: New Food Media', in Kathleen LeBesco and Pater Naccarato (eds), *The Bloomsbury Handbook of Food and Popular Culture*, 54–65, London: Bloomsbury Academic.

Diemer, Stefan, Marie-Louise Brunner and Selina Schmidt (2014), '"Like, Pasta, Pizza and Stuff" – New Trends in Online Food Discourse', *CuiZine: The Journal of Canadian Food Cultures*, 5(2). Available online: https://www.erudit.org/en/journals/cuizine/2014-v5-n2-cuizine01533/1026769ar/

Herring, Susan (2013), 'Discourse in Web 2.0: Familiar, Reconfigured, and Emergent', in Deborah Tannen and Anna Marie Trester (eds), *Discourse 2.0: Language and New Media*, 1–25, Washington, DC: Georgetown University Press.

Jenkins, Henry (2004), 'The Cultural Logic of Media Convergence', *International Journal of Cultural Studies*, 7(1): 33–43.

Jurafsky, Dan, Victor Chahuneau, Bryan R. Routledge and Noah A. Smith (2014), 'Narrative Framing of Consumer Sentiment in Online Restaurant Reviews', *First Monday*, 19. Available online: http://firstmonday.org/ojs/index.php/fm/article/view/4944

Lang, Tim and Michael Heasman (2004), *Food Wars: The Global Battle for Mouths, Minds and Markets*, London: Earthscan.

Lewis, Tania (2018), 'Digital Food: From Paddock to Platform', *Communication Research and Practice*, 4(3): 212–228.

Locher, Miriam A., Brook Bolander and Nicole Höhn, eds. (2015), 'Relational Work in Facebook and Discussion Boards/Fora', Special Issue, *Pragmatics*, 21(1).

Lupton, Deborah (2018), 'Cooking, Eating, Uploading: Digital Food Cultures', in Kathleen LeBesco and Peter Naccarato (eds), *The Bloomsbury Handbook of Food and Popular Culture*, 66–79, London and New York: Bloomsbury.

Norberg-Hodge, Helena (2016), *Ancient Futures*, 3rd edn, Local Futures.

Riley, Kathleen C. and Amy L. Paugh (2018), *Food and Language: Discourses and Foodways across Cultures*, New York: Routledge.

Rousseau, Signe (2012), *Food and Social Media: You Are What You Tweet*, Lanham, MD: AltaMira Press.

Schneider, Tanja, Karin Eli, Catherine Dolan and Stanley Ulijaszek, eds. (2018), *Digital Food Activism*, New York, NY: Routledge.

Sneijder, Petra and Hedwig F.M. te Molder (2005), 'Moral Logic and Logical Morality: Attributions of Responsibility and Blame in Online Discourse on Veganism', *Discourse & Society*, 16(5): 675–696.

Thurlow, Crispin (2013), 'Fakebook: Synthetic Media, Pseudo-Sociality and the Rhetorics of Web 2.0', in Deborah Tannen and Anna Marie Trester (eds), *Discourse 2.0: Language and New Media*, 225–249, Washington, DC: Georgetown University Press.

Vásquez, Camilla and Alice Chik (2015), '"I am not a foodie . . .": Culinary Capital in Online Reviews of Michelin Restaurants', *Food and Foodways*, 23(4): 231–250.

Vercelloni, Luca (2016), *The Invention of Taste: A Cultural Account of Desire, Delight and Disgust in Fashion, Food and Art*, trans. Kate Singleton, New York: Bloomsbury.

Zappavigna, Michele (2014), 'CoffeeTweets: Bonding Around the Bean on Twitter', in Philip Seargeant and Caroline Tagg (eds), *The Language of Social Media: Identity and Community on the Internet*, 139–160, Basingstoke: Palgrave Macmillan.

Notes on Contributors

Ahad Al Hinai is an undergraduate student in the Department of English Language and Literature (College of Arts & Social Sciences) at Sultan Qaboos University (Oman). Her research interests focus on Arab identity. For her 2019 Research Project class, she wrote an unpublished paper entitled: *What are the cultural features of Arabs?*

Einas Al Moqbali is an undergraduate student in the Department of English Language and Literature (College of Arts & Social Sciences) at Sultan Qaboos University (Oman). Her research interests focus on Omani (Arab) identity and political dissent. For her 2019 Research Project class, she wrote an unpublished paper entitled: *How do Omanis on Twitter negotiate unemployment in Oman?*

Najma Al Zidjaly is Associate Professor of Sociolinguistics in the Department of English Language and Literature (College of Arts & Social Sciences) at Sultan Qaboos University (Oman). She is the author of *Disability, Discourse and Technology: Agency and Inclusion in (Inter)action* (Palgrave Macmillan, 2015) and the editor of the Special Issue on Society in Digital Contexts: New Modes of Identity and Community Construction (*Multilingua*, 2019). Al Zidjaly has additionally published articles in scholarly journals such as *Language in Society; Discourse & Society; Discourse, Context & Media; Visual Communication; Communication & Medicine; Multimodal Communication; Linguistik Online; Russian Journal of Linguistics* and *Multilingua*. Al Zidjaly's research interests focus on social media and Arab (Omani) identity, and she serves in the directorial board of the *Journal of Multimodal Communication*. She is further an Associate Editor (for the Arab World) of the *IPrA Bibliography of Pragmatics Online*.

Isidoropaolo Casteltrione is Lecturer and researcher at Queen Margaret University, Edinburgh. He holds a PhD in Political Communication and New Media from Queen Margaret University (2015). His PhD project examined the contributions of Facebook to citizens' political participation in Italy and United Kingdom and his main research interests include social media, online self-presentation, the internet and information, media and political communication, persuasion, and citizens' political behaviors. He has published in several international peer-reviewed academic journals and is a reviewer for a number of journals such as *Computers in Human Behaviour* and *Social Media + Society*.

Hanwool Choe is a discourse analyst primarily interested in digital communication, language and food, multimodal interaction, and life stories. She received her PhD in Linguistics from Georgetown University. Her publications have appeared in journals such as *Language in Society, Discourse Studies*, and *Journal of Pragmatics*.

Jana Declercq is Assistant Professor of Discourse and Communication at the Center for Language and Cognition Groningen at the University of Groningen. She is interested in discourses of health and illness, both in mass and social media texts, and in clinical contexts. In her current research, she focuses on food and eating, and chronic pain.

Cornelia Gerhardt is Senior Lecturer of Linguistics in the English Department of Saarland University, Germany. Her main research areas include (digitally) mediated discourse and language use around food. She published a monograph *Appropriating Live Televised Football through Talk* (2014) as well as two edited volumes *The Appropriation of Media in Everyday Life* (2012, together with Ruth Ayass) and *Culinary Linguistics: The Chef's Special* (2014, together with Maximiliane Frobenius and Susanne Ley). Also, she edited a special issue (*Participation Framework Revisited: (New) Media and their Audiences/Users*) of the *Journal of Pragmatics* (2014, together with Volker Eisenlauer and Maximiliane Frobenius). Her current works both in linguistic food studies and in technologically-mediated communication include handbook, review, and research articles.

Cynthia Gordon is Associate Professor in the Department of Linguistics at Georgetown University. She is the author of *Making Meanings, Creating Family: Intertextuality and Framing in Family Interaction* (Oxford University Press, 2009), and co-editor (with Deborah Tannen and Shari Kendall) of *Family Talk: Discourse and Identity in Four American Families* (Oxford University Press, 2007). She is on the editorial boards of *Language in Society*, the *Journal of Language and Social Psychology*, and the *Journal of Sociolinguistics*.

Didem İkizoğlu is a PhD candidate in the Department of Linguistics at Georgetown University. She is the co-editor (with Anna De Fina and Jeremy Wegner) of *Diversity and Super-Diversity: Sociocultural Linguistic Perspectives* (Georgetown University Press, 2017). Her research interests include language and identity, medical discourse, family discourse, and multimodal interaction analysis. Her work has appeared in *Discourse Studies* and *Journal of Pragmatics*.

Geert Jacobs is Professor at the University of Ghent and received a PhD in Linguistics from the University of Antwerp. His research focuses on media linguistics, the discourse of news production processes, and on language use in professional settings.

Gwynne Mapes is a postdoc researcher in the Department of English at the University of Bern, Switzerland. As a critical discourse analyst, she addresses issues of social class and elitism in the context of food/material culture consumption. She has recent papers published in *Journal of Sociolinguistics*; *Discourse, Context & Media*; and *Language in Society*, as well as a forthcoming book with Oxford University Press.

Nadine Pierce is an MSc Gastronomy graduate of Queen Margaret University (2017) and author of two award-winning blogs. "A Pentland Garden" blog focuses on her own GYO and gardening activity. Based in the Scottish Borders, she writes about food and organic and sustainable methods in kitchen gardening. She also writes for other publications about environmental and food issues.

Ana Tominc (PhD, Lancaster, 2012) is interested in contemporary food discourses related to lifestyle and class (especially in cookbooks and on TV), food and media in socialism (Yugoslavia), and critical discourse analysis. She is currently a lecturer and a researcher at Queen Margaret University Edinburgh, where her teaching focuses on food, communication, and the media. She is currently working on an edited collection on food and cooking on early European television (Routledge). She is the author of *The Discursive Construction of Class and Lifestyle: Celebrity Chef Cookbooks in Post-Socialist Slovenia* (John Benjamins, 2017). In 2018, she founded the Biennial Conference on Food and Communication.

Alla Tovares is Associate Professor in the Department of English at Howard University in Washington, DC. Her main research interests include Bakhtin's theory of dialogue and carnival, language ideologies, and digital communication. She is the co-author of *How to Write about the Media Today*; her recent articles have appeared in *World Englishes*; *Discourse & Society*; *Discourse, Context & Media*; and *Multilingua*.

Stéphan Tulkens is a PhD researcher at the Institute for Computational Linguistics and Psycholinguistics (CLiPS) at the University of Antwerp

(Belgium). He works on models of language processing in bilinguals, focusing specifically on word reading and the phonological and semantic ambiguity bilinguals face during reading.

Camilla Vásquez is Professor of Applied Linguistics at the University of South Florida. Camilla is the author of *The Discourse of Online Consumer Reviews* (Bloomsbury, 2014) and *Language, Creativity and Humour Online* (Routledge, 2019). Her research about online review language has also been published in journals such as *Current Issues in Tourism*; *Discourse, Context & Media*; *Food & Foodways*; *Journal of Pragmatics*; *Language@Internet*; *Narrative Inquiry*; and *Visual Communication*.

Index

Headings in italics are titles of blogs and newspapers. # is ignored in the filing order.

accountability 22, 28
activism. *See* digital activism
acts 15, 16, 61
adjectives 16, 254
   in complaints 118–19, 124
   derived from animal products 99–102, 103
   vegan/plant-based 94–8, 102
adults
   eating habits 30, 255
   as picky eaters 13, 18–25
Afreeca TV 139, 143–4, 151
ambiguous/polysemous words 203, 204, 208
Anconc software 37
apologies 16, 121, 124–5, 128, 130
   requests for 205–6, 218
Arabic culture 198, 199, 202–6, 208–9, 218–20
Arabic language 205–6
   indirectness 198, 203–4, 208
   insults 211–12, 218–19
   pronouns 217, 220
   use of repetition 210
   varieties of 206, 209, 212–13, 219
   verbs 213–14, 217
Arab Spring 198–9, 219
askesis 16
Association internationale de linguistique appliquée research network (AILA ReN) 89
audiences 244
   engagement of 184–5
   food related TV 34–6, 48
   knowledge 35, 41, 43–4
   viewer participation 144, 151
authenticity 70, 79, 174

Bakhtin, Mikhail 59, 226, 230–1, 238, 244

Belarusian Parmesan 232–4, 234–9, 243, 244
Belgium 34, 36
blogs 171–2
   activism 175–7, 179, 181, 182–3
   food 88–90, 172, 176
   Grow Your Own (GYO) 172–3, 189, 254
   health 182–3
   vegan food 87–8, 93–5
Bourdieu, Pierre 30, 70, 89, 101, 200, 227, 228
bread making 183–5, 186
broadcast jockeys (BJs) 137, 139, 151
businesses. *See also* complaints; response strategies (to complaints)
   online reputation management 111, 114, 132, 252
   promotion 63

call to action 114, 212
capitalism 172–3, 175, 181, 185
captions 64–5, 72–5
category-bound activities 14, 18–23
ChangHyun 143–4, 149–50, 152–61
chat messages 138, 143, 149–51
children 30
   as picky eaters 13, 19, 24–5, 27, 28
#Chips_Oman 202, 204, 220, 254
   attitudes to Emiratis 207–9
   attitudes to fellow Omanis 210–14
   creation of 197–8
   and Omani government 213–17
   piñata incident 197, 205
Chomsky, Noam 216
chronotope 59, 79–80
cochineal 45–7
co-construction 60, 142–3, 156, 161, 162
code-switching 212–13
collocation 37, 45–7
   emoji/emoticons 50, 52

commensality 137–8, 140–2, 162
  online 142–3, 146, 151–62
communication 3, 227
  through food 2–4, 200–2, 220, 251, 256
community identity 183, 189
  blogs 173–5
complaints 112, 116
  food-related 117–18, 123–4
  private responses 117, 120–1
  public response strategies 113–14, 118–23, 124–31
compost 187–8
concordances 37, 51
#Consciencerelieved 215
constructed actions 152
consumers
  and food related TV 34–5
  schooling of 60
content analysis 64–5
controversy 51, 52
corpus-assisted discourse studies (CADS) 37
corpus linguistics analysis 37, 93–4
corruption, government 199, 201–2, 210–11, 213, 219
Cowspiracy (documentary) 42
Crimea. *See* Ukraine
critical discourse analysis (CDA) 172, 177–8
cultural capital 227–8, 242
cultural values 33, 45, 48, 51–2
customers. *See also* complaints
  expectations 124–5
  involvement strategies 114
  schooling of 60

deproblematization 236–7. *See also* problematization
dialogicality 226, 230–1
digital activism
  blogs 172–3, 175–7, 182–8, 254
  in Oman 198–9, 201–2, 214–17
digital media 3
  mixing with offline activities 149, 188, 255
direct identity claims 18–19
directives 151–2, 156, 161, 187

discourse analysis methods 17–18, 37, 64–5, 116–17, 144–5, 202, 232–4
  corpus linguistics analysis 37, 93–4
  critical discourse analysis (CDA) 172, 177–8
discussion forums 13, 30
  FriendInFitness (FIF) 14, 15–16, 17, 25
dispersion 37
distraction strategy 216–17
drinking, mukbang 146–9, 151
Du Bois, John 60–1, 76, 231
Dutch language
  food related TV 34, 36
  reference corpora 37–8, 48, 54 n.1
  vegan online forum 93

eating
  emotions of 48–52
  mealtimes 138, 140–2, 151
  mixing on and offline 149, 255
  virtual eating together 151–62
  virtual togetherness 145–51
economic capital 227–8, 241–2
economic factors 13–14
economics, blogs 179, 181
elitism 59, 60–2. *See also* status
  stancetaking 65–6, 70, 72–7, 79–80
Emirati. *See* UAE (United Arab Emirates)
emoji/emoticons 74, 81 n.5
  comments on TV 37, 48–52
  mukbang 146, 149
  political dissent 198
emotions 53
  emoji/emoticons 48–52
  linguistic expression of 14, 29
English language
  American 14, 17, 22, 27–8, 116, 120
  British 178, 184–5, 189
  Canadian 88, 93–4, 94–5, 98, 101–2
  in Dutch corpus 36
environmentalism 179, 180, 185
  herbicides 187–8
  self-sufficiency 172
  and veganism 42, 43–4, 182–3
ethics
  animals 47–8, 182–3
  meat eating 41–2, 43, 44–8
  veganism 91
ethnographic studies 202–3

eWOM (electronic Word of Mouth) 111
exhortative forms 138, 146, 150
expired food scandal 199, 201–2
extreme case formulations 128, 131

Facebook
    emoji/emoticons 48–52
    and food related TV 35–6, 54 n.1
    meat eating 42, 45
    Russian food 232
    smoothies 40
face saving 204–5, 208, 218, 220, 238
fashion 253–4
    authenticity 68–70
    food 59–60, 64, 72–5, 77–80
food. *See also* healthy eating
    avoided foods 19–20, 21–2, 30
    communication through 2–4, 200–2, 220, 251, 256
    expired food scandal 199, 201–2
    fashion 59–60, 64, 68–75, 77–80
    and politics 200–2, 217–20, 227–8
    preferences 3–4, 21–2, 33–4, 47–8
    preparation 20
    sharing 151–62
footing 138, 142, 152, 161
framing 175
    controversy 51
    customer perspective 121, 124–5, 128–9
    mukbang 138, 142, 149
French cuisine 201, 225
French language
    adjectives 88, 96–7, 98, 100, 101–2
    modifiers 95
    vegan food blog 88, 93–4
FriendInFitness (FIF) 14, 15–16, 17, 25
Fristi 45–7, 50, 53
front stage 174, 182

gender politics 69–70, 78
genres 65. *See also* social media
    blogs 89, 90, 93, 175, 183
    discussion forums 13, 14, 17, 30
    photographs 66–71
    user comments 64–5, 75–8
    video 230–1, 232–3, 244
    webcare 112, 132
    written captions 72–5

German language
    adjectives 95–6, 97, 99–101, 102
    modifiers 94–5
    vegan food blog 88, 93–4
Goffman, Erving 16, 26, 114, 142, 174, 203, 217
group identities 173–5
Grow Your Own (GYO) 171, 188–90
    digital activism 172–3, 176–7, 254
    organic food 187–8
Gulf States 220 n.1

Haetnim 143–4, 146–50
hashtags 63
    political dissent 201–2
    in stancetaking 73–5
healthy eating 33–4, 38–9
    Grow Your Own (GYO) blogs 181–2
    picky eaters 13–14, 24, 26
    self transformation 25–9
    specific foods 40, 41, 47
    veganism 91–3, 182–3
Herman, Edward 216
heteroglossia 213, 226, 230–1, 234, 243, 244
hummus 185–7, 201
hyper hedging 18, 28, 29

identities 34
    collective 2, 173–5, 176
    construction of 14, 18–25, 66, 251, 255
    digital activist 183–8
    direct identity claims 18–19
    ethnic 33
    indexing of 15, 225, 228, 231
    national 199, 200, 202, 220
    negotiation of 231–2, 243–5
    problematization 23–5, 29, 255
    self-presentation 174–5
identity politics 200–2, 217–20
ideologies 176
    construction of 251, 254
    negotiation of 231–2, 237–8, 243–5
    normalizing 62
implicit referencing 204–5
impoliteness 198, 202–3. *See also* offensive language
impression management 111, 132, 252
indexical order 65–6

indexing
    of identities 15, 225, 228, 231
    master narratives 19
    national identity 200
indirectness 203, 208–9, 218–19, 220
    language use 198, 203–4, 208
informality 187
information 231–2
    audience knowledge 35, 53
    blogs as resources 174, 177
    as commodity 34–5
insects 45–8
Instagram 80
    and food related TV 35
    @nytfood 59, 60, 62–3, 65–6
    Russian food 232
    stancetaking 61
instructions 151–2, 156, 161, 187
insults. *See* offensive language
involvement 142–3, 145

Just, Nicole 94

keyness analysis 37–8, 39, 48–50
Korean culture 137, 138, 139, 140
    table manners 140, 151
Korean language
    exhortative forms 138, 146, 150
    online language 145

Al-Lawati, Haider 215–16
lexical analysis
    Parmesan in Russia 234–5, 239–40, 243, 254
    veganism 90, 94–103, 118–19, 254
Life on a Pig Row (blog) 178, 181, 183–5, 186

Mark's Veg Plot (blog) 178, 179, 187–8
master narratives 18, 19, 24–5, 27
mealtimes 138, 140–2, 151
meaning
    co-constructed 142–3
    of emoji/emoticons 49–51
    implied 204, 209
    polysemous/ambiguous words 203, 204, 208
meat eating 41–8, 103
mediatization 35–6, 60

membership categorization 14, 15–16, 23
Middle East 220 n.1
Al-Mishiqri, Saeed 206
modals 14, 18, 22, 29
modifiers 18, 94–5, 254
moves 113–16, 120, 121–2
mukbang 137–40, 162, 253
    BJs 143–4
    drinking 146–9
    togetherness interactions 145–51
    virtual feeding interactions 151–62
multidimensionality 34, 35, 52–3, 253
multimodal interaction 138, 142–3, 151, 201, 213

nationalism 237–8, 240, 243
negation 14, 18, 29
negative evaluation 22–3, 50, 51, 77–8, 111
New York Times (NYT) 59–60, 66, 72, 76–7, 253
    @nytfood 60, 62–6, 69–70, 72–3, 76, 79–80
    status 62–3
Nicole Just (blog) 94
Novorossiya (New Russia) 233
nutrition 33, 92, 93. *See also* healthy eating

Odnoklassniki (Classmates) 232
offensive language
    Arabic 198, 203–4, 211–12, 218–19
    Russian 238
Oh She Glows (blog) 88, 93–4
Oman 197–8
    Arab Spring 198–9
    attitudes to fellow Omanis 210–14
    culture 197–8
    government 199, 201–2, 206, 210–11, 213–17, 219
    and UAE (United Arab Emirates) 199–200, 207–9
omnivore cuisine 88
online activism. *See* digital activism
online reputation management 111, 132, 252
Open Rice 113
organic food 89, 187–8
organic products 188
Orlov, Andrei (Orlusha) 233

Index

Parmesan 226, 229–30, 232–3
   Belarusian Parmesan 232–4, 234–9, 243, 244
   Russian Parmesan 239–43, 241, 244
participation framework 198, 203–4, 217
Pattern Python Package 36
personalization 121–2
photographs 59, 64–5, 66–71
picky eaters 13–14, 18–25, 29, 255
   children as 13, 19, 24–5, 27, 28
plant-based eating. *See* veganism
polarization 235
politics 233, 235
   dissent 198–9, 201–2, 214–17
   manipulation 204
polyphony 230, 244
polysemous/ambiguous words 203, 204, 208
predicational strategies 172, 189
problematization 23–5. *See also* deproblematization
pronouns 131
   alternation of 120, 130
   inclusive 183, 184–5, 187–8
   indirectness 198
   political dissent 204–5, 217, 219
pseudo-social interactions 62, 252–3
Putin, Vladimir 233, 234, 235, 239, 240, 244

questions 138, 187, 211–12
   rhetorical 42, 181, 237

rabbits 44–5
recipes 87, 93, 95–7, 98
referential strategies 172, 189
reflexivity 14, 18, 26, 27
response strategies (to complaints)
   apologies 121, 124–5, 128, 130
   counter-claim 119–20, 125–6, 127–8, 131
   educate 122–3
   elicit information 121, 126–7, 129
   generic 124–5
   ignore 118–19
   privacy 117, 120–1
restaurant reviews 112–16. *See also* complaints

rhetorical devices 113–16
   personalization 121–2
   questions 42, 181, 237
   repetition 186–7, 210
ritual 174, 200
   Arabic culture 202–4
   Korean culture 162
Russia 226
   banned Western food 225–6, 236, 240
   import substitution 229, 232–3, 241
   nationalism 229, 237–8
   traditional food 228–30
Russian language 235–42
Russian Parmesan 239–43, 244

safety, food 182, 241
sarcasm 72, 73–5, 205–6, 213
saving face 204–5, 208, 218, 220, 238
search engine optimization 98, 102
self
   image 174
   positioning 61
   presentation 174–5, 188–9
   split sense of 18, 22, 25, 26, 27–8, 29
   transformation 16–17, 22, 25–9, 29
semiotic genres 64–5
   photographs 66–71
   user comments 75–8
   written captions 72–5
Sirota, Oleg 233
smoothies 40
snack food. *See* #Chips_Oman
sociality 62–3, 137
   pseudo-sociality 62, 252–3
social media 225, 255–6. *See also* blogs; Facebook; Twitter; YouTube
   monetization 139, 151, 252
   pseudo-sociality 252–3
   social practices 3, 174
social structures 4–5, 80–1, 113, 253
Sonar new media corpus 37
stacking 14
   verbs 26, 27–8
stances 23
   collective 204
   elitism 60–2
   evaluative 226, 235
   stancetaking 15–16, 65–6, 70, 72–7, 230–1, 238

stance triangle 61, 76, 231
us-versus-them 208
star balloons 139, 151
status 60–2, 79–80. *See also* elitism
   modernity 77–8
   picky eaters 13–14
supermarkets 185–7, 190 n.2

table manners 151
Tannen, Deborah 114, 138, 142, 203, 208
taste 30, 89, 253, 254
   elitism 61, 66, 72, 74, 75, 77–9
   and food preferences 20, 27, 43, 53
   as marker of class 89, 227
   necessity/luxury 226, 228–30, 232, 234, 236–7, 241–5
   subjectivity 120, 127, 128, 132
#tbt (#throwbackthursday) 63–4, 72, 78, 80
   photographs 68–70
television 35
   food related shows 34–6, 51–2
traditional media 53, 253
TripAdvisor 111, 114, 116–17
Tumblr 172
Twitter
   attitudes revealed on 207–14
   #Chips_Oman 197, 204–7
   emoji/emoticons 48–50
   food related TV 36
   meat eating 44–5
   political dissent 198–9, 201, 214–17
   reference corpus 37
   smoothies 40

UAE (United Arab Emirates) 197
   and Oman 199–200, 207–9
Ukraine 229, 233, 235, 236, 238, 244
Urban Veg Patch (blog) 178, 185–7
user comments 64–5, 75–8

vegan (adjective) 94–8, 102
veganism 43, 90–3, 98, 103 n.2, 182, 254
   blogs 87–8, 93–5
   Facebook 42–3
   healthy eating 91–3
   membership categorization 15
vegetables 21–2, 23–4
Végétal – Cuisine Vegan (blog) 88, 94
vegetarianism 43, 44, 91
verbs
   modals 14, 18, 22, 29
   passive 213–14, 217
   reflexivity 14, 18, 26, 27
   stacking 26, 27–8
virtual togetherness 145–51
   eating together 151–62
visual cues 213

WhatsApp 198–9
word of mouth 111
written captions 64–5, 72–5

Yefremov, Mikhail 233, 235
Yelp 111, 113, 114, 116–17, 133 n.2
YouTube
   mukbang 139, 143
   Parmesan 226, 230–2, 234–44, 254

www.ingramcontent.com/pod-product-compliance
Lightning Source LLC
Chambersburg PA
CBHW072130290426
44111CB00012B/1846